More Saintly Solutions
to Life's Common Problems

Also by Fr. Joseph M. Esper
from Sophia Institute Press®:

Saintly Solutions
to Life's Common Problems

Fr. Joseph M. Esper

More Saintly Solutions
to Life's Common Problems

SOPHIA INSTITUTE PRESS®
Manchester, New Hampshire

Sophia Institute Press®
Box 5284, Manchester, NH 03108
1-800-888-9344
www.sophiainstitute.com

Library of Congress Cataloging-in-Publication Data

Esper, Joseph M.
    More saintly solutions to life's common problems / Joseph M. Esper.
        p. cm.
    Includes bibliographical references and index.
    ISBN 1-928832-67-9 (pbk. : alk. paper)
    1. Christian life — Catholic authors. 2. Christian saints. I. Title.
    BX2350.3.E86 2004
    282′.092′2 — dc22   2004001280

04 05 06 07 08 09 10 9 8 7 6 5 4 3 2 1

Contents

More Saintly Solutions
to Life's Common Problems

Appendix

The Canticle of Mary

My soul magnifies the Lord,
and my spirit rejoices in God my Savior,
for He has regarded the low estate
of His handmaiden.
For behold, henceforth all generations
will call me blessed;
for He who is mighty has done great things for me,
and holy is His Name.
And His mercy is on those who fear Him
from generation to generation.
He has shown strength with His arm;
He has scattered the proud in the imagination of their hearts;
He has put down the mighty from their thrones,
and exalted those of low degree;
He has filled the hungry with good things,
and the rich He has sent empty away.
He has helped His servant Israel,
in remembrance of His mercy,
as He spoke to our fathers,
to Abraham and to His posterity forever.

Luke 1:46-55

Introduction

As we enter into the third millennium, human technological progress has reached dizzying and unprecedented heights; advances in science, medicine, engineering, transportation, and communication continue at a relentless pace, with breakthroughs occurring in these or related fields almost every day. Our accomplishments in these areas would have been unimaginable just one hundred years ago — and if a visionary from the earliest days of the Church had been granted a glimpse into the twenty-first century, he would have been hard-pressed even to find the words to describe the wonders he saw, let alone explain how they were possible.

In so many fields of endeavor, the ancient world cannot begin to compare with our own, but there's at least one vitally important exception: the realm of spiritual growth and holiness. Beginning two thousand years ago, the followers of Jesus Christ — starting in the most perfect way with the Blessed Virgin Mary — began ascending new heights of religious and moral achievement, and in the centuries that followed, men, women, and children of every race and culture gave the world new and inspiring demonstrations of sanctity and self-giving. These heroes of human holiness — the saints — successfully faced many of the same struggles, and discovered the answers to many of the same questions, that we face today. Therefore, we citizens of our technologically wise and powerful twenty-first century can benefit immensely by reflecting humbly on their words and deeds and learning from their wisdom.

In its *Dogmatic Constitution on the Church*, the Second Vatican Council declared, "All Christians in any state or walk of life are called to the fullness of Christian life and to the perfection of love." In this way, the council said, earthly society will be transformed, and through the use of Christ's gifts by the members of the Church for the glory of God and the service of their neighbor, "the holiness of the People of God will grow in fruitful abundance, as is clearly shown in the history of the Church through the life of so many saints."[1] The council also stated, "To look on the life of those who have faithfully followed Christ is to be inspired with a new reason for seeking the city which is to come, while at the same time we are taught to know a most safe path by which, despite the vicissitudes of the world . . . we will be able to arrive at perfect union with Christ."[2]

This "universal call to holiness" stressed by Vatican II is by no means a new idea; the Church has always emphasized the importance of responding to God's invitation to an ever-deepening relationship with Him — an invitation extended to all Christ's faithful. Near the end of the fourth century, for instance, St. John Chrysostom wrote, "Is it perhaps only monks who are obliged to please God? No, God wishes that all should become holy and that none should neglect the practice of virtue." Because the saints who populate the Church's "Hall of Fame" come from every culture, status, age, and way of life, they serve as a continuing source of inspiration and guidance through their words and example.

None of us can claim, "Holiness isn't for me; I'm just a sinner," for indeed, striving for holiness — through active cooperation with God's grace — is the only possible way of overcoming or

[1] *Lumen Gentium*, par. 40.
[2] Ibid., par. 50.

transcending our weak and sinful human nature. Moreover, the great English convert to Catholicism Gilbert Keith Chesterton wrote, "There are saints indeed in my religion; but a saint only means a man who really knows that he is a sinner." With the glorious and divinely decreed exception of the Virgin Mary, all the saints were profoundly aware that they were sinners, in constant need of God's mercy and assistance. The perfect life they now enjoy in Heaven can be a source of hope and inspiration for us here and now; the struggles and difficulties they faced on earth can be a source of consolation and encouragement in our own journey through life.

The heroes of God faced many of the same problems and weaknesses that afflict us today; they had to struggle with such things as anger, lust, pride, laziness, and uncertainty, enduring hunger, tiredness, and poor health; they were often unappreciated, misunderstood, and resented. The saints experienced grief, worry, and failure; they knew what it was to cope with little irritations and to bear heavy crosses. Thus, their words of advice and encouragement to us today bear the ring of truth and express a wisdom purchased at great cost — and we can do ourselves a great favor by seriously considering, and whenever possible, acting upon, their suggestions.

Mother Teresa of Calcutta — now declared Bl. Teresa of Calcutta (one step removed from saintly canonization) — once attempted to minister to persons suffering from a natural disaster, but was overwhelmed by their grief and misery. "What can I say to these people who have suffered so much?" she asked the local bishop. "How can I tell them about God's love?" The bishop, no doubt inspired by the Holy Spirit, gave her a simple but profound answer: "Don't try to tell them about God's Love. *Be* God's love."

This is what the saints seek to do for us today — not only to demonstrate God's love by the way they lived, but, through their continuing intercession and prayers, to help us live in this spirit, growing ever more deeply in holiness and peace. It's my hope that this book, a companion to my earlier *Saintly Solutions to Life's Common Problems*, will not only help you learn about the saints, but, more important, will help you become like them, hearing God's unique call to you more clearly, and answering it more wholeheartedly — in particular, by being God's love to the people around you.

Rev. Joseph M. Esper

As You Read This Book

As you read this book, whether you wish to learn about the saints for your own edification or entertainment, or whether you seek help or advice for a particular problem or life situation you're experiencing, keep in mind the following:

+ *Remember that, whatever you're facing, you're not alone.* Jesus has promised to remain always with those who trust in Him,[3] offering strength and refreshment to those who are burdened or weary[4] — and all the saints have experienced this divine help firsthand. The stories contained in these chapters remind us that the saints, too, had to struggle with life's problems, and their example of perseverance and trust may inspire you to remain faithful to your own efforts to answer the Lord's call.

+ *Cultivate a devotion to particular saints* — those who experienced the same weaknesses or temptations you do and those whose lives illustrate the corresponding virtues. It's natural and fitting that you feel a particular attraction to those saints who had similar occupations, difficulties, or life

---

[3] Matt. 28:20.
[4] Matt. 11:28-29.

experiences as your own; they have a special understanding of your needs and are particularly eager to assist you if you ask for their help.

• *Don't assume that traveling the path of perfection was easy for the saints, but will be impossible for you.* By and large, these holy men and women were not born saints; they became saints as a result of their willingness to cooperate with God's grace.

• *In seeking to overcome your personal weaknesses, choose only one, or at most two, to work on at a time.* As the saints discovered, overcoming faults requires not only divine assistance, but humble dedication and perseverance. Don't attempt to do too much at once; after all, as long as you're honestly trying to come closer to the Lord, He'll be very patient with you.

• *If you don't see immediately the changes you seek — either in your personality or in your life — don't grow discouraged.* Some of the saints were recipients of miracles, and others underwent dramatic conversions, but most of them, using God's grace, overcame their faults or problems one day at a time. Even the holiest of saints — our Lady excepted — if asked whether they were holy, would have insisted on their own sinfulness. Nevertheless, God's grace was at work in them in a wonderful manner. In the same way, your openness to God allows Him to bring about beneficial changes in you, even though you're unaware of them.

• *Read each of the points in each chapter under "For Further Reflection."* One or more of these quotations, ideas, or suggestions may offer you insight, inspiration, or encouragement. Ask the Holy Spirit to make you receptive to whatever message you need to hear.

• *Consider the advice given under "Something You Might Try."* If this isn't practical and useful to you now, continue reflecting and praying about your situation for at least several days, asking particular saints of your choice to help you find the answer.

• *Read the Scripture passages suggested in each chapter under "Further Reading."* Ask the Lord to speak to you through His Word, and to give you an openness to His truth as it applies to your life right now.

• *Pray the prayer given at the end of each chapter.* If necessary, make it your own, modifying it to fit your situation; if you wish, write out your own prayer on this subject, and begin praying it each day.

• *Consider using one or more of the novenas (over a period of nine days) given in the Appendix.* Many people have found novenas to be a powerful and effective way of seeking heavenly assistance.

The saints are those men, women, and children who have successfully arrived home at our heavenly Father's kingdom, and, eternally rooted as they are in the love of Jesus Christ, they're eager to help us and rejoice with us as we, too, seek to complete our lifelong journey.

More Saintly Solutions
to Life's Common Problems

Abuse and Neglect

Whoever causes one of these little ones who believe in me to sin,
it would be better for him to have a great millstone fastened
round his neck and to be drowned in the depth of the sea.

Matthew 18:6

In 1579, a girl was born to a family in the French town of Pibrac. Named Germaine, the child was weak, ill, and afflicted with a withered and paralyzed right hand. Her mother died when she was very young, and her father, Laurent Cousin, remarried. Germaine's new stepmother, Hortense, despised her and taught her own children to do the same (having them, for instance, put ashes in her food and tar on her clothes). The girl received only cruelty and abuse, and her father — a man weak in character — did nothing to defend her; for example, he pretended not to notice that his young daughter had been given so little food that she had to learn to crawl over to the dog's dish and eat there to satisfy her hunger.

One time Hortense left Germaine wedged in a drain outside while she went to care for the chickens — and then forgot about the child for three days. Later Hortense expressed her hatred by deliberately pouring boiling water on Germaine's legs, and when the girl became ill with tuberculosis, she despised her all the more — and, to safeguard her own children, she made Germaine sleep out in the stable. On cold winter nights, Germaine's only source of warmth came from the sheep that slept there, and the only food she received consisted of scraps that her stepmother, depending upon her mood, might throw to her.

When Germaine was a bit older, her father and stepmother gave her the task of caring for the sheep — and out there, in the fields, she was at peace; instead of feeling lonely or neglected, Germaine prayed and expressed her love for God. Her simple prayers ("Dear God, please don't let me get too hungry or thirsty. Help me to please my mother. And help me to please You") and her daily attendance at Mass — during which time she left her flock in the care of God — helped her achieve a great degree of holiness in a short time (further angering her stepmother, who tried unsuccessfully to prove that the girl was nothing but a fraud).

As Germaine's reputation for sanctity spread, and as stories circulated about the miracles worked through her prayers, Hortense's hatred lessened to the point where she invited the girl back into the house — but Germaine politely declined; she had become used to living in the stable, and preferred to be alone there with God. It was there in the stable that she was discovered dead one day, worn out after twenty-two years of suffering and penance.

We are right to be horrified and angered that an innocent child should have to suffer such cruelty and hatred — just as the world today is right to respond with indignation to the many instances of sexual abuse of the young (both within the Church and elsewhere in society) that have come to light. Violating the sanctity and dignity of any of God's children is a grave and inexcusable sin, one that contemporary society is quick to condemn — unless it falls under a politically correct category (such as abortion or homosexuality). Jesus, of course, rejects such hypocrisy, and warns that all evil deeds performed in secret will one day be brought to light,[5]

[5] See Luke 12:2.

thus providing a standard of conduct for Christians of every age. None of the saints, of course, were ever guilty of this sort of grave sin, but many of them suffered from abuse or neglect to one degree or another, and in terms of a response to evil, there's much we can learn from their example.

St. Germaine, who had so much to suffer, never gave in to resentment or self-pity (the way almost any of us would); instead, she developed a simple but very deep faith, forgiving her unloving family and constantly praying on their behalf. Something similar occurred to a young girl named Odilia in the eighth century. Because the future saint was born blind, her father, Adalric, a nobleman, wished for her to be "exposed" — that is, left outside to die from the elements or starvation. Odilia's mother, however, secretly entrusted the child to a peasant woman, who later took her to be raised in a convent. Upon being baptized there at age twelve, she immediately received her sight. When the story of this miracle, and of Odilia's true identity, reached her brother, he asked his father that she might be brought home, but Adalric, in a fit of rage, killed him.

Then, having a temporary change of heart, Adalric welcomed his daughter with a show of joy, and even arranged her engagement to a suitable candidate. Odilia, however, had vowed to remain a virgin, and when she fled her father's castle to avoid being married against her will, he attempted unsuccessfully to have her killed. Afterward Adalric once more repented, this time sincerely, and was reconciled to his daughter; when Odilia entered into religious life, he not only accepted her decision, but even assisted her financially in the foundation of two convents.

Not all cases of abuse are this dramatic, but many of the saints have suffered greatly at the hands of family members or relatives. In the fifth century, when St. Sabas was quite young, his father — a military officer — was transferred to a different post and, taking his wife with him, left the boy in the care of an aunt and uncle.

The aunt, unfortunately, was so cruel to the child that, at the age of eight, he ran away to another uncle. The two uncles thereupon engaged in a series of lawsuits over who was entitled to the income from Sabas's family estate. The holy youth was quite upset by the noise and discord, and ran away to a monastery. (Afterward the uncles repented and invited Sabas home, but he had become attracted to the monastic way of life, and remained where he was — later becoming a great abbot.)

Sometimes abuse comes not from family members, but from those who are supposed to be our brothers and sisters in Christ. This was the case with St. Jeanne de Lestonnac, a widow who, after raising her four children, founded a religious order in the seventeenth century. One of her own nuns, motivated by jealousy, eventually had Jeanne deposed as superior, and maneuvered herself into this position; she thereupon abused this wrongly gained authority and cruelly mistreated Jeanne. The saint endured these trials patiently and without complaint, and when her rival finally repented and offered to restore her position, Jeanne refused, desiring instead to spend her remaining years in prayer and meditation.

A similar experience happened to St. Peter Claver, who had spent his life ministering to black slaves in the New World. At the age of seventy, Peter suffered from partial paralysis and constant pain and, for the final four years of his life, was confined to his room. During this time, everyone forgot about him, and even his nurse, Manuel, frequently mistreated him; for instance, the servant ate most of Peter's food himself, and when full, insolently tossed the remainder into the saint's mouth. Peter, for his part, didn't complain, but simply stated, "My sins deserve more punishment than this."

Abandonment and neglect was also the fate of the great Jesuit missionary St. Francis Xavier, who spent many years preaching the Gospel, first in India, and then in Japan. It had long been his dream to evangelize in China, but Christians weren't welcome there, and it was difficult and dangerous to gain entry into that forbidden land. Finally, in 1552, Francis was able to arrange for a Portuguese ship to take him to the Chinese coast, where he would be transferred to a Chinese boat whose captain had agreed to smuggle him ashore. However, the saint became ill on the journey, and the Portuguese — fearing discovery — dropped Francis off on a small island. During his final two weeks, the saint lay in a primitive hut, praying continuously until he died, with no one other than a solitary faithful companion to care for him.

In the thirteenth century, St. Contardo was taken ill on a pilgrimage, and his comrades left him in a hostel for travelers. The landlord, fearing that the saint's groans would frighten away the other customers, had him removed to a miserable hut, where he died destitute and abandoned — all the while humbly resigning himself to God's will.

The seventh-century abbot St. Maximus the Confessor also died far from home, banished by the emperor due to a theological dispute. Maximus, an elderly man of seventy-five, suffered terribly from cold, hunger, and neglect before finally dying seven years later.

Other saints who suffered from abuse or neglect include St. Elizabeth of Hungary, St. Edwin, St. Godelive, and Bl. Margaret of Castello. Some of God's holy ones have undergone neglect by choice. The bishop St. Cuthbert, realizing his end was near and wanting to use a final opportunity for penance, wouldn't allow anyone to stay with him and care for him in his illness during his last three weeks on earth.

It's very easy to fear that others will abandon or even abuse us in our time of need — and so we can have great appreciation for someone who, like St. Leo the Great, remains faithful to his duties and loving toward the people around him. In the fifth century, the Roman Empire in Western Europe was undergoing a major crisis; in the face of warfare and barbarian invasions, civil authority broke down, and the far-off Eastern Emperor in Constantinople was unwilling or unable to intervene. Leo, who had been elected Pope in 440, stepped into the vacuum of leadership that developed. When Attila the Hun invaded Italy in 452, the authorities fled in fear. Pope Leo went out to meet the warlord and convinced him, in exchange for the payment of a ransom, to leave the city untouched. (When later asked why he had agreed to such generous terms, Attila explained that he had seen a fierce angelic warrior standing next to Leo, threatening to attack him should any harm befall the Pope.)

Three years later, when the fiercely destructive Vandals occupied Rome, Leo persuaded them to forgo their normal practice of massacring the city's inhabitants. St. Leo earned the admiration and loyalty of the common people, for they saw that he — unlike the leaders of government — did not abandon them in their darkest hour or attempt to exploit the situation to his own benefit. His intercession, like that of all the saints, can be very valuable and consoling when we're called upon to bear the cross of neglect or abuse in our own lives.

For Further Reflection

"Forgotten! . . . Yes, I want to be forgotten, not just by humans, but also by myself. I would like to be so reduced to nothing that I would have no desires [except] . . . the glory of my Jesus; that's all." — St. Thérèse of Lisieux (Even when others neglect us, we must never neglect God; loving Him even when it seems as if no one loves us is a wonderful and powerful way of sanctifying our sufferings.)

"Nothing has done so much harm to a healthy friendliness as the belief that we ought to do one good act a day. Why one good act? What about all the other acts? Charity is a habit, not an isolated act." — Archbishop Fulton J. Sheen

"The biggest disease today is not leprosy or tuberculosis, but rather the feeling of being unwanted, uncared for and deserted by everybody. The greatest evil is the lack of love and charity." — Bl. *Teresa of Calcutta*

Something You Might Try

♦ According to Archbishop Fulton J. Sheen, "Whether we know it or not, the actions of our daily life are fixing our character for good or for evil. The things you do, the thoughts you think, the words you say are turning you either into a saint or a devil, to be placed at either the right or the left side of the Divine Judge." Taking this perspective can motivate us to treat others as we wish to be treated, and to fulfill those moral and religious duties we might otherwise neglect (especially those acts of compassion we're bound by charity to perform for our neighbor). It can be helpful to remind ourselves each morning, "The decisions I make today will help determine what happens to me on Judgment Day."

♦ If you've been the victim of any form of abuse, God does not expect you to bear this burden alone. It's important, first of all, that you not blame yourself for what happened, and that you then seek whatever form of counseling or other assistance may be needed. If you, or someone known to you, have suffered abuse (whether by a representative of the Catholic Church or another religion, a teacher, a counselor, an athletic coach, a family member or a relative, or anyone else), contact the appropriate authorities (e.g., the local Department of Social Services) as soon as possible.

Further Reading

Scripture: Sirach 7:35; Sirach 51:10; Hebrews 12:2-3; Hebrews 13:16.

Classics: St. Teresa of Avila, *The Way of Perfection*.

Contemporary Works: Matthew Linn, Sheila Fabricant, and
Dennis Linn, *Healing Spiritual Abuse and Religious Addiction*;
Mary E. Latela, *Healing the Abusive Family: Beyond Survival*;
Fr. Benedict J. Groeschel, C.F.R., *From Scandal to Hope*.

Lord God,
because You are my Father,
I know that You will never
abandon me or forget me,
nor will You ever show me anything
but a gentle and abiding love.
This, however, has not been my
experience with the people in my life;
many times I feel unloved, neglected,
unfairly treated, robbed of my dignity,
and even made to feel unworthy of life.
My life contains many hurts
that have yet to be fully healed;
I struggle with unresolved anger,
unhealthy guilt, a sense of depression,
and a deep and constant sadness.
Help me, O Lord.
Help me to trust in You wholeheartedly,
even though my trust has been abused by others;
help me to remember You always,
even though I am so often forgotten by others.
Help me to avoid feeling sorry for myself,
and above all, keep me from
becoming bitter or unforgiving.
I know that I have at times taken
Your love for granted and even
abused Your goodness and mercy;

Abuse and Neglect

*I admit that I have neglected You
far more often than anyone has neglected me.
I'm sorry, and I ask for Your help.
Please bless all those who have hurt me,
neglected me, or abandoned me,
and help me to remember always
that my faith in You will never be disappointed.*

Academic Difficulties

I will instruct you and teach you in the way you should go;
I will counsel you and watch over you.

Psalm 32:8

Imagine, if you can, that one of the greatest professional athletes of our times absolutely hated to play sports as a boy, and was clumsy and uncoordinated. Imagine that one of our greatest and most popular movie stars was very shy and self-conscious as a girl. Imagine that a great chef had sworn, as a child, never to have anything to do with cooking. All these hypothetical situations could well have happened (and, if so, they'd illustrate the importance of perseverance and the resiliency of the human character). They're mentioned here to introduce someone who did have this sort of remarkable and unexpected turnaround in life: the seventh-century Spanish bishop St. Isidore of Seville.

Isidore, who was named a Doctor of the Church almost 1,100 years after his death, was one of the great scholars of his age. As archbishop of Toledo, he decreed that a seminary or cathedral school be established in every diocese of Spain, and as the most learned man of the country, he drew up a very impressive and wide-ranging curriculum for the education of students. Isidore even compiled his own encyclopedia, called the *Etymologies* (or

Origins), which gathered into a unified form all the knowledge of his age.

Impressive achievements, to be sure — but how do they fit into a discussion on difficulties in gaining an education? For the simple reason that, as a student, Isidore hated learning and studying.

St. Isidore came from a very holy family; his sister and two of his brothers were eventually canonized. One of these brothers, St. Leander, was much older than Isidore and was placed in charge of his education. Leander was very intelligent and well educated, and this may have influenced his high expectations for his younger brother — for Leander was a very demanding schoolmaster. In fact, he was so strict that one day Isidore ran away. The youth took refuge in the woods, and, while resting, noticed a stone that was being worn down by water, one drop at a time. Isidore pondered this, and then the "lesson" hit home: if he approached his studies in the same manner, he would succeed; it wasn't necessary for him to learn or understand everything all at once, but merely to proceed with persistence, step by step, learning a little bit at a time, until mastery of the subject finally came about. Isidore returned to his studies, and, with his new attitude and sense of determination, succeeded far beyond what he could have imagined.

This isn't to say that every student can become a great scholar, but it's true that God wants us to do our best in our efforts to learn, and as long as we make the effort, He will gladly assist us. As St. Isidore himself later stated, "One who is slow to grasp things but who really tries hard is rewarded; equally he who does not cultivate his God-given intellectual ability is condemned for despising his gifts and sinning by sloth." In other words, the Lord looks not at our level of success in academics (or in any other field), but at how hard we've tried.

As one would expect, many of the saints are to be numbered among the greatest thinkers and scholars of history, and quite a few of them did much to advance the methods and availability of education for others. Such saints include St. Angela Merici, who was ahead of her time, early in the sixteenth century, in creating a teaching order of religious women (the Ursuline Sisters); the English monk and scholar St. Bede the Venerable, who was the first known writer of English prose and an expert in many fields of learning; St. John Bosco, the nineteenth-century Italian priest who upset professional educators by successfully teaching and guiding delinquent boys using a mixture of gentleness, firmness, and practicality, combined with an effort to make learning enjoyable; St. Ephrem, a fourth-century Scripture scholar who also taught uneducated Christians the truths of the Faith by setting religious verses to the melodies of popular tunes of the day; St. Albert the Great, the "Universal Teacher" known for his expertise in a vast number of subjects, and today considered a patron saint of students; and Albert's famous student St. Thomas Aquinas, perhaps the greatest theologian in the Church's history, who is also considered a patron of students.

Other noted educators in the Church's history include St. Lawrence of Brindisi, a great Scripture scholar whose fluency in ancient languages made it possible for him to study the Bible in the original texts; the sixteenth-century bishop St. Turibius of Mongrovejo, who was a brilliant scholar and successful professor of law before being ordained; St. John Baptist de La Salle, the French priest who — like St. John Bosco two hundred years later — devoted himself to the education of poor, underprivileged boys (even though this work was at first distasteful to him); and St. Jerome, the brilliant but cantankerous biblical scholar who was very gentle with the local children as he taught them basic grammar, and of whom the great St. Augustine said, "What Jerome is ignorant of, no mortal has ever known." (St. Jerome took great care in advising the mother of the young St. Paula on how to teach her daughter; he suggested the importance of combining learning with play, fostering friendly competition between the child and her classmates or companions, and arousing her ambition for learning by praising her accomplishments.)

Still other important scholars include Jerome's contemporary St. Augustine, one of the greatest thinkers in the history of Western civilization; the eleventh-century bishop St. Anselm, who is known as the "Father of Scholasticism" (scholasticism being the attempt to uncover religious truths through rational arguments and propositions); St. Francis Xavier, an instructor at the prestigious University of Paris, until St. Ignatius of Loyola convinced him that success in this world counts for nothing compared with serving God; St. John of Kanty, whose brilliance as a student and instructor prompted jealous colleagues to have him sent away to one of the poorest parishes of the diocese; St. Thomas More, who in sixteenth-century England taught his daughters Greek and Latin even though educating girls was considered a waste of time; and St. John Neumann, who, as bishop of the important American diocese of Philadelphia, emphasized the importance of a Catholic school system (to preserve the faith of Catholic immigrants in the face of Protestantized public schools), and who soon increased the number of Catholic students in his diocese twentyfold.

Impressive as this list is, however, it should not obscure an important fact: not all the saints enjoyed school or had an easy time learning. St. Augustine, for instance — although a brilliant student — hated having to attend classes. (Ironically, during his long search for the truth, he became a popular and successful teacher himself.) Some saints had to struggle with their studies. This was the case with the famous patron saint of parish priests, St. John Vianney. The future Curé d'Ars, as he was later known, greatly desired to become a priest, but his academic difficulties seemed destined to prevent this. Only the assistance of a tutor, and much diligence and prayer on his part, overcame this obstacle — and even then, he was ordained more because of his devoutness and growing holiness than for any other apparent qualifications.

A young girl named Bernadette, to whom the Blessed Virgin appeared within a year of St. John Vianney's death, was considered a very slow student and, although fourteen, hadn't yet made her First Communion. Indeed, it was Bernadette's unintelligent disposition that lent authenticity to her claim to have seen Mary; when she told her parish's pastor that the Lady in question had referred to herself as "the Immaculate Conception," the priest realized it would have been impossible for Bernadette to have imagined or made up such a term.

In the seventeenth century, the parents of St. Charles of Sezze desired a priestly vocation for their son, but it wasn't to be — Charles was barely able to read and write, and found learning quite difficult; however, his great sanctity caused the Franciscans to accept him as a lay brother.

Still another struggling student was St. Vincent Pallotti, an Italian priest during the same era as St. John Vianney. His schoolmaster once stated, "He's a little saint, but a bit thick-headed." His mother suggested he make a novena to the Holy Spirit, and after he did so, his grades improved dramatically.

All the saints found prayer to be very important in achieving academic success — but there's at least one instance of a saint almost praying *too much* during his studies. As a Dominican novice, St. Louis Bertrand greatly enjoyed the year-long period of prayer and contemplation. Following his solemn profession, however, a much greater emphasis was placed on academics. Louis found the new routine tedious, and greatly desired to set aside his studies for increased prayer — until he realized this was a subtle temptation from the Devil to dissuade him from his ultimate goal. Chastened by this insight, Louis applied himself with renewed dedication, and successfully completed the order's required course of study.

The Church has always valued education, but has also recognized that many times what the Lord has hidden from the learned

and clever, He has revealed to the merest children.[6] Bl. Jordan of
Saxony, the successor of St. Dominic as master general of the Dominican Order, was once informed that some of the novices were
so unintelligent that they could barely be taught to read. Jordan
responded, "Let them be. Despise not one of these little ones: I tell
you that many among them will become excellent preachers" —
and so it happened.

Furthermore, education wasn't always available to those who
desired it. As a girl, Bl. Osanna of Mantua was eager to learn about
religion, so she asked to be taught to read, but her father refused,
explaining that learning was a dangerous thing for women. Osanna
learned to read nonetheless, supposedly taught by our Lady herself
(who, of course, wasn't bound by the chauvinism of the fifteenth
century).

Early in the twentieth century, the Spanish gypsy Bl. Ceferino
Gimenez Malla lived as an illiterate horse dealer, but rich and
poor alike sought his advice, due to his integrity and common
sense. The same thing was true of the lay brother Bl. Silvester of
Valdiseve; although totally uneducated, his infused wisdom was so
great that he was often consulted by learned men, including the
prior of his monastery. In the sixteenth century, the shepherd boy
St. Paschal Baylon received no formal education, but he was so
determined to use a prayer book in honor of the Virgin Mary that
he taught himself to read and write.

Education was a source of humiliation for several of the saints.
As a youth, the great theologian Thomas Aquinas was called by
his fellow students "the Dumb Ox," for his usual silence in the
classroom kept them from realizing what a brilliant intellect he
possessed. Both St. Ignatius of Loyola, the founder of the Society
of Jesus, and a later Jesuit, St. Alphonsus Rodriguez, got a late start
on their academic careers — which meant that, although grown

[6] Cf. Matt. 11:25.

men, they had to attend grammar school and learn Latin with boys half their age before being ordained.

However, humility is not out of place when it comes to learning, for no matter how much we learn, our knowledge is slight compared with that of the angels, and as of nothing compared with an all-knowing God. Moreover, our legitimate efforts to study and learn must be kept in proper perspective. A great scholar and Doctor of the Church, St. Bonaventure, once remarked that a poor, uneducated person might very well know and love God more than a theologian or Church leader, and St. Vincent de Paul noted, "It is on humble souls that God pours down His fullest light and grace. He teaches them what scholars cannot learn, and mysteries that the wisest cannot solve He can make plain to them."

A good education can make life easier and more satisfying (although there's no guarantee of this), but it's certainly not a requirement for holiness. As St. Pius X pointed out, "To praise God well, it is not necessary to be learned." Education is but a means to an end — that of knowing and loving God with all our hearts — and our struggles to learn and understand should fit into this process. In a letter to his younger brother, the nineteenth-century priest and martyr St. Théophane Vénard wrote, "You will be glad one day of these days that you learned your lessons. They will fit you better to do what God wants you to do, so as to win Heaven at the end of it all. For that alone must be the object of all we do. Work hard, work steadily, not for praise or honor or prizes, but simply to please God."

If we are seeking academic success primarily for our own glory, it doesn't matter how successful we might be; all our achievements will end up leaving us unsatisfied. If, however, we're trying to learn and develop our minds primarily for God's glory, it doesn't matter whether we succeed; His presence will bless us. The Lord wants us to do our best, and He promises that, if we seek to please Him, He will smile upon our efforts.

For Further Reflection

"The man who is slow to grasp things but who really tries hard is rewarded; equally he who does not cultivate his God-given intellectual ability is condemned for despising his gifts and sinning by sloth." — *St. Isidore of Seville*

"Do not plunge straight into the sea [of learning], but rather enter it by way of little streams, because it is wise to work upward from the easier to the more difficult. . . . See that you thoroughly grasp whatever you read and hear. Check up on doubtful points. And do your best to hoard up whatever you can in that little bookcase of your mind; you want to fill it as full as possible." — *St. Thomas Aquinas*

"After hearing that they should be humble, some persons do not wish to learn anything. They think they will be proud if they have anything. It has been made clear to us where God wishes us to be in the depths and where He wishes us to be in the heights. He wishes us to be humble to avoid pride, and He wishes us to be on high to grasp wisdom." — *St. Augustine*

Something You Might Try

◆ Three of the Church's greatest scholars, St. Albert the Great, St. Thomas Aquinas, and St. Bonaventure, all stated that they gained more learning by prayer than by study. (Indeed, one of St. Thomas's contemporaries wrote, "Thomas did not acquire his knowledge by natural ingenuity, but rather through the revelation and infusion of the Holy Spirit, for he never began to write without previous prayer and tears. Whenever a doubt arose, he had recourse to prayer. After shedding many tears, he would return to his work, now enlightened and instructed.") Thus, it's important to begin all our academic efforts (studying for a test, reading an assignment, writing a paper, taking a quiz, and so forth) with a silent prayer. Not only can this help relax us (enabling us to do our best), but — more important — it's a way of calling down God's blessing upon our efforts. According to Pope St. Pius V, "The most powerful aid we can bring to [our] study is the practice of earnest prayer. The more closely the mind is united to God, the richer will be the stores of light that follow its researches." Prayer is no substitute for studying (for God helps those who help themselves), but it can definitely help us improve our results, for God wants us to succeed when we seek to do our best for His glory.

◆ According to St. Ignatius of Loyola, "Learning will always be necessary, or certainly useful, and not only that which is infused [revealed to us by the Holy Spirit], but that also which is acquired by study. . . . Try to keep your soul always in peace and quiet, always ready for whatever our Lord may wish to work in you." Thus, we should undertake our studies in a spirit of trust, doing our best to avoid all anxiety.

Further Reading

Scripture: Psalm 119:73; Colossians 3:16; James 1:5.

Classics: St. Alphonsus Liguori, *Thoughts on the Holy Spirit.*

⌒

You who make the mouths
of the speechless skillful in speech:
Teach our mouths;
pour upon our lips
the grace of Your benediction.
Give us keenness of understanding,
ability to remember,
discernment in exposition,
readiness in learning,

and abundant grace in utterance.
Bestow upon us,
at the outset of our journey, gifts;
as we journey, guide us;
and bring to a perfect end our course,
through Jesus Christ our Lord.

St. Thomas Aquinas

Anger

Be angry, but do not sin; do not let the sun go down
on your anger, and give no opportunity to the Devil.

Ephesians 4:26-27

Many of the Church's saints were highly unlikely candidates for holiness before their conversions. A foremost example is the African hermit and martyr known to us as St. Moses the Ethiopian. Born around 330, he was a servant in the household of an important Egyptian official. Moses had a big, muscular physique and an even bigger temper. Because of his vicious nature, and his habit of stealing his master's property (a habit not curbed by the lash), he was eventually dismissed by his employer. The huge, ferocious man thereupon became the much-feared leader of a gang of thieves who terrorized the area, but some time later, he converted to Christianity. (The exact circumstances of his conversion are unknown; it's possible that he sought refuge from pursuing authorities by hiding in a monastery and was genuinely moved by the monks' example of prayer, sacrifice, and charity.)

Moses made great efforts to conquer his fierce temper — fortunately for four robbers who foolishly accosted him while he was praying in his cell. The saint easily overcame the robbers, and, unable to dispose of them as he would have previously done, he tied them up, slung them over his shoulder, and dumped them in front of the priests of a nearby church, asking what should be done with them. (It's said that the unsuccessful robbers — perhaps reasoning that "if you can't beat 'em, join 'em" — repented and went on to become monks themselves.)

In spite of successes like this, St. Moses feared he'd never fully master his temper, so his abbot, a holy man named Isidore, took him up to the roof of the monastery at dawn. Pointing to the sky, he said, "See, my son. The light only gradually drives away the darkness. So it is with the soul." Reassured by these words, Moses continued to make slow but steady progress in gaining a peaceful spirit — so much so that eventually the Archbishop of Alexandria insisted upon ordaining him a priest. Many years later Moses the Ethiopian died as a martyr, for when his monastery was attacked by nomadic raiders, he refused to defend himself, quoting instead Christ's words, "All who take the sword will perish by the sword."[7]

Anger is a common emotion, experienced by almost everyone at one time or another — saints included. There were some holy men and women known for never displaying a temper, such as Bl. Fra Angelico, the famous Renaissance painter. It was said by a contemporary that "he was never seen in anger by the friars, which is a great thing, and seems to be almost impossible to believe." (Thus, the twenty-first century has no monopoly on temperamental people, nor on the difficulty in believing that a person's temper can be perfectly controlled.)

Many saints, however, had an ongoing struggle in this area — including some, such as St. Francis de Sales and St. Vincent de Paul, who became known for their gentle nature. Francis, for instance, once claimed that it had taken him more than twenty years to gain full control of his temper. (That he learned this lesson well

---

[7] Matt. 26:52.

is shown by the fact that in his successful efforts to convert Protestants back to the Church, he chose not to attack their religious beliefs directly, but to bear witness to the truths of Catholicism. Francis himself often said, "A spoonful of honey attracts more flies than a barrelful of vinegar.")

A gentle spirit didn't come naturally to all the saints. For instance, St. Hyacintha Mariscotti entered the convent for a rather surprising reason. Her older sister was already a nun. Hyacintha had no desire for such a life herself, but her parents forced her to enter because of her uncontrollable temper. (After a number of setbacks, the future saint — with the help of God's grace — prevailed in her struggle against anger.)

St. Bernard of Clairvaux was zealous in his service of God, but this single-mindedness often came across in an unfavorable way. Before he moderated his dominating personality, he tended to be quick-tempered, harsh with his monks, and somewhat narrow-minded.

Quite often God's servants have a way of provoking anger on the part of others. St. Basil the Great, who was capable of willfulness himself, faced opposition when chosen as bishop of Caesarea, which he sadly acknowledged in a homily, saying, "The bees fly in swarms, and do not begrudge each other the flowers. It is not so with us. We are not at unity. More eager about his own wrath than his own salvation, each aims his stings at his neighbor." The bishops of the area — including Basil's own uncle — were united in their opposition to him; they refused to come to Caesarea, until they heard a false report of the saint's death. Basil, rather than expressing anger, used the opportunity to speak to them on the importance of unity and peace.

Some saints who were very successful in keeping their own tempers in check, had to learn — like Basil — how to handle the anger of others. For instance, in the fifth century St. Volusian was married to a woman with a fearsome temper. When he worried aloud about a threatened invasion by the Goths (a barbarian tribe), someone remarked that a person enduring such hostility in his own household had more than enough to handle without worrying about enemies from without.

More successful in calming troubled marital waters was St. Margaret of Scotland, who was married at a young age to King Malcolm III — a good man who had a rough personality and was quick to anger. Her loving influence over the years softened his temper and helped him to become holy (and this, indeed, is the most important thing one can do for a spouse).

A similar success was earlier achieved by St. Monica, the mother of St. Augustine, whose unfailing patience gradually calmed her quick-to-anger pagan husband Patricius and even led to his eventual conversion. (Monica herself, undoubtedly speaking from experience, offered this advice to Christian wives: "Guard your tongue when your husband is angry.")

A more daunting challenge was faced by St. Hugh of Lincoln, who had to contend with the stormy temper of King Henry II of England. (It was Henry's frustrated lament, "Will no one rid me of this troublesome priest?" that led to the murder of the archbishop St. Thomas Becket in Canterbury Cathedral.) Hugh coped with royal fits of rage in a surprising way: by laughing at the king. (The fact that he survived and even prospered doesn't necessarily make this a recommended approach in our own dealings with angry people.) It's said that St. Rose of Lima used this same method when physically assaulted by the Devil. Satan, whose pride cannot allow him to be the object of ridicule, is supposed to have screamed in impotent fury before angrily departing the saint and leaving her in peace.

Several amusing ways of dealing with anger were demonstrated by the holy priest St. Vincent Pallotti, who sought to hear the confession of a dying man who had threatened — in all seriousness — to shoot any priest who came near him. Vincent dressed up as an old woman, gained access to the man's room and, after revealing his identity, withstood the man's anger and succeeded in reconciling him to the Church. On another occasion, before going to the deathbed of a public enemy of the Church, St. Vincent purchased a box of cookies. He then awakened the man and began urging him to repent. When the sinner began shouting at him, Vincent shoved a cookie into his mouth, and as the man paused to chew and swallow the cookie, the holy priest used the interval to continue his urgent message. The process had to be repeated several times, but in the end Vincent overcame the dying man's anger and stubbornness, and was finally able to hear his confession.

The saints had various ways of dealing with difficult people. For instance, if someone angered or upset the holy bishop Alphonsus Liguori, his custom was to remark, "God make you a saint." (Even if uttered in frustration, such a remark on our part would certainly be more edifying and helpful than other things we might normally say.)

In the nineteenth century Bl. Agostina Pietrantoni worked as a nurse in the tubercular ward of a Roman hospital. When frustrated by her patients — many of whom were prisoners and who had been transferred there after becoming ill in a local prison — she would express her feelings in writing to the Virgin Mary, and then "mail" the letters by placing them behind a painting of our Lady in one of the hospital hallways.

Through her total devotion to her family, Bl. Anna Maria Taigi had a knack for calming her easily angered husband, Domenico. After her death, he testified, "I often came home tired, moody, and cross, but she always succeeded in soothing and cheering me. And due to her, I corrected some of my faults."

Many saints have spoken on the importance of gaining control of one's temper, for, as St. Catherine of Siena notes, "There is no sin or wrong that gives a man such a foretaste of Hell in this life as anger and impatience." St. Thomas More referred to "this deadly cancer of anger from which so much harm grows: it makes us un-like ourselves, makes us like timber wolves or furies from Hell, drives us forth headlong upon the points of swords, makes us blindly run forth after other men's destruction as we hasten toward our own ruin." St. John Chrysostom gives us the following vivid description: "Imagine your anger to be a kind of wild beast . . . be-cause it, too, has ferocious teeth and claws, and if you don't tame it, it will devastate all things. . . . It not only hurts the body; it even corrupts the health of the soul, devouring, rending, tearing to pieces all its strength, and making it useless for everything."

According to St. Alphonsus Liguori, "All the days of their life, persons addicted to anger are unhappy, because they are always in a tempest." Anger makes it impossible to relate to God in a hum-ble, trusting way or to offer Him our sincere prayers. Indeed, as St. Ephrem states, "It is blasphemy if you pray before God while you are full of wrath." St. Augustine tells us that the terrible condition of hatred is nothing more than ingrained and deep-rooted anger, and St. John Climacus, in a vivid description of anger's effects, warns us that it "keeps alive sin, hates justice, ruins virtue, poisons the heart, rots the mind, defeats concentration, paralyzes prayer, puts love at a distance, and is a nail driven into the soul." Re-flecting on the likely cause of habitual anger, St. Thomas More suggests that it results from people having too high an opinion of themselves, causing them to be easily offended when others fail to give them what they consider their due.

In addition to diagnosing the problem, the saints have much to say regarding its cure. According to St. John Climacus, "The first step toward freedom from anger is to keep the lips silent when the heart is stirred; the next, to keep thoughts silent when the soul is upset; the last, to be totally calm when unclean winds are blow-ing." Achieving this balance is, for many of us, a long-term proj-ect, as the saint himself acknowledges: "Freedom from anger is a triumph over one's nature. It is the ability to be impervious to insults, and comes by hard work and the sweat of one's brow." The saint also tells us, "It is impossible to achieve freedom from anger without humility."

Thus, learning to control one's temper involves humility, perseverance, and also prayer, for as St. John Chrysostom teaches, "As water extinguishes fire, so prayer does extinguish the heat of the passions." St. John was himself known to express anger (usually righteous) on occasion; imparting some hard-won wisdom, he wrote while in exile, "Conquer your rage with wise, rational thought. Offer it up as a sacrifice to God."

St. Maximus the Confessor warns us of the danger of brooding over insults, saying, "Don't recall to your memory anything your neighbor may have said in a moment of acrimony, whether he insulted you to your face, or spoke evil of you to another and that person has come and reported it to you. If you let yourself become angry, it is but a short step from anger to hatred." Instead, in the words of St. Seraphim of Sarov, "Maintain a spirit of peace, and you'll save a thousand souls." In other words, because anger — one of the Seven Deadly Sins — can give rise to so many evils, preventing it from taking hold in our hearts can prove to be a great blessing for ourselves and others.

Many of us wrongly assume that getting angry makes us appear strong and decisive, but as St. Francis de Sales notes, "Nothing is so strong as gentleness, nothing so gentle as real strength." Moreover, when our expression of anger provokes an angry response from someone else, we're less likely to solve our problem or obtain what we want. St. Angela Merici tells us, "You will effect more by kind words and a courteous manner than by anger or sharp rebuke, which should never be used but in necessity." A similar point is made by the twentieth-century priest St. Josemaría Escrivá, who advises, "Say what you have just said, but in a different tone, without anger, and your argument will gain in strength and, above all, you won't offend God."

Anger can indeed be very offensive to the Lord, for it often represents our ignoble attempt to take revenge; and Scripture tells us that vengeance belongs to God, not to us. Therefore, our attempts to control our tempers are actually a very practical and important way of cooperating with divine justice, and our efforts in this regard, no matter how halting and incomplete, will surely be blessed.

For Further Reflection

"We are never justified in being 'bitter' toward anyone except ourselves. In very deed, if we were only one-tenth as appreciative as we have every reason to be, our gratitude for what God has done for us . . . would be such that we would be perfectly content with what we are and what we have." — Ven. *Solanus Casey*

"Anger never travels alone. It is always accompanied by plenty of other sins." — *St. John Vianney (Thus, we'll never make true and lasting progress in overcoming our other faults unless we also sincerely seek God's help in overcoming our temper.)*

"If we should see two men fighting together over serious matters, we would still think them both crazy if they did not leave off fighting when they saw a ferocious lion coming toward them, ready to devour them both. Now, considering that we surely see that death is coming on us all, and will undoubtedly within a short time devour us all — how soon, we don't know — isn't it worse than insanity to be angry and bear malice to one another, more often than not over trivial matters, in the same way children fight over cherry stones?" — *St. Thomas More*

Something You Might Try

◆ According to St. Peter Chrysologus, God "wants us to smother anger when it is still only a spark. If it grows to the full flame of its fury, it does not get checked without bloodshed." Therefore, it's important to face anger immediately, rather than brooding and letting it take root in our hearts. As soon as we feel angry, for whatever reason, we should pray for God's help, saying something like this: "Lord, help me bear this injustice calmly. Remind me of all that You suffered on my behalf. Let me see this event in the light of Your truth."

♦ St. Maximilian Kolbe, who had a great devotion to the Immaculate Heart of Mary, advises, "We should make it a point never to do anything when we are 'hot and bothered,' but strive first of all to calm down, to hand ourselves over to the will of God and of the Immaculate, and then to act with serenity so that we may not commit blunders." Thus, instead of responding to injuries according to our own inclinations — a response that will usually be rooted in anger — we must form the habit of asking ourselves, "What does God want me to do in this situation?"

Further Reading

Scripture: Proverbs 19:11; Matthew 5:22; 1 Corinthians 13:5; James 1:19-20.

Classics: St. Francis de Sales, *An Introduction to the Devout Life*; St. Alphonsus Liguori, *The Practice of the Love of Jesus Christ*.

Contemporary Works: Charles J. Keating, *Dealing with Difficult People*; Marilyn Gustin, *Facing Anger* (pamphlet); Priscilla J. Herbison, *God Knows We Get Angry*.

It's troubling to admit it, Lord,
but my temper is sabotaging my happiness
and keeping me from coming closer to You.
Anger is a big part of my life — too big.

There are certain people and
certain situations that set me off,
and even though I know I need
to keep myself under control,
I find it hard to do so.
I need Your help, O Lord;
my anger is too much
for me to handle alone.
Increase my patience,
humility, and trust,
and help me to remember
that I'm not always right,
that I don't always know what's best,
and that I don't always have
to have my own way.
Touch my heart, and make it calm
and gentle, and give me the grace
to live always in a peaceful spirit.

Criticism

*Do not find fault before you investigate;
first consider, and then reprove.*

Sirach 11:7

Few American presidents have faced challenges of the magnitude of those Abraham Lincoln confronted — and few were more disparaged and criticized during their term of office. Lincoln, of course, is today revered as an American hero, but at the time of his presidency, many people were dissatisfied with his leadership and conduct. For instance, he delivered what most Americans consider one of the greatest speeches in our nation's history, but the day after he delivered the Gettysburg Address, a newspaper in Chicago editorialized, "The cheek of every American must tingle with shame as he reads the silly, flat, and dishwatery utterances of a man who has to be pointed out to intelligent foreigners as the President of the United States."

Lincoln was undoubtedly hurt by these and similar remarks, but he didn't let himself be influenced or discouraged by them; instead, he described his philosophy in these words: "If I were to try to read, much less answer, all the attacks made on me, this shop [the White House] might as well be closed for any other business. I do the very best I know how — the very best I can — and I mean to keep doing so until the end. If the end brings me out all right, what is said against me won't amount to anything. If the end brings me out wrong, ten angels swearing I was right would make no difference."

For better or worse, the experience of being misunderstood, unappreciated, and criticized is part of life — and that's especially true for Christians. Jesus warned His followers, "If the world hates you, know that it has hated me before it hated you. If you were of the world, the world would love its own; but because you are not of the world, but I chose you out of the world, therefore the world hates you."[8] Criticism is often hard to bear; it has been said that it can take up to nine compliments or positive affirmations to restore our peace of mind after receiving just one critical remark. The saints, for all their holiness, were not immune to receiving criticism or, on occasion, giving it, so, when we find ourselves being criticized, we can at least console ourselves that we're in good company.

A partial list of criticized saints includes St. Cyprian, for going into hiding during a time of persecution; Sts. Cyril and Methodius, for insisting on the right of Slavic people to have their culture respected within the Church; St. Turibius of Mongrovejo, for opposing the exploitation of the Indians of South America; St. Anthony Claret, for trying to improve the living conditions of the poor in Cuba; St. Bernardine of Siena, for renewing the faith of tens of thousands of people through his preaching and teaching; St. Columban, for insisting upon Church discipline within religious monasteries; St. Teresa of Avila, for working to restore the original ideals of the Carmelite Order; St. Ludger of Münster, for giving money to the poor instead of spending it on the decorating of churches; and Bl. Damien de Veuster, for his work among the lepers of Hawaii.

[8] John 15:18-19.

St. Cyril of Jerusalem, a great fourth-century bishop, was faulted by his contemporary St. Jerome for supposedly gaining his bishopric through political maneuvering and ambition. In his role as Bishop of Jerusalem, Cyril was caught in the middle of the Arian controversy (involving the heresy of Arianism, which denied the divinity of Christ). Cyril, while upholding the true teaching of the Church, took a moderate and conciliatory course with the heretics, hoping to bring them back to the true Faith. This succeeded only in gaining him criticism and suspicion from both sides.

Another holy bishop of the same name, St. Cyril of Alexandria, gave and received much criticism during his efforts to oppose the later heresy of Nestorianism. Perhaps the most severe comments directed against him, however, were contained in a pointed letter circulated after his death: "Behold, at long last this wicked man is dead. . . . His demise brings great joy to the living, but must terrify the dead; there is danger that they will quickly tire of him and get rid of him. It is imperative to place a very heavy stone on his grave, so that he will not show himself to us again."

St. Basil the Great was no stranger to harsh words and misunderstandings, and he had a difficult time handling the experience. Basil writes (perhaps a bit overdramatically), "My heart was constricted, my tongue was unnerved, my hand grew numb, and I experienced the suffering of an ignoble soul. . . . I was almost driven to misanthropy. Every line of conduct I considered a matter of suspicion, and I believed that the virtue of charity did not exist in human nature, but that it was a specious word which gave some glory to those using it. . . ."

Similarly, St. Peter Damian stated that he endured a "painful confusion" at the jokes and unfavorable stories told at his expense, and St. Albert the Great was no doubt hurt at being nicknamed "Boots the Bishop" for his habit of walking everywhere (instead of traveling by horse) throughout his diocese, but he chose to ignore the insult.

Scripture tells us that those who live as true Christians can expect to be persecuted,[9] so it's not surprising that good deeds are often met with criticism and rejection. Nevertheless, we're called to persevere in our efforts to practice Christian charity. The life of St. Catherine of Siena gives an inspiring example of this. A woman named Tecca suffered so badly from leprosy that no one dared approach her. Upon hearing of this, Catherine hurried to the leper hospital, embraced the neglected woman, and offered to help her. The saint began coming to tend to her needs every morning and evening. Tecca, however, soon became very demanding and unappreciative, and even began taunting her, sarcastically calling her a queen who was too busy to care for a poor subject like her. Catherine's mother insisted that she stop wasting her time helping such a critical and ungrateful soul, but Catherine continued ministering to Tecca until the woman died, and the saint's prayers and good example helped Tecca to die a holy death.

Some saints had to oppose people because of their morally dangerous ideas or actions. This opposition often involved giving criticism — which meant finding the right balance between strong words and Christian compassion. St. Bernard of Clairvaux, in opposing the mistaken ideas of Peter Abelard, had difficulty achieving this balance at first; he referred to Peter's theology as "foolology" and his reasoning as "raving." When Bernard was called to refute Abelard, however, he first spoke to him in private, hoping to spare him a public denunciation of his writings; when this attempt failed, Bernard eventually succeeded in having Abelard's teachings condemned by Rome, but was himself personally kind to the misguided theologian; and this made possible a reconciliation of the two men and an admission of error by Abelard.

On another occasion St. Bernard had to correct the Duke of Aquitaine, a man of fierce pride with a violent temper. Duke

---

[9] See 2 Tim. 3:12.

William had cast out the Bishop of Poitiers from his diocese and, as a result, was excommunicated. The duke thereafter sacrilegiously entered a church where Bernard was presiding at Mass. After the consecration, the saint walked toward the duke and ordered him to repent. Duke William fell to the floor; his men helped him stand upright, but because of the force of Bernard's words, he was unable to remain on his feet. Bernard again ordered him to repent and told him to give the kiss of peace to the deposed bishop and restore his rights. The overmatched duke agreed to do this, and his repentance lasted.

Some of the saints could be quite blunt in pointing out people's failings. St. Anthony of Padua, for instance, was invited by an archbishop to preach at a national council in France. The saint used the opportunity to urge various reforms, and to make sure the message was received, he turned directly to his host and said, "And now I have something to say to you who wear the miter," and he proceeded to point out those faults of the archbishop which were hindering the desired reforms and improvements.

Honesty is said to be the best policy, but that doesn't mean there's never room for tact and discretion, and it was the latter approach that St. Francis de Sales preferred. He tried never to criticize others, and if he heard someone being criticized, he tried to make excuses on that person's behalf. If no excuse was possible, he would simply shrug his shoulders and say, "Human misery, human misery! This is but to remind us that we are men."

St. Francis's point is an obvious one: none of us is free of sin, and therefore none of us is exempt from being criticized. It's very easy for us to forget this, however. As the fourth-century hermit St. Pior noted, "We are too fond of flinging our own faults behind our backs, so that we may fix all our attention on the foibles and failings of others."

Sometimes critics claim to be speaking for the person's own good, but this excuse carried little weight with St. John Climacus.

He once stated, "I have rebuked slanderers, and in self-defense these evildoers claimed to be acting out of love. My answer was, 'If, as you insist, you love that person, then don't make a mockery of him, but pray for him in secret, for this is the kind of love that is acceptable to the Lord. Do not start passing judgment on the offender, Judas was in the company of Christ's disciples and the robber [the Good Thief] was in the company of killers. Yet what a turnabout there was when the decisive moment arrived!' "

Taking criticism, even when well-intentioned, is never easy, but we must be willing to receive it humbly and, if it's valid, to modify our behavior accordingly. If instead we respond angrily or defensively, we may be unknowingly rejecting a message from God or an opportunity for true spiritual growth. Moreover, as St. Philip Neri warns us, "Very often the fault we commit by too great sadness when we are rebuked is greater than the fault which drew on us the rebuke."

Even when criticism is unfair or unwarranted, we shouldn't be too insistent on defending ourselves. Instead, we should strive to imitate the example of Jesus, who, when brought before Pontius Pilate, didn't defend Himself against the accusations of His enemies.[10] This, of course, is a hard thing to do, as the saints themselves realized. St. Augustine, for instance, prayed, "O Lord, deliver me from this lust [or fierce desire] of always vindicating myself."

All things must be evaluated in the light of God's truth — including the praise, and criticism, we receive from other people. St. Gregory the Great, in writing to a friend who was upset over being criticized, said, "Amid the words of flatterers and revilers, we should always turn to our soul, and if we do not find there the good that is said of us, sorrow should arise; and again, if we do not find there the evil that men speak of us, we should break forth into great joy."

[10] See Mark 15:5.

As Christians, we're called to love those who criticize us or treat us unfairly, and as St. Anthony Zaccaria notes, "We should love and feel compassion for those who oppose us, since they harm themselves and do us good. . . ." To speak unkindly of others is sinful. To bear such wrongs patiently helps us grow in grace; and in that sense, we can say our critics are doing us a favor, for they're giving us an opportunity to follow Christ more closely. Being criticized is an unavoidable part of life. With God's help, we can also make it an occasion of grace.

For Further Reflection

"It is a man's duty to do his best to alleviate human enmities by kindly speech, not to excite and aggravate them by the repetition of slanders." — *St. Augustine (Thus, any criticism we make of others should have a serious and worthwhile purpose; otherwise, our speech will worsen a situation rather than improve it.)*

"Be as blind to the faults of your neighbors as possible, trying at least to attribute a good intention to their actions." — *Ven. Solanus Casey*

"To criticize, to destroy, is not difficult; any unskilled laborer knows how to drive his pick into the noble and finely hewn stone of a cathedral. To construct: that is what requires the skill of a master." — *St. Josemaría Escrivá*

Something You Might Try

◆ St. Peter Claver devoted his life to ministering to the physical and spiritual needs of black slaves in South America, and his efforts to secure better treatment for them resulted in bitter criticism from the slave owners. In response, he said, "The humble ass is my model. When he is evilly spoken of, he is dumb. Whatever happens, he never complains, for he is only an ass. So also must be God's servants." It's very difficult for us to remain silent in the face of criticism, but making this effort can be a great act of humility and self-denial — and God always blesses such efforts. If you're honestly attempting to do what God wants of you, remind yourself that any criticism you receive is actually directed toward God, not you (since it's His will you're doing, not your own); and thus, you can remain silent, as it's up to Him to respond if He chooses.

♦ According to St. Josemaría Escrivá, "Whenever you need to criticize, your criticism must seek to be positive, helpful, and constructive. It should never be made behind the back of the person concerned. To act otherwise would be treacherous, sneaky, defamatory, slanderous even, as well as utterly ignoble." Thus, we should make a point of saying only positive things about persons who are absent; if we need to share a criticism or rebuke, we should do so only person to person (and preferably in private). It's also helpful to present our criticism in terms of asking a favor; for instance, instead of saying to a family member, "Why are you always such a slob? Don't you care how hard I have to work to keep this house clean?" you might say, "May I please ask a favor? If you could take these bowls and cups back to the kitchen when you're done with them, that would be a big help to me." People are more likely to respond favorably to this approach, for being asked a favor is less threatening than receiving criticism, and gives them more of a sense of control and security.

Further Reading

Scripture: Sirach 19:9; Sirach 41:22, 24; 1 Peter 3:9.

Classics: St. Thérèse of Lisieux, *The Story of a Soul*; St. Francis de Sales, *An Introduction to the Devout Life*; St. Alphonsus Liguori, *The Practice of the Love of Jesus Christ*.

Contemporary Works: Rudolf Allers, *Self-Improvement*; Charles J. Keating, *Dealing with Difficult People*.

Heavenly Father,
give me the grace to be
gentle in the words I speak to others
and humble in receiving the words they direct at me.
Remind me that You alone are the Source of truth,
that my judgments of others may be wrong,
and their criticisms of me are unimportant
so long as I am trying to please You.

Difficulties in Praying

If we hope for what we do not see, we wait for it with patience.
Likewise the Spirit helps us in our weakness; for we do not
know how to pray as we ought, but the Spirit Himself
intercedes for us with sighs too deep for words.

Romans 8:25-26

True or false: The saints all believed in the importance of praying. True.

True or false: The saints can rightly be considered experts in prayer. True.

True or false: The saints always found prayer to be easy and enjoyable. False.

There were indeed some saints who found it very easy to be absorbed in prayer. It's said, for instance, that once when St. Dominic was praying in church, he didn't even notice when a stone came loose from the ceiling and landed next to him after grazing his ear. When someone asked the sixteenth-century Capuchin friar St. Felix of Cantalice how he managed to pray without being distracted by the hustle and bustle of life, he answered, "All earthly creatures can lift us up to God if we know how to look at them with an eye that is single." One saint who would definitely be considered single-minded in that regard was the young Jesuit

St. Aloysius Gonzaga; when asked by his spiritual director if he experienced distractions at prayer, Aloysius responded, "If I were to sum up all the distractions I have had during the past six months, there wouldn't be enough to fill the time of saying a Hail Mary."

Experiences like these, however, are relatively uncommon, even among the saints. Many of them, at one time or another, found praying to be difficult and tiresome. The great mystic St. Teresa of Avila, for instance, was plagued by distractions (which she likened to wild horses pulling the mind in one direction and then another), and for eighteen years she experienced aridity and restlessness. Describing one period of her life, she writes, "I was more occupied in wishing my hour of prayer were over and in listening whenever the clock struck, than in thinking of things that were good. Again and again, I would rather have done any severe penance that might have been given me than practice recollection as a preliminary to prayer. It is a fact that, either [because of] the intolerable power of the Devil's assaults or because of my own bad habits, I did not at once betake myself to prayer; and whenever I entered the oratory, I used to feel so depressed that I had to summon up all my courage to make myself pray at all."

This is a startling admission from one of the Church's greatest saints — and, quite possibly, a reassurance for the rest of us that our own struggles in prayer needn't be an impediment to spiritual growth and holiness. Moreover, we have the opportunity to learn from the successes, and failures, of those who have gone before us. In this regard, St. Teresa noted that a priest of her acquaintance made more progress in prayer in just four months than she did in seventeen years. She attributed this to his superior preparation in what she considered the three essential foundations for prayer: love of neighbor, detachment from worldly things, and humility.

Teresa's namesake St. Thérèse of Lisieux, also experienced difficulties in praying. After her religious profession, although she felt a deep inner peace, she found it hard to be recollected during community prayer, and praying the Rosary — which she had done since childhood — became burdensome.

St. Bernard of Clairvaux had difficulty praying for a different reason. He once wrote that his life was "overrun everywhere by anxieties, suspicions, and cares. There is scarcely an hour free from the crowd of discordant applicants, and the troubles and cares of their business. I have no power to stop their coming and cannot refuse to see them, and they do not leave me even time to pray."

Examples like these make it readily apparent that prayer isn't always an experience of sweetness and light; sometimes it can be quite burdensome and unsatisfying. Nevertheless, it's an essential part of a true Christian life, and the saints have many helpful things to teach us. In regard to prayer's importance, St. Ephrem reminds us, "Virtues are formed by prayer. Prayer preserves temperance. Prayer suppresses anger, prevents emotions of pride, or envy, and it draws into the soul the Holy Spirit, and raises man to Heaven."

According to St. Bonaventure, if our prayer is to be fruitful, we must be profoundly aware of our ongoing need for God's mercy and protection, truly grateful for the forgiveness of our sins, won for us through Christ's death and Resurrection, and genuinely desirous of spending time in God's presence.

To these basic prerequisites, St. Bernard adds a practical note: "Anyone who wishes to pray must choose not only the right place, but also the right time. A time of leisure is best and most convenient. The deep silence when others are asleep is particularly suitable [although not possible for everyone], for prayer will then be freer and purer."

Different saints have had their preferred methods of prayer. For instance, St. Faustina Kowalska — the Polish nun whose private revelations from Jesus in the 1930s (as recorded in her *Diary*) form the basis of the Divine Mercy devotions — was taught by the Lord to use the Chaplet of Divine Mercy. Overwhelmed by its effective-ness in converting sinners, she wrote, "Never before had I prayed with such inner power."[11]

In the fourteenth century, St. Gregory of Sinai suggested the use of the Jesus prayer: "Lord Jesus Christ, Son of God, have mercy upon me." According to him, "Some of the fathers taught that the prayer should be said in full . . . others advised saying half . . . or to alternate, sometimes saying it in full and sometimes in a shorter form. Yet it is not advisable to pander to laziness by changing the words of the prayer too often, but to persist a certain time as a test of patience."

Patience in prayer is certainly important, but we also need to recognize our physical limitations. St. John Fisher tells us, "Our chief labor in prayer must be to . . . set our hearts on fire with fer-vent love of God, and then to spin our prayer, so long until we have attained unto this end. But when, through weariness of our frail body, we find this fervor grows cold, then we must desist and pray no longer, but then apply ourselves to some other work of virtue."

Sometimes a person having difficulty praying should seek relief in legitimate forms of recreation; St. Teresa of Avila writes, "At such times, the soul must render the body a service for the love of God, so that on many other occasions the body may render ser-vices to the soul. . . . Sweet is His yoke, and it is essential that we should not drag the soul along with us, so to say, but lead it gently, so that it may make the greater progress."

St. Teresa has many other valuable things to say about praying: "Anyone who has not begun to pray, I beg, for the love of the Lord, not to miss so great a blessing. There is no place here for fear, but only desire. For even if a person fails to make progress, or to strive after perfection, so that he may merit the consolations and favors

---

[11] *Diary*, no. 474.

given to the perfect by God, yet he will gradually gain a knowledge of the road to Heaven." Even those who abandon praying after falling into serious sin should not lose heart; St. Teresa states, "I can say what I know by experience — namely, that no one who has begun this practice, however many sins he may commit, should ever forsake it. For it is the means by which we may amend our lives again. . . . If we repent truly and determine not to offend Him, He will resume His former friendship with us and grant us the favors that He granted aforetime, and sometimes many more, if our repentance merits it."

In regard to mental prayer, or silently conversing with God (as opposed to reading Scripture or using formal, or recited, prayers), St. Teresa notes that the Devil, wanting to block our spiritual growth, tries to convince people to avoid mental prayer on the grounds of supposed weakness or sickness. At one point, Teresa herself was deceived in this way, but then she found that the less she worried about her health, the more it improved.

When it comes to mental prayer, is there a "right" way to pray? Not according to St. Jane Frances de Chantal. She writes, "The great method for mental prayer is simply this: that there *is* none when the Holy Spirit has taken charge of the person who is meditating, for then He does with the soul as it pleases Him, and all rules and methods vanish away. In the hands of God the soul must become like clay in the hands of a potter, who from it can form any sort of dish; or, if you like, the soul must become like soft wax receptive to the impression of a seal, or like a blank sheet upon which the Holy Spirit writes His divine will. If, when entering upon prayer, we could make ourselves a mere capacity for receiving the Spirit of God, this would suffice for all method. Prayer must be carried on by grace, and not by deliberate art."

A desire to make our prayer pleasing to God is far more important than the particular means or approach we use. St. Bonaventure warns that half-hearted prayer is no prayer at all, and St.

Bernard asserts, "A person who prays carelessly, and still expects his prayers to be heard, is like unto a man who pours into the mill bad grain, and expects to receive good flour in return." Conscious of our Lord's words that "where your treasure is, there will your heart be also,"[12] St. Caesarius of Arles states, "A person worships whatever captivates his mind during prayer. Whoever in his prayers thinks of public affairs, or the house he is building, worships them rather than God." Thus, it's important to enter into prayer with the right priorities — namely, a desire to please God and to worship Him alone.

Reflecting on the difficulties of remaining focused in prayer, St. Thomas More notes (somewhat facetiously), "Our minds do not go wandering while we address an earthly prince about some important matter or even while we speak to one of his ministers who might hold a position of some influence with his master. So surely it could never happen that our minds should stray even a little while we pray to God — surely not, that is, if we believed with a strong, lively faith that we are truly in the presence of God."

Because prayer is so important and spiritually beneficial, St. Albert the Great advises us, "Banish from your heart the distractions of earth. Turn your eyes to spiritual joys so you may learn at last to rest in the light of the contemplation of God. Indeed, the soul's true life and repose are to abide in God, held fast by love and refreshed by divine consolations."

All of us who love God would certainly agree with each of the points made above, and we would all like to be able to pray wholeheartedly all the time; yet, in spite of our best efforts, distractions never seem very far off. Does this invalidate our prayer? Not according to Ven. Solanus Casey. The holy Capuchin friar wrote, "Do such distractions displease the good God? For myself, I do not think that they do. I would answer, as I have occasionally done

<hr>

[12] Matt. 6:21.

now and then to assure scrupulous souls: No, Jesus is no crank. He knows that we are not angels, but poor sinners."

Further words of reassurance come from St. Jane Frances de Chantal: "So when we pray and have a multitude of distractions like troublesome flies, as long as they displease us and we do what lies in our power to turn from them faithfully, our prayer doesn't stop being good and acceptable to God. We may be sure of this. When we have a sense of our sinfulness at prayer, there is no need to make speeches to our Lord to inform Him. It is better to remain quietly in this state, which speaks to God for us sufficiently. . . . Draw near to God with the greatest simplicity you can, and be certain that the simplest prayer is the best."

In addition to fighting against distractions, almost everyone who prays faithfully will sooner or later undergo a time of spiritual aridity, in which praying seems to be a dry, lifeless experience. Many saints experienced this, some for prolonged periods — numbered not in months, but in years. These sometimes involved severe feelings of doubt, restlessness, and a sense of being abandoned by God. While we ourselves may never undergo overwhelming experiences of spiritual desolation, it's likely we'll gain some personal familiarity with dryness in prayer. In this regard, St. Claude de la Colombière reassures us, "Do not be either astonished or discouraged at the difficulties you find in prayer. Only be constant and submissive, and God will be pleased with you."

Similarly, St. Pio advises us, "Do not be surprised at your distractions and spiritual aridity. This derives partly from the senses and partly from your heart, which is not entirely under your control. But your courage, which God granted you, is irremovable and constantly determined. Therefore, live tranquilly. You must not be anxious, however long this evil lasts."

All the saints agree on the need to persevere when prayer becomes difficult. Giving up accomplishes nothing and may even rob us of spiritual benefits taking place without our awareness.

According to St. Teresa of Avila, "There must be many who have begun [their spiritual journey] some time back and never manage to finish their course, and I believe it is largely because they do not embrace the cross from the beginning that they are distressed and think that they are making no progress. When the understanding ceases to work, they cannot bear it, although perhaps even then the will is increasing in power and putting on new strength without their knowing it." Jesus told us to persist in asking for what we need,[13] and so St. Louis de Montfort advises us, "We ought not to act as many do when praying for some grace: after they have prayed for a long time, perhaps for years, and God has not granted their request, they become discouraged and give up praying, thinking that God does not want to listen to them. Thus they deprive themselves of the benefit of their prayers and offend God, who loves to give and who always answers, in some way or another, prayers that are well said."

The importance of perseverance was emphasized by a great expert in prayer, St. John of the Cross, who tells us, "Never give up prayer, and should you find dryness and difficulty, persevere in it for this very reason: God often desires to see what love your soul has, and love is not tried by ease and satisfaction." Similar advice is given by the holy bishop St. Francis de Sales: "Let us persevere in prayer at all times. For if our Lord seems not to hear us, it is not because He wants to refuse us. Rather, His purpose is to compel us to cry out louder and to make us more conscious of the greatness of His mercy." Lastly, the fifteenth-century mystic Bl. Julian of Norwich offers us these words: "Our prayer brings great joy and gladness to the Lord. He wants it and awaits it. So He says this: 'Pray inwardly, even though you find no joy in it. For it does good, even though you feel nothing, see nothing, yes, even though you think you cannot pray. For when you are dry and empty, sick and

---

[13] See Matt. 7:7-11.

weak, your prayers please me, even though there be little enough to please you. All believing prayer is precious to me.' "

True or false: The saints all believed in the importance of praying. True.

True or false: The saints can rightly be considered experts in prayer. True.

True or false: The saints teach us that, no matter how many difficulties or distractions we face, our sincere efforts to pray are always pleasing to God and spiritually beneficial to us. True.

For Further Reflection

"Since we find it difficult to pray because our souls are hard and dry and devotionless, then let us do as the parched earth does which yawns open and in a manner cries out for the rain. A humble recognition of our need is often more eloquent to the ears of God than many prayers." — *St. Robert Bellarmine*

"Seven characteristics are required in prayers. Prayer should be *faithful,* in accordance with the Scripture: 'Whatever you pray for, believe that you already have it, and it will be yours' (Mark 11:24). Then prayer should be *pure,* after the example of Abraham, who drove the birds away from his sacrifice (Genesis 15:11). Third, it should be *just.* Fourth, it should be *heartfelt,* since 'the heartfelt prayer of a just person works very powerfully' (James 5:16). Fifth, it should be *humble.* Sixth, it should be *fervent* (these last two characteristics you see in the mustard seed). And seventh, it should be *devout.*" — *St. Bernard of Clairvaux*

"If you want faith, pray. If you want hope, pray. If you want charity, pray. If you want poverty [of spirit], pray. If you want obedience, pray. If you want chastity, pray. If you want humility, pray. If you want meekness, pray. If you want fortitude, pray. If you want any virtue, pray." — *Bl. Angela of Foligno*

Something You Might Try

◆ It's sometimes difficult to find time and opportunities for formal prayers, but it's always possible to speak to God silently in our hearts, no matter what we're doing and no matter how we're feeling. St. Alphonsus Liguori suggests, "Acquire the habit of speaking to God as if you were alone with God. Speak with familiarity and confidence as to your dearest and most loving friend. Speak of your life, your plans, your troubles, your joys, your fears. In return, God will speak to you — not that you will hear audible words in your ears, but words that you will clearly understand in your heart."

◆ According to St. Philip Neri, "It is an old custom of the servants of God to have some little prayers ready and to be frequently darting them up to Heaven during the day, lifting their minds to God out of the mire of this world." To act upon this advice, we simply need to choose our favorite short prayer, and try to form the habit of using it (silently) as many times as possible throughout the day. A good suggestion for such a prayer are the simple, powerful words popularized by the Divine Mercy devotion: *Jesus, I trust in You.*

For Further Reading

Scripture: Ecclesiastes 11:4-5; Matthew 6:6-8, Colossians 3:16.

Classics: Lorenzo Scupoli, *Spiritual Combat*; St. Thérèse of Lisieux, *The Story of a Soul*; St. Francis de Sales, *An Introduction to the Devout Life*; Fr. Gabriel of St. Mary Magdalen, O.C.D., *Divine Intimacy*.

Contemporary Works: Archbishop Anthony Bloom, *Beginning to Pray*; Fr. Benedict Groeschel, C.F.R., *Listening at Prayer*; Eugene McCaffrey, *Patterns of Prayer*; Gloria Hutchinson, *Six Ways to Pray*; Rev. Bartholomew O'Brien, *Primer of Prayer*.

O supreme and unapproachable light!
O whole and blessed truth!
How far You are from me,
who am so near to You!
How far are You removed from my vision,
though I am so near to Yours!
Everywhere You are wholly present,
and I see You not.
In You I move, and in You I have my being,
and cannot come to You;
You are within me, and about me,
and I feel You not.

St. Anselm

Distrust in God

*I trust in the Lord; my soul trusts in His word. My soul
waits for the Lord more than sentinels wait for the dawn.*[14]

Psalm 129:5-6

St. Charles Borromeo, the holy sixteenth-century archbishop of
Milan, was known to relax sometimes by playing chess. Once he
was asked what he would do if he were told by an angel that he
would die within the hour. The saint replied that he would continue his game of chess, for — even as a form of relaxation — he
had begun it for the glory of God, and he knew of nothing better
than to be called from this world while performing an action for
that purpose.

This is a wonderful example of trust, which simply means believing in our heavenly Father's ever-present and eternal love for
us, and then acting upon this belief. Most of us, if we learned that
we had but one hour to live, would probably stop whatever we
were doing, and in addition to sharing tearful farewells with our
loved ones, we would seek to offer fervent prayers to God and
hurriedly search for a priest to hear our last confession. These are
all good and proper things, but it would be even better to have

---

[14] Douay-Rheims translation (RSV = Ps. 130:5-6).

lived in such a way that all these wonderful, last-minute actions might be considered unnecessary.

Many people realize the importance of expressing their love and gratitude to their families and friends, so that sudden and unexpected death might not cause these important things to remain unsaid. The same idea applies in a far more important way to our relationship with God: we should always live so as to be ready for the moment when we see Him face-to-face. If we're living in such a manner, we'll be able to show it by placing our trust completely in Him.

A wonderful story about St. Pio of Pietrelcina shows how those who trust in the Lord aren't disappointed. The holy Capuchin served as a chaplain in the Italian army during part of World War I, but he was frequently sent home on leave due to his poor health. On one such occasion, wearing an oversize uniform and feeling cold and miserable, he took a train to Benevento, but then found he had less than half the amount of money needed to buy a bus ticket for the remainder of the journey back to Pietrelcina. Deciding he had no choice but to trust in God, although still feeling great unease, Padre Pio entered the bus and deliberately took a seat in the rear, so that as few people as possible would witness his embarrassment when he confessed his plight to the conductor. After seating himself, he noticed a fashionably dressed man carrying a small new suitcase get on board. This gentleman came all the way to the back and sat next to Padre Pio. The stranger then opened his case, brought out a thermos of steaming hot coffee, and offered a cup to the soldier-priest.

At first Padre Pio refused out of politeness, but his traveling companion insisted, so he gratefully took the offered cup of coffee. It proved to be just what he needed, but the saint couldn't really enjoy it, as he was fearfully watching the conductor steadily make his way toward the back of the bus, checking everyone's ticket. Padre Pio prayed silently and fervently, and decided that he'd beg to be allowed to pay his fare as soon as he reached his destination, but before he could say anything, the conductor turned to him and said, "Soldier, your ticket has already been paid for." Astounded at this, the saint looked suspiciously at the well-dressed passenger seated next to him, but his companion stared straight ahead and said nothing. Upon arriving at Pietrelcina, Padre Pio, convinced that his ticket had been paid for by the man sitting next to him, stepped off the bus and turned to thank his traveling companion, but he wasn't anywhere in sight; he had completely disappeared. It was evident to the holy Capuchin that God had sent his guardian angel in visible form to help him in his moment of need.

Bl. Teresa of Calcutta once said, "Where there is great love, there are always great miracles," and this truth is borne out by a number of stories about the saints, including one about St. Brigid, an abbess in sixth-century Ireland. Once she and her sisters had just eaten the last of their food in the convent, and then learned that seven bishops were on their way to visit them and join them for dinner. Brigid, unlike her sisters, wasn't worried. She told everyone that God would provide, and then she said, "Go ask the hens kindly if we might have an egg or two. See if the cow might be persuaded to give a bit more milk, and ask the trees if they might have more ripe fruit tonight." As the sisters went off on these unlikely errands, Brigid herself went into the kitchen to stir up the fire, and discovered loaves of bread in the oven that hadn't been there earlier; a short time later, her sisters returned with plenty of eggs, milk, apples, and pears.

The Lord provided a similar and equally if not more miraculous meal for St. Dominic and his brothers over six hundred years later. One day the community was completely out of food. Several brothers were sent out to beg, but because they then gave away the few loaves of bread they received to some needier persons, they returned to the monastery empty-handed. When Dominic was informed of this, he blessed God and joyfully ordered the bell to be rung, summoning the brothers to dinner as usual. After the brothers recited grace and sat down, two young men, never before seen in the monastery (and afterward never seen again) entered the dining hall carrying baskets full of bread. They silently placed loaves at the lowest table, and worked their way up to the one where St. Dominic himself was seated. Then they left the room without saying a word. Once again, trust in God — and a generous sharing with the poor — was rewarded.

The saints understood that in their efforts to serve the poor, they were ministering in God's Name, and they knew they could rely upon Him to make their efforts successful. St. Frances Xavier Cabrini once remarked, "I have started houses [for orphans or the poor] with no more than the price of a loaf of bread and prayers, for with Him who comforts me, I can do all things."

In the sixteenth century, St. John of God opened and ran a shelter for the homeless, in spite of many difficulties. He once said, "I work here on borrowed money, a prisoner for the sake of Jesus Christ. And often my debts are so pressing that I dare not go out of the house for fear of being seized by my creditors. Whenever I see so many poor brothers and neighbors of mine suffering beyond their strength and overwhelmed with so many physical or mental ills which I cannot alleviate, then I become exceedingly sorrowful; but I trust in Christ, who knows my heart."

Another expert in serving God's people with very little in the way of material resources was St. John Bosco, the nineteenth-century priest famous for his work with delinquent boys. He established work-homes and schools for boys (and later girls), and was always willing to make additional efforts to help the poor as an expression of his trust in God's providence. Because he was attempting to do so much with so few material resources, many people — whose faith in the Lord's ability to provide didn't match his own — began to doubt the saint's sanity. Several fellow priests, deciding Fr. Bosco would benefit from a temporary visit to the asylum, arranged one day to take him for a "ride in the country." John, having been warned of what was actually afoot, pretended to agree. He was about to step into the carriage when he suddenly "remembered" his manners, and stepped aside so the others could enter first. When they had done so, he slammed the door shut and shouted to the driver, "To the asylum!" — allowing the surprised and bewildered priests to make that journey without him.

This story about St. John Bosco is not only amusing, but it makes an important point: God does not want worries over money and material things to rob us of the joy of life; when we gratefully experience life as something good and enjoy it as a valuable gift, we express our trust in Him and give Him great honor.

The same thing is true when we confidently trust in His mercy and humbly seek the forgiveness of our sins. This was the message given to St. Faustina Kowalska. Jesus said to her, "The graces of my mercy are drawn by means of one vessel only, and that is trust. The more a soul trusts, the more it will receive. Souls that trust boundlessly are a great comfort to me. . . . I pour all the treasures of my graces into them."[15]

Even for the worst of sinners, trust is the key that unlocks God's mercy. According to St. Catherine of Genoa, "When God sees that man distrusts himself, and places his whole confidence in Providence, He immediately stretches forth His holy hand to help him. He stands ever at our side, He knocks, and, if we open to Him, He enters; He drives forth our enemies one after another, and restores to the soul its baptismal robe of innocence; and all this God does in different modes and ways, operating according to the state in which He finds His creature."

The Lord is happy to forgive our sins and help us in our needs, but we have to take the first step of surrendering ourselves to Him, and then use the graces He gives us. As St. Francis de Sales says,

[15] *Diary*, no. 1578.

"The past must be abandoned to God's mercy, the present to our faithfulness, the future to divine providence."

The Devil can be expected to interfere in this process whenever possible, and one of his favorite tactics is to use our concern over the material needs of the present to distract us from our spiritual preparations for the future. As St. Francis of Assisi notes, "By the anxieties and worries of this life Satan tries to dull man's heart and make a dwelling for himself there." The best defense against this attack, of course, is trust. Ven. Solanus Casey states, "In my opinion, there is hardly anything else that the enemy of our soul dreads more than confidence — humble confidence in God. Confidence in God is the very soul of prayer." Those who place their hopes in the Lord are never disappointed, nor are they overcome by the enemy. That's why St. Catherine of Siena advises us, "Be trustful, firmly believing that God always provides for souls who trust in Him. Then the Devil is powerless, because [of] the power of the trust in Him."

Because it's obvious to Christians that they can't meet their own spiritual needs, turning to the Lord for these things comes quite naturally. When it comes to material needs, however, even Christians can get caught up in the trap of self-reliance. According to St. John Baptist de La Salle, "The more you abandon to God the care of all temporal things, the more He will take care to provide for all your wants; but if, on the contrary, you try to supply all your own needs, Providence will allow you to continue to do just that, and then it may very well happen that even necessities will be lacking. God is thus reproving you for your lack of faith and reliance on Him." This doesn't mean, of course, that we shouldn't work hard and make careful plans for the future. We need to fulfill our responsibilities, but in a way that always gives the final word in our lives to God.

We'd like life to be worry-free, at least as much as possible, but the Lord often uses our problems and anxieties to remake us in His image. As St. Francis Xavier tells us, "God in His good Providence allows so many terrors, sorrows, and dangers to be put in our way by our enemy, that He may break down our spirit, give us lowly hearts, and train us to submissiveness of mind and humility, so that we may never in the future feel any trust in our own prudence, but [put our] entire trust in His divine providence." In this same spirit, St. Jane Frances de Chantal reassures us, "Whatever good or evil befalls you, be confident that God will convert it all to your good."

St. Faustina Kowalska writes, "I do not understand how it is possible not to trust in Him who can do all things. With Him, everything; without Him, nothing. He is Lord. He will not allow those who have placed all their trust in Him to be put to shame." According to St. Josemaría Escrivá, "God's ordinary providence is a continual miracle; but He will use extraordinary means when they are required."

Thus, we're never beyond the range of God's care for us, even when we ourselves can't conceive of a solution to our problems. In one way or another, God will provide for our needs. For this reason Padre Pio tells us, "Your soul is in the arms of your divine spouse, like a baby in its mother's arms. You may sleep in peace, therefore, for this heavenly spouse will guide you in the way which is to your greatest advantage."

Worry and fear over the future are endemic in our society, but these things have no legitimate place in the lives of Christians, for God is very concerned for the well-being of His children. St. Louis de Montfort suggests, "Be at peace and trust in divine providence and the Blessed Virgin, and do not seek anything else but to please God and love Him," and St. Robert Bellarmine tells us, "Let your one worry be that you never fall away from His grace and that you try to please Him alone, always and everywhere." If we follow this advice, we will have peace of mind in this life, and unending happiness in the next.

For Further Reflection

"Entrust yourself entirely to God. He is a Father, and a most loving Father at that, who would rather let Heaven and earth collapse than abandon anyone who trusted in Him." — *St. Paul of the Cross*

"Entire conformity and resignation to the divine will is truly a road on which we cannot go wrong, and it is the only road that leads us to taste and enjoy the peace which sensual and earthly men know nothing of." — *St. Philip Neri*

"Christ does not force our will; He only takes what we give Him. But He does not give Himself entirely until He sees that we yield ourselves entirely to Him." — *St. Teresa of Avila*

Something You Might Try

♦ According to St. Julia Billiart, "However severe God's guidance may seem to us at times, it's always the guidance of a Father who is infinitely good, wise, and kind. He leads us to our goal by different paths. And after all . . . let's be honest — isn't it true that we tend to spoil the work of grace in us? So it's to our advantage to experience the withdrawal of grace and abandonment by God. Then we must act as little children do in the dark — clasp the hand of father or mother, and go where we are led." When we have doubts about God's personal care for us, we might think of someone whom we trust completely: a parent, a spouse, a friend or relative, or anyone else; then we might simply remind ourselves that if we can rely upon this fallible, imperfect person, our all-knowing and all-powerful heavenly Father is infinitely more deserving of our trust.

♦ Referring to God's miraculous provision of food for the Israelites during the Exodus from Egypt, St. Pio advises, "We must imitate the people of God when they were in the desert. These people were severely forbidden to gather more manna than they needed for one day. Do not doubt that God will provide for the next day, and all the days of our pilgrimage." Laziness and fear are both to be avoided. Just as the Israelites had to gather the manna they needed, so we must do our part in working and fulfilling our duties; and just as they were to gather only as much as they actually needed, so we're supposed to trust that if we put God first in our lives, He will provide for all our needs.

Further Reading

Scripture: Psalm 23; Psalm 25:1-3; Psalm 37:3; Matthew 6:8-13, 25-34; Luke 16:10; 1 Corinthians 13:7.

Classics: St. Alphonsus Liguori, *The Practice of the Love of Jesus Christ*; Thomas à Kempis, *Imitation of Christ*; Lorenzo Scupoli, *Spiritual Combat*.

Contemporary Works: Joseph Ciarrocchi, *Why Are You Worrying?*; Carolyn Thomas, *Will the Real God Please Stand Up*.

I trust in You, Lord.
I desire to forget myself
and leave my own cares
until I trust You with all,
and nothing worries me.
Give me peace because
in Your mercy I put my hope.

St. Henry de Osso

Eccentricity

*I give You thanks that I am
fearfully, wonderfully made.*[16]

Psalm 138:14

Do people sometimes act as if you're a little strange? Do you feel as if you're rather different from everyone else, or do you perhaps have some very unusual habits or personality quirks? Do you have a reputation for marching to the beat of a different drummer? If so, you might well be considered eccentric — and so it will be re-assuring to know that you're hardly unique. In fact, some of the saints are numbered among your companions. This should be no surprise, for the closer we come to God, the more fully are we alive, and all the unique features and surprises of our character have a chance to come into their own. Revelation 2:17 states that the Lord will give each of His children "a white stone, with a new name written on the stone which no one knows except him who receives it." This stone may be seen as symbolizing our unique character and personality — something in which, assuming we live in a spirit of love, God takes great delight. The Lord is infi-nitely interesting, and He shares this gift with those who seek

---

[16] Douay-Rheims translation (RSV = Ps. 139:14).

Him. Contrary to popular belief, holiness isn't lifeless or boring; the saints comprise some of the most colorful people who ever lived.

As an example of unusual behavior, we might begin with St. Joseph of Cupertino, a seventeenth-century Italian priest. As a young man, Joseph wandered aimlessly about his village with his mouth open all the time — a habit that earned him the nickname "the Gaper" (*Boccaperta* in Italian). He was also known for quite often forgetting to eat. Perhaps his withdrawal into his own world was a defense mechanism learned during his unhappy childhood. At any event, he was eventually accepted by the Franciscans, although even after Ordination, he was known for unusual (indeed, miraculous) activities, such as levitating (literally rising from the ground and flying unaided), having ecstatic experiences (during which it was impossible to awaken him), and going five years without tasting bread or wine. As a result of such highly unorthodox behavior, his superiors forbade him to celebrate public Mass, to walk in processions, and to eat with the rest of the community (a prohibition that lasted thirty-five years).

In the eleventh century, the hermit St. Godric was an extraordinary animal lover. He kept a number of vipers as pets — until their hissing began to distract him during his prayers. St. Francis of Assisi, who is far better known than Godric for his love of all God's creatures, isn't recorded to have experienced this particular difficulty (but then, vipers aren't listed among the animals with whom he interacted). Francis, of course, had his own colorful reputation; one of his contemporaries, Thomas of Celano, wrote, "Sometimes he used to do this: a sweet melody of the spirit bubbling up inside him would become a French tune on the outside; the thread of a divine whisper which his ears heard secretly would break out in a French song of joy. Other times — as I saw with my own eyes — he would pick up a stick from the ground and put it over his left arm, while holding a bow bent with a string in his right hand, drawing it over the stick as if it were a viola, performing all the right movements, and in French would sing about the Lord." As Francis himself said, "The Lord told me what He wanted: He wanted me to be a new fool in the world."

Saints, because of their profound awareness of the temporary nature of this life, are frequently inspired to act in ways that may seem eccentric to persons with a more worldly perspective. St. Rose of Lima definitely had her own way of looking at things. She wanted a religious life, but her parents opposed this idea. Because she feared they might try to arrange a marriage for her, she used to rub her face with pepper so as to produce disfiguring blotches, in the hopes of scaring away potential suitors. On one occasion, someone remarked on the beauty of her hands, so she rubbed them with lime to make them unattractive. (In the process, she also rendered them unusable for the next month; the pain and rawness made it impossible for her to dress herself or to perform other daily duties.)

Sometimes otherwise-normal people become fixated on an unusual idea. This happened to the eighth-century cleric St. Virgil, who — for reasons unknown — began proclaiming that another entire world exists beneath ours, complete with its own sun, moon, and inhabitants. St. Boniface, archbishop of Mainz, was not amused by this fanciful notion and had Virgil censured by the pope. (St. Virgil seems to have gotten the message, for he was soon afterward appointed Bishop of Salzburg.)

Eccentricity may also be expressed by a joyful reaction to what many people would call a misfortune. St. Anthony Grassi was struck by lightning; not only did he survive, but he cheerfully claimed the experience had cured the indigestion that had been plaguing him.

On at least a few occasions, saints have deliberately sought to be known as strange or unusual. The sixth-century monk St. Simon Salus, after living as a hermit for many years, returned to his

hometown and began caring for prostitutes and other social outcasts. So as to understand and share in the contempt they experienced, he deliberately acted in an outrageous manner — giving
him his nickname "Salus" (which means "the crazy"). Simon's example was consciously imitated by St. Basil the Blessed, a sixteenth-century figure honored by the Russian Orthodox Church,
who was known for his care for the destitute. (The famous St. Basil's Church, within the Kremlin in Moscow, is named after him.)

Probably the most unusual of all the saints, however, is a virgin
who lived in the eleventh century. Even her nickname points to
her highly unlikely and surprising character: St. Christina the Astonishing. She suffered a seizure at twenty-two and was assumed to
have died. Her open coffin was carried into church, but during her
funeral Mass, Christina sat up, soared or levitated to the ceiling,
and perched on one of the rafters of the church. The congregation, except for her older sister and the priest, fled in terror and
confusion. According to legend, she stated that she had actually
been dead and had visited Hell, Purgatory, and Heaven before being restored to life; because of her brief experience of perfection in
Heaven, she could no longer abide the smell of sinful humanity
(accounting for her vaulting up to the ceiling). Christina came
down from the church rafters at the command of the priest, but after that, she felt no need to conform to anyone's expectations.
During the remaining fifty-two years of her life, Christina wore
rags, lived by begging, performed extreme acts of penance (such
as handling fire and jumping into icy rivers), prayed while curled
up on the ground, ran about wildly in the streets, and went to extreme lengths to avoid human contact (such as climbing towers
and trees and hiding in ovens). A local count welcomed her to his
castle, patiently accepting her rebukes of his sinfulness and allowing her to live there until his death. After this, Christina spent her
remaining years in a convent (evidently somehow coping with the
sisters who resided there).

The twentieth-century American novelist Flannery O'Connor was once asked, "Why are your characters so bizarre?" She responded, "When you're talking to the deaf, you have to shout." Perhaps God is using some of His children for this same purpose.

For Further Reflection

"For a husband to enter religious life and leave to his wife the care of the children is hardly advisable. Such a life is holy, but it is not practical. If God ever wants such a thing, He will open the way. But for now, bury yourself in God's will and give Him your desires." — *St. Paul of the Cross (It's not good to act on every whim or impulse that comes to us; eccentricity is acceptable, but irresponsibility isn't.)*

"He who marries the spirit of the age is sure to be a widower in the next." — *G. K. Chesterton (Thus, excessive conformity is not a good long-range approach to life.)*

"Democracy cannot survive where there is such uniformity that everyone wears exactly the same intellectual uniform or point of view." — *Archbishop Fulton J. Sheen*

Something You Might Try

◆ As a penance, St. Benedict Joseph Labre used to refrain from washing; and thus, his clothing was infested with vermin. We shouldn't imitate this practice, but we should imitate his response to the criticism he received for it: remaining humble and uncomplaining, without feeling a need to defend or explain himself.

◆ The farther we advance in morality, the more unique our personality becomes, for it is by living in God that we ourselves become most truly ourselves. Therefore, rather than deliberately going out of our way to cultivate an eccentric reputation (which may in fact be little more than a form of pride, or a desire for attention, or a form of rebellion), we should place the focus on God, instead of on ourselves.

Further Reading

Scripture: Ephesians 2:10.

If only I possessed the grace, good Jesus,
to be utterly one with You!
Amidst all the variety of worldly things around me,
the only thing I crave is unity with You.
You are all my needs.
Unite, dear Friend of my heart,
this unique little soul of mine
to Your perfect goodness.
You are all mine;
when shall I be Yours?
Lord Jesus, my Beloved,
be the magnet of my heart;
clasp, press, unite me forever
to Your Sacred Heart.
You have made me for Yourself;
make me one with You.
Absorb this tiny drop of life
into the ocean of goodness whence it came.

St. Francis de Sales

Failure

*We preach Christ crucified, a stumbling block to Jews and
folly to Gentiles, but to those who are called, both Jews and
Greeks, Christ the power of God and the wisdom of God.*

1 Corinthians 1:23-24

Once there was a girl named Catherine who had a very deep and
intimate relationship with the Lord. As a result, she wanted more
than anything else to give her life to God, and she was convinced
this meant becoming a religious sister. She had two important advantages when it came to acting upon this desire: first, her parents
understood and accepted it; and second, her uncle was a priest and
the spiritual director for a nearby convent of Dominican nuns.
With his approval and help, Catherine, while still a teenager, was
allowed to enter the convent as a novice. It seemed her dream had
come true, but then there were unexpected problems — caused,
surprisingly enough, by her deep spirituality.

Catherine firmly intended to follow the rule of her order as
closely as possible, but her rich prayer life and constant spiritual
conversations with the Lord Jesus made it very difficult to focus on
her daily duties. Catherine had a deep awareness of Christ's presence, but this blessing made it hard for her to be aware of what was
happening around her. She seemed to be clumsy in her chores,

absent-minded, and constantly distracted; she even had trouble keeping up with everyone else in community prayer. Sr. Catherine was rebuked again and again, but she never spoke in self-defense. She happily accepted correction as an integral part of what she considered her calling from God.

Then something happened that Catherine considered unthinkable: the community, in consultation with her uncle, concluded that she was a failure at religious life and not meant for such a vocation; because of her apparent dullness and inability to follow conventual discipline, it was deemed best to release her. As soon as Catherine learned of this devastating news, she fell to her knees in fervent prayer, begging the Lord to help her — and her prayers were heard.

The Lord in effect "turned down the volume" of His spiritual gifts to her, allowing her to pay more attention to the world around her. She found it easier to participate in chant and other community prayers and was now able to adhere very closely to the convent's routine. As a result, the other sisters slowly came to recognize and appreciate her many virtues. The decision to send her away was set aside, and eventually Catherine was allowed to make her religious profession.

As time went by, it became known why Sr. Catherine had at first always appeared so distracted: the Lord was granting her many visions and mystical experiences, and carrying on a nearly continuous spiritual conversation with her — experiences that would have made it difficult for anyone to focus on mundane matters. Catherine lived a life of great holiness — so much so that she was canonized within two centuries of her death.

This is the story of the sixteenth-century Dominican St. Catherine de Ricci. It may seem strange that a person who wanted to give herself entirely to God nearly failed at this because she was too spiritual, but the Lord's purposes were served by letting her undergo this trial. Allowing her to be misunderstood and requiring her to make special efforts to fulfill her vocation were part of His plan for her continuing sanctification. God's ways are not our ways, and the unfolding of divine providence doesn't necessarily require that we be successful in everything we do in the Lord's Name. Many of the saints experienced what the world calls "failure," but in remaining faithful to God, they succeeded in the way that matters most.

St. Bernard of Clairvaux was one of the greatest religious figures of the twelfth century, and so it was only natural that when the Latin Kingdom of Jerusalem (established after the first of the Crusades) was besieged by the Muslims, the Pope called upon him to promote a new Crusade to rescue the Christians in the Holy Land. Bernard threw himself heart and soul into this mission, using all his eloquence to persuade men to enlist in such a noble cause, and the Crusade was launched in 1147. However, it failed disastrously, and Bernard himself was blamed because he had seemingly assured its success. The saint defended himself by explaining that it was the Crusaders' own misconduct and sinfulness that caused God to withdraw His blessing from the undertaking, and he asked, "Who could judge the true success or failure? How is it that the rashness of mortals dares to condemn what they cannot understand?" Bernard insisted that somehow God would use this unexpected setback for His own glory — and when this failed to silence his critics, the saint consoled himself that at least it was better for the people to be angry at him than at God.

Great efforts, even when sincerely intended for God's glory, have no guarantee of success, and saints are just as capable of failure as anyone else. This was true for St. Albert the Great, who, roughly one hundred years after Bernard's failure, was entrusted by the Pope with the duty of promoting another Crusade. In spite of Albert's best efforts, the people, perhaps remembering the earlier failures, largely ignored this latest summons to defend Christendom. Albert was one of the most learned men, and greatest scholars, of all history (and is especially remembered as the teacher of St. Thomas Aquinas), but he failed in another important assignment: serving as Bishop of Regensburg. The saint didn't have the temperament for church politics and the imposition of necessary reforms in his diocese; it's to his credit, however, that he himself recognized this and therefore resigned from his position two years later.

Not everyone is capable of coming into a difficult situation and imposing order, but surely those who are present at the very beginning of a great religious undertaking — such as the founding of a religious order — are likely to succeed and to remain true to their original ideals. That, at least, is what we might expect — but this expectation might be mistaken. When he established the Order of Friars Minor, St. Francis of Assisi was quite clear in what he expected of his followers: a willingness to embrace poverty and trust completely in God's care. However, when Francis resigned as the order's superior (so as to devote his final years to prayer and contemplation), his brothers lost sight of their original ideals. Some Franciscan communities began accepting gifts of property, built monasteries and chapter houses, and took on teaching positions at universities and various Church appointments. Soon the order was criticized for hypocritically preaching poverty while many of its members lived quite comfortably.

St. Francis was greatly distressed by these developments, but due to his poor health and his limited official status in his own order, he had little influence on the course of events. He knelt in prayer, begging the Lord to show him how to keep his vision for the order from collapsing. It's said that the Lord gently rebuked him, telling him that He — the Lord God — was the true founder of the order, and the One who would sustain it through the coming centuries. Francis was consoled (and chastened) by this message, and after his death, the order recovered much of its earlier spiritual identity and direction.

Jesus expects us to share our light with others,[17] but that doesn't mean everyone will be open to receiving it — and even saints can fail in this regard. St. Catherine of Siena, for instance, boldly advised kings and popes, and her words were usually taken seriously, but she was unable to bring an end to the Great Western Schism (a division in the Church of the fourteenth century, centering on two rival popes), which occurred shortly before her death. There was also a tragic case involving the suicide of one of her own disciples, a man who despaired of God's mercy (perhaps after falling in love romantically with Catherine).

Similarly, St. Alphonsus Liguori — the Church's greatest moral teacher, and a constant advocate of trusting in divine mercy — failed in his efforts to get a fallen-away Catholic to repent and confess his sins while on his deathbed.

There are times when God's will becomes evident only as a result of apparent failure. Soon after his conversion, St. Ignatius of Loyola — perhaps inspired by the story of St. Francis of Assisi's journey to the Holy Land, where he unsuccessfully attempted to convert the sultan — decided to go to Jerusalem himself and there boldly preach the gospel to the Muslims. When he arrived there in 1523, however, the local Franciscans turned him away, warning him that the sort of evangelization he intended wasn't allowed and would only endanger the Christians living there. Disappointed but undaunted, Ignatius returned to Europe, completed his studies, and was ordained a priest.

Still not abandoning his dream of converting the Muslims, he and his first Jesuit companions went to the Pope in 1538 and offered their services as missionaries to the Holy Land, but the Pope gently vetoed this idea, urging them instead to form a religious order and devote themselves to renewing the Church within Europe — which they did.

[17] See Matt. 5:16.

More Saintly Solutions

Some of the saints devoted their lives to the building up of Christ's Church, only to have their accomplishments largely fade away or disappear after their deaths. This was true of the great bishop St. Augustine. His many teachings and writings have come down to us, but the Church in North Africa, for which he had labored unceasingly, largely withered away after his passing. For instance, at the time of his death, there were about five hundred bishops in the province (with each small city or community having its own); just two decades later, there were fewer than twenty.

Sometimes this sort of failure occurred even before the death of someone who has labored for the gospel, as happened to the eighth-century bishop St. Willibrord. His missionary activities in Germany were bearing great fruit, but Willibrord decided that even greater success in preaching the gospel awaited him in Denmark. In this he was greatly disappointed, for he managed to make only thirty converts and, while attempting to return home, ended up landing on an island whose hostile inhabitants murdered one of his companions.

It's very common for things to work out quite differently from what we had hoped and expected. Even saints have had this experience. A Jesuit missionary to India, Bl. Rudolph Aquaviva, wrote to one of his superiors, "You know how I longed for this mission, and how delighted I was when it was granted me. I have been able to do what I wished for — to bear witness to the Name of Jesus Christ before kings and rulers of this world. And thus to hope for winning the prize of such a death as Scripture calls precious in the sight of the Lord.[18] You may be sure that many desire for us this death. Meantime, while it is deferred, there is no lack of thousands of opportunities of suffering from within and without, so that sometimes I grow weary of life." Rudolph's life as a missionary was

[18] See Ps. 116:15.

harder than he had expected, but his wish for martyrdom was eventually fulfilled.

St. Rose Philippine Duchesne and her sisters didn't face the same degree of danger during their missionary work among American Indians, but their success in preaching the Gospel was quite limited at first. As the saint remarked, "Perhaps God wants His missionary nuns to sanctify themselves on failure."

Other saints who experienced failure include St. Lawrence O'Toole, who was unable to negotiate peace between his Irish countrymen and an invading English army; St. Anthony of Padua, who failed in his efforts to obtain the release of certain prisoners from a local warlord; St. Edmund, King of England, whose army was defeated by Viking invaders and who, after offering himself to the victors in hopes of sparing his people, was tortured and beheaded; St. Adalbert of Prague, who offered sanctuary in his church to an adulteress, only to have a mob break in and kill her; and St. Leonard of Port Maurice, who, in his efforts to preach peace in Corsica, was shouted down by hostile mobs. St. John Vianney, the famous patron of parish priests, almost didn't make it to Ordination. He began his studies for the priesthood at age twenty-five and finished last in a class of two hundred. Not only was he mocked by other students, but he was dismissed from the seminary and forced to find a private tutor.

God doesn't promise us success in this life, even when we're laboring on His behalf. In fact, by telling us to take up our cross each day,[19] Jesus made it very clear that following Him will inevitably involve a certain amount of sacrifice and suffering — often in the form of misunderstanding, persecution, and failure.

As Bl. Henry Suso reminds us, however, "After big storms there follow bright days" — and those who faithfully seek to do God's will in this life, regardless of the results, have the assurance

[19] See Luke 14:26-27.

of succeeding in the most important thing of all: attaining eternal life in Heaven.

For Further Reflection

"Don't be discouraged when you fall. . . . Your becoming discouraged and disheartened after the fall is the work of the enemy. . . . You will not do this, therefore, because the grace of God is always vigilant in coming to your aid." — *St. Pio of Pietrelcina* (*There's no shame in failing, but when we do fail, we must beware of one of Satan's favorite tricks: tempting us to give up entirely.*)

"You haven't failed; you have gained experience. On you go!" — *St. Josemaría Escrivá*

"If I succeed, I bless God; if I do not succeed, I bless God, for then it will be right that I should not succeed." — *St. Elizabeth Ann Seton*

Something You Might Try

◆ According to St. Alphonsus Liguori, "By tribulations we atone for the sins we have committed, much better than by voluntary works of penance." Thus, we can offer up everything we suffer, including our failures, in reparation for our sins. Instead of "wasting" our failures, we should present them to God, not only for His glory, but for our own spiritual benefit.

◆ St. Clare of Assisi tells us, "Gladly endure whatever goes against you, and do not let good fortune lift you up: for these things destroy faith." In other words, we should try to maintain a balanced approach to life, not becoming too elated over success or too depressed over failure. Whenever we have either experience, we might pray, "Lord, help me to see and understand this event in the light of Your unchanging truth."

Further Reading

Scripture: Sirach 24:21; Matthew 25:20-21; Romans 8:18; Philippians 3:11-17.

Classics: St. Thérèse of Lisieux, *The Story of a Soul.*

Contemporary Works: Rudolf Allers, *Self-Improvement*; Rev. Robert DeGrandis, *Failure in Your Life*; Kathleen Fischer and Thomas Hart, *Facing Discouragement.*

Father, sometimes it seems I have
the "Midas touch" in reverse: every
good thing I undertake fails to bear fruit,
every noble dream I pursue turns to ashes,
and every attempt to get ahead leaves me further behind.
I have become accustomed to failure in so many things,
but it's not easy for me to accept.
I want to be successful and respected,
I want to have a sense that I'm making a difference,
and I want to know that I'm doing
worthwhile things in Your name.
Please help me, Father.
Show me the way, make known Your will to me,
and help me to persevere in taking up my cross each day.
I will always believe that my life has a purpose,
and I will never give up my hope that,
in achieving this purpose,
I will find satisfaction and happiness.
Please strengthen me, O Lord,
and fulfill my hope in You.

False Accusations

*Soldiers also asked him, "And we, what shall we do?"
And he said to them, "Rob no one by violence or by
false accusation, and be content with your wages."*

Luke 3:14

Early in the twentieth century, a faithful and devout young pastor
was assigned to a parish near Washington, D.C. The woman who
cleaned his rectory, herself relatively young, felt a strong physical
attraction toward him, and as a result, tried to seduce him. Like
the innocent maiden Susanna in the Old Testament Book of
Daniel,[20] victimized by detraction after refusing to sin, the priest
rejected these advances — and then found himself accused of attempted rape. Even though there was no evidence against the
priest aside from the woman's testimony, his bishop believed this
accusation, removed him from ministry, and forced him to leave
his parish. The slandered priest had to support himself in the secular world, but he remained true to his Catholic Faith and, badly
treated as he was, didn't turn against the Church. Years later his
accuser summoned the bishop and, on her deathbed, confessed the
truth, resulting in the priest's immediate reinstatement.

[20] Dan. 13:1-27.

The scandals that have afflicted the Catholic Church in the United States over the past few years, in which more than three hundred priests have been removed from active ministry as a result of well-founded accusations of sexual misconduct with children and young people, shouldn't blind us to the fact that sometimes the charges leveled against God's servants are nothing more than malicious slander. Jesus called Satan "the father of lies,"[21] so it's no surprise that the Devil and his servants use innuendoes and false accusations in their efforts to prevent the spread of the gospel and hinder the ministry of the Church. After all, Christians forced to defend themselves against serious charges, no matter how untrue and outlandish, have less time and effort for the work of God, and the accusations themselves — if sensational enough — are a good way (from the Devil's perspective) of distracting people from the gospel message. The truth always comes out in the end, but sometimes only after great suffering on the part of the innocent. There are many examples of this in the lives of the saints.

The fourth-century heresy of Arianism denied the divinity of Christ, and due to political and various other considerations, it quickly became powerful and popular, especially in the Eastern Empire. St. Athanasius was the leading figure in opposing Arianism and upholding Church teaching, and as a result, he soon found himself involved in controversy. His opponents resorted to the underhanded but often effective tactic of accusing him of practicing magic, bringing forth a box containing the withered hand of a dead man. This, they claimed, was the hand of the deceased bishop Arsenius, whom Athanasius had allegedly poisoned and whose hand he had then — so they claimed — used in demonic rituals. At a council of bishops held in 335, St. Athanasius presented the supposedly dead bishop, who wore a long-sleeved robe

---

[21] John 8:44.

for the occasion. With a dramatic flourish, Athanasius asked Arsenius to remove and show first one hand, then the other; thereupon the saint said to the assembly, "You see, he has two hands. Where is the third, which I cut off? God has created men with two hands only."

Athanasius' opponents were thwarted for the moment, but they didn't give up. At that same council, they bribed a woman to come forward and profess to have knowledge of sexual immorality on the part of the saint. However, a quick-thinking priest, believing in the holy bishop's innocence, came up to the woman and confronted her: "Do you really accuse me of this crime?" Not realizing the trap that had been laid for her, the woman answered, "Certainly," thus proving that she didn't know Athanasius by sight and discrediting her own testimony.

A similar experience of vindication was granted to St. John of the Cross when a woman publicly accused him of fathering her child. "How old is the baby?" he asked, and upon being told by the mother that her child was a year old and that she herself had lived in that area for many years, the saint happily pointed out that he had come to the town less than a year earlier himself. The woman was shamed into silence, while the bystanders amused themselves at her expense.

On another occasion a sinful woman solicited John while he was staying at an inn and, when he refused her advances, threatened to denounce him. The saint merely responded, "That does not matter to me," and thereupon ignored her. The woman, having expected him to make a scene that she could thereupon turn to her advantage, instead left him alone and went away.

Not all false accusations are handled so quickly and easily. The fourth-century hermit St. Macarius the Elder was wrongly accused of rape by an unmarried woman desperately seeking an explanation for her pregnancy, and the woman's relatives and friends dragged the saint through the streets and beat him. Macarius accepted this treatment without complaining, trusting that God would make the truth known at the time of His choosing. This hope was well founded: when the woman was in labor a few months later, she was unable to deliver her child until she cleared the saint's name. (Thereafter Macarius was so admired for his virtue that he had to escape to the desert to find the solitude he desired.)

A more complicated situation was faced by Bl. Henry Suso when a woman accused him of fathering her child and demanded that he take responsibility for the infant. To Henry's great distress, her charge was widely believed, damaging his reputation and robbing him of his peace of mind. As if that weren't enough, another woman came to him and offered to "solve" the problem by destroying the child, arguing that unless the baby were killed, Henry would be forced to accept and raise the baby as his own. Naturally, Henry rejected this loathsome idea and instead arranged for an upright woman to take care of the baby. His efforts to do the right thing, however, only increased the gossip against him, causing many of his friends to desert him and almost resulting in his expulsion from religious life.

Still another man of God wrongly believed for a time to be guilty of sexual misconduct was Bl. Damien de Veuster. The holy priest of the lepers was accused of violating his vow of celibacy after contracting leprosy himself — for leprosy was widely viewed as a punishment for immorality.

Some accusations can be hard to defend against, and so the experience of vindication can be particularly sweet. Perhaps the most amusing instance of this occurred when St. Arnulf of Metz was publicly accused by a drunk named Noddo of being lustful and accustomed to immoral pleasures. That night, while Noddo was in bed, his pants caught fire (although whether this was divine punishment for lying, the result of the saint's prayers for justice, or mere coincidence, isn't recorded).

A more public form of vindication was granted early in the eleventh century to St. Cunegund, the wife of the emperor St. Henry II. When accused of scandalous behavior, the empress willingly underwent "trial by fire" by successfully walking barefoot on a bed of red-hot coals — much to the delight and relief of her husband.

In the nineteenth century, the religious foundress St. Thérèse Couderc was removed as superior of her own order due to various false allegations, and for thirteen years she was assigned to do the community's hardest manual labor. The saint bore this injustice with patience, and eventually her innocence was recognized and her position restored.

Often saints have chosen to imitate their Master, who remained silent when many false charges were leveled against Him.[22] St. Catherine of Siena, for instance, cared for a number of elderly and neglected persons, including a widow named Andrea, who suffered terribly from breast cancer. Andrea's self-pity eventually turned into hatred for the saint, whom she accused of immoral living. Catherine bore this unjustified reproach without complaint, and when her mother urged her to abandon her care of the woman, she answered, "Dearest Mother, do you expect God to stop showing His daily mercies to sinners because of human ingratitude? Did the Savior refuse to accomplish the salvation of the world when He was on the Cross because of the insults that were hurled at Him? . . . She [Andrea] has been practiced on by the Devil; now perhaps she will be enlightened by the Lord and will see the error of her ways." Catherine's optimistic prophecy came true, in part because Andrea saw her surrounded by a holy light as she continued caring for her. The elderly woman confessed her sins and freely admitted she had been a victim of the Devil's deceptions.

A similar degree of resignation in the face of unjust charges was manifested by St. Pio. As news circulated of his spiritual gifts

[22] See Mark 15:4-5.

and mystical experiences, including the stigmata, some people, whether through ill will or honest misunderstanding, accused him of being a charlatan and an impostor. At Rome's insistence, his superiors conducted a series of investigations, questioning his spiritual children, confining him to a small area of the monastery, and forbidding him to hear confessions, receive visitors, or say Mass in public. It was many years before these restrictions were lifted, but Padre Pio never complained about this treatment. All he ever said regarding these restrictions was, "Let God's will be done."

Other saints victimized by false accusations include St. William of York, a twelfth-century bishop whose election was challenged on the grounds of unchastity; St. Sunniva, a tenth-century virgin accused, with her companions, of stealing cattle; St. Margaret Mary Alacoque, whose claims to have received revelations from Jesus regarding devotion to His Sacred Heart were rejected by others as delusions or deliberate fraud; Bl. Juliana of Mount Cornillon, whose reward for proposing a feast to honor the Most Blessed Sacrament was to be driven out of the convent for supposedly mishandling funds entrusted to her care; St. Vincent de Paul, who was wrongly suspected of theft; and the twentieth-century cardinal Bl. Aloysius Stepinac, falsely accused of war crimes by the Communist government of Yugoslavia.

Witnesses in court are sworn to tell "the truth, the whole truth, and nothing but the truth," but often injustices occur nonetheless. Being falsely accused can be a terrible ordeal, and we're certainly within our rights to defend ourselves as best we can. We must remember, however, that true justice will be found only in the life to come, and our willingness to avoid giving in to the hatred of our accusers plays an important part in preparing us for this new life.

For Further Reflection

"Has So-and-so slandered you? Do not give in to hatred. If you hate the slanderer, you are hating a person and therefore breaking the commandment to love. The evil done with words you are now doing with your deeds. On the other hand, if you keep the commandments, you are helping the other as much as you can to become free from this sin." — *St. Maximus the Confessor*

"If, then, it is said that, because you are of a devout habit, you are a hypocrite, or if having forgiven an injury, you are called a coward, take no heed of such things. They are the judgments of foolish, trifling people. And if you were thus to lose your good name, still you are not justified in forsaking virtue or in turning aside from its path, for this would be to prefer mere foliage to fruit — that is to say, external gain to inward and spiritual good. We should be jealous of our good name, but not idolize it; and as we would not offend the eyes of good men, neither must we wish to please those who are bad." — *St. Francis de Sales (In other words, being falsely accused doesn't give us the right to lash out or respond in sinful ways. Doing so would harm us spiritually, and it might be just the reaction our accusers desire.)*

"The most common sins of the tongue are lying, false testimony and detraction. As to this last, it is a mortal sin to make known a serious fault which is not public, if done with a bad intention or with a notable prejudice to our neighbor's reputation. If the fault revealed be less serious, the sin is only venial." — *St. Ignatius of Loyola (Thus, we need to be very careful in making charges against other people; even if it's not a case of false accusation, our unflattering words can easily lead us into sin.)*

"As they who always speak well of others are loved by all, so he who detracts his neighbor is hateful to all — to God and to men, who, although they take delight in listening to detraction, hate the detractor, and are on their guard against him." — *St. Alphonsus Liguori*

Something You Might Try

◆ According to St. Francis de Sales, "A good reputation is one of the foundations of society, without which we are not only useless, but actually hurtful to the public welfare, and a cause of scandal; therefore, charity demands and humility consents that we should seek and studiously preserve a good name." The holy bishop, however, warns us that a good reputation must not become an end in itself, but only a means of glorifying God. Therefore, he advises, "Let us keep our eyes fixed on our crucified Savior, and go on in His service in simple-hearted confidence, with discretion and prudence. He will watch over our reputation, and if He permits it to be lost, He will restore it tenfold, or else cause us to advance in that blessed humility, one grain of which weighs more than all worldly honors. If we are unjustly blamed, let us calmly oppose the calumny with truth; but if it perseveres, let us persevere in our humility, for we cannot better protect our reputation than by trusting it wholly in the hands of God." Having given us this uplifting advice, the saint then offers a practical consideration: "There are some exceptions — such as horrible and infamous crimes which no one should endure to have imputed to him falsely; and certain persons on whose good reputation the edification of others depends. In such cases, following the opinion of divines [theologians], we must calmly seek reparation of the evil."

◆ We want others to assume the best about us and to interpret our words in the most charitable way possible — and so we must be willing to do this for them. According to St. Ignatius of Loyola, "Every good Christian ought to be more ready to give a favorable interpretation to another's statement than to condemn it. But if he cannot do so, let him ask how the other understands it. And if the latter understands it badly, let the former correct him with love. If that does not suffice, let the Christian try in all suitable ways to bring the other to a correct interpretation so that he may be saved." As Ignatius emphasizes, the spiritual well-being of the other person should be our primary concern in any controversy or dispute. Moreover, if we develop a reputation for being fair and honest in our judgments, not only will we glorify God, but we ourselves are more likely to be given the benefit of the doubt should we be falsely accused.

Further Reading

Scripture: Psalm 37:6; Matthew 5:11-12; Ephesians 4:2; 1 Peter 2:20-21.

Classics: St. Francis de Sales, *An Introduction to the Devout Life;* St. Alphonsus Liguori, *The Practice of the Love of Jesus Christ.*

Lord Christ,
let me not be put to shame.
Christ, I beseech You,
let me not be put to shame.
Christ, come to my aid,
have pity on me,
let me not be put to shame.
Christ, I beseech You,
give me the strength
to suffer what I must for You.

St. Dativus

Family Difficulties

Whoever does the will of God is
my brother, and sister, and mother.

Mark 3:35

In her autobiography, St. Thérèse of Lisieux tells us much about the wonderful upbringing she received. The youngest of five children, Thérèse Martin was greatly influenced by the holy example of her parents and her sisters. Mr. and Mrs. Martin attended Mass almost every day, carefully observed Sunday as a day of complete rest, and enjoyed each other's company while engaged in spiritual reading. They prayed together and taught their daughters to do so. Even after his wife's death (when Thérèse was only five), Mr. Martin was known for his charitable concern for others. Thérèse frequently observed him help the poor and the homeless. Speaking of her father's reaction to a sermon at Mass, Thérèse writes, "As he listened to the eternal truths, he seemed no longer of this earth; his soul was observed in the thought of another world." Thérèse was equally influenced by her sisters, who took over the responsibility of raising her after Mrs. Martin's death. From them she learned the importance of generosity and self-sacrifice.

Most would agree that St. Thérèse of Lisieux was quite fortunate in her experience of family, and there would be equal agreement that many people today do not grow up in such a loving home atmosphere. It has been said that Satan's primary attacks on the Church over the past century have focused on two targets in particular: the priesthood and the family. The scandals experienced by the Church in the United States over the last few years bear painful witness to the former. Equally serious, if not more so, is the terrible extent of familial disintegration in our society — so much so that a family similar to the Martins' would today be considered an oddity. Our divorce rate is very high, there are many single-parent homes, and jobs and other outside activities place limits on family togetherness. Moreover, societal influences tend to undermine parental authority and promote values contrary to the gospel.

Many people are confronted by such a reality, but this isn't part of God's plan. The family is meant to be a "domestic church," with its members encouraging and supporting one another in their efforts to travel the path of holiness. Parents in particular are intended by God to raise their children in the ways of truth and righteousness. As Jesus warned, however, quite often families are divided because of Him,[23] and this was often the experience of the saints. For every St. Thérèse of Lisieux who knew the tender love of a father, there's also a St. Martin de Porres, whose father abandoned him and the rest of the family, or a St. Dymphna, executed by her own pagan father for refusing to compromise her Christian beliefs. Many of the saints achieved holiness not because of, but in spite of, the efforts of their families, and their example can inspire those of us who face similar struggles.

Living as part of the family of God may mean opposing a member of our earthly family — often at terrible cost. For instance, the ninth-century martyrs Sts. Flora and Mary were denounced as Christians by Flora's Muslim brother, and both were beheaded.

[23] See Luke 12:52-53.

A similar price was paid by St. Hermenegild, one of two sons of Leovigild, a barbarian king in sixth-century Spain. Leovigild was an adherent of Arianism, the heretical teaching that denied the divinity of Jesus, and he raised his sons in this mistaken belief. As a young man, Hermenegild was converted to Catholicism by his new wife and by St. Leander, the archbishop of Seville. A furious Leovigild ordered his son to resign his princely authority. Hermenegild refused and for a time even went into revolt against his father, but eventually the two were reconciled, and the issue seemed to be resolved.

Leovigild's second wife, however, managed to turn the king against his son. Hermenegild was imprisoned at his father's orders, but his freedom was offered to him if only he would renounce Catholicism and accept Arianism. The saint, of course, refused to do this. On Easter, Leovigild sent an Arian bishop into his son's cell, promising to release and reward him if he'd accept Communion from the Arian. When Hermenegild again refused, his father went into such an uncontrollable rage that he ordered his son's immediate execution. St. Hermenegild thus died as a martyr of the Eucharist, murdered at the command of his own father.

Our loved ones might turn against us because of our Faith, but rejection might occur for other reasons as well. St. Germaine of Pibrac was slightly deformed when born, and in poor health; her mother — the one person in her family who truly seemed to have loved her — died when Germaine was an infant. Her new stepmother, and the stepmother's children, treated Germaine cruelly, and her father ignored her plight; the saint suffered many physical difficulties and expressions of contempt until her death at the age of twenty-two.

Perhaps an even sadder case was that of Bl. Margaret of Castello, who was born blind and severely deformed. Her embarrassed parents tried to ignore her until age six, then actually had her walled up in the alcove of a church for a number of years. Later they took her to a pilgrimage site and prayed that she would be cured; when this didn't happen, they abandoned her.

Rejection of a different sort was experienced by St. Margaret of Cortona, who ran away from home as a teenager and lived in sin with her lover, bearing him a son. When her consort was murdered, however, Margaret underwent a conversion; she repented of her sins, but when she returned home with her little boy, her father refused to forgive her or allow her and her son into his house. Margaret, almost in despair, sought assistance from the Franciscans, who generously cared for her and her child and helped her discover and respond to her calling from God.

Parents and family members are supposed to support and assist young people in their efforts to answer God's call (even if that response is quite delayed, as in St. Margaret's case), but the reality is often quite different. St. Francis Xavier Bianchi, the virgin Bl. Diana d'Andalo, St. Hypatius, and St. Mary Frances of Naples all experienced great opposition from their parents (especially fathers) when they announced their religious vocations. St. Leonard of Port Maurice was disowned by a wealthy uncle for choosing a religious vocation rather than becoming a physician, and in the seventh century, when St. Amand went to a monastery at age twenty, his father threatened to disinherit him. To this Amand replied, "Christ is my only inheritance."

Grown children have often brought much heartache to their saintly parents. For instance, the married son of St. Bridget of Sweden had an affair with Queen Joanna of Spain, causing his mother considerable shame and anguish — and, of course, grave concern for the state of his soul. Similar distress was experienced by St. Elizabeth Ann Seton, St. Clotilda, St. Matilda, and, of course, St. Monica. Monica at least had the joy of seeing her son Augustine undergo a profound religious conversion shortly before her death. She died very peacefully, knowing her example and prayers played a major role in the conversion of her husband, her mother-in-law, and her son.

It's a wonderful thing when righteous parents help irreligious children come to know and love God, but sometimes it works the other way around. A dramatic example of this occurred in the lives of the sixth-century hermits Sts. Gundleus and Gwladys. According to legend, Gundleus was a Welsh chieftain who desired to marry a young woman named Gwladys. When her father refused, Gundleus kidnaped her and made her his bride. (The legend even states that King Arthur helped them escape from Gwladys's pursuing father, although afterward he had to be dissuaded from taking Gwladys for his own bride.) The happy couple thereupon devoted themselves to making other people unhappy, practicing banditry and various forms of violence and criminal behavior. Many years later, it was their son, St. Cadoc, who finally convinced them to repent and to follow a religious way of life together; later the two penitents separated and spent the rest of their lives performing penance as hermits.

When "Heaven's family album" is made available for everyone to see on Judgment Day, there will surely be many fascinating and amazing images and stories. In the meantime, we're called to do our best to make our families on earth a reflection of the joy and peace that awaits us in Heaven. This may often be difficult, and sometimes even impossible, but the Lord will surely bless our attempts to help our family members, and will certainly hear our prayers on their behalf. As Ven. Solanus Casey said, "How merciful is the good God in making us dependent on one another." We need our families, and our efforts to be there for them can be a sign and source of God's grace.

For Further Reflection

"In our own time, in a world often alien and even hostile to faith, believing families are of primary importance as centers of living, radiant faith. For this reason the Second Vatican Council, using an ancient expression, calls the family the *Ecclesia domestica* ["domestic church"]. It is in the bosom of the family that parents are bound by word and example . . . [to be] the first heralds of the Faith with regard to their children. They should encourage them in the vocation which is proper to each child, fostering with special care any religious vocation." — *Catechism of the Catholic Church, par. 1656*

"As with a general whose troops are so well organized on the front that the enemy cannot find a place to penetrate for an attack, so it is with husband and wife: when the concerns of everyone in the house are the same, harmony reigns in the family, but if not, the entire household is easily broken up and destroyed." — *St. John Chrysostom*

"Let married people remain on their cross of obedience, which is in marriage. It is the best and most practical cross [for] them and one of the most demanding, in that there is almost continual activity — and occasions for suffering are more frequent than in any other state. Do not desire, therefore, to descend from this cross under any pretext whatever. Since God has placed you there, remain there always." — *St. Francis de Sales*

Something You Might Try

♦ According to St. Francis de Sales, "Among all those who are included under the title of neighbor, there are none who deserve it more, in one sense, than those of our own household. They are nearest of all to us, living under the same roof and eating the same bread. Therefore they ought to be one of the principal objects of our love, and we should practice in regard to them all the acts of a true charity, which ought to be founded not upon flesh and blood, or upon their good qualities, but altogether upon God." In other words, we must relate to our family members not on the basis of our own strength or their loving reasonableness, but through divine grace. This means we must set a good example for them when it comes to practicing the Faith, even if that example doesn't seem to be having an effect. It also means that if members of our family reject us, we must not reject them; instead of responding to them harshly, we must remain peaceful and forgiving, while keeping them always in our prayers.

◆ The great artist Michelangelo carved his masterpiece statue of David from a stone that had been rejected by many other great artists of the day; he was able to see something within it that they missed. In the same way, being rejected by our loved ones, especially our families, because of our Faith, is a frightening prospect, but those who have faith are able to look beyond surface appearances, and recognize that such a great sacrifice will help us grow in grace and gain us everlasting membership in God's family. Moreover, we can — if we choose — offer the pain of rejection as a prayer on behalf of the very people who rejected us.

Further Reading

Scripture: Psalm 133:1; Matthew 10:34-36; Matthew 12:46-50; Mark 3:21.

Classics: St. Alphonsus Liguori, *The Glories of Mary* and *The Practice of the Love of Jesus Christ*.

Contemporary Works: Marilyn Spaw Krock, *Building a Family;* Dan A. Myers, M.D., *Golden Rules for Parenting;* Patricia McLaughlin, *Rooted in Jesus*.

☞

Dear Jesus,
I'm willing to follow You
no matter what it costs me.

I don't say these words lightly,
because discipleship is costing me a great deal —
especially my relationship with
some of the people I love most.
They don't understand, Lord;
they can't seem to realize why it's so important
that I place my life entirely in Your hands.
"A little bit of religion, yes, but don't overdo it" —
or "What's the matter? You can't cope with your problems,
so you're trying to escape into all this religious stuff?"
They say these and similar things to me,
not even beginning to see what the truth is:
I need You. I need You, Lord,
even more than the people who are dearest to me,
the people to whom I owe so much.
I love them, but I love You more.
Out of love for You,
I'm willing to embrace this cross —
this painful, sorrowful cross —
and follow in Your footsteps.
Please help me, Lord;
above all, please help my family.
Enlighten them, and show them Your truth.
I forgive them for all the pain
and hurt they've caused me,
whether intentional or not,
and I ask You to forgive them, too, Lord.
May my efforts to serve You be pleasing in Your sight,
and — through the workings of Your grace —
may they one day assist in the conversion of my family members.
O Lord Jesus, I claim You as my Brother and Mary as my Mother,
and I pray with all my soul that
my loved ones may one day do this, too.

Forgetfulness

Bless the Lord, O my soul,
and forget not all His benefits.

Psalm 103:2

Bring any ten people together, and at least nine of them will prob-ably confess to sharing the same problem: a poor memory. We tend to forget things: where we put a certain item, the punch line of a joke, the reason we came into a particular room, what we were going to say to someone when we saw him or her, an important job that we needed to do at a certain time, and so forth. Our memories tend to become weaker as we grow older, but that doesn't mean they were anywhere near perfect at a younger age. Almost every one of us forgets things, sometimes out of laziness or carelessness, but quite often through no real fault of our own. (Chalk it up as one more negative result of Original Sin.) Some of the saints had this same problem; others had excellent memories. In either case, it makes sense to seek their assistance.

As everyone knows, St. Anthony of Padua is the saint to turn to when you're trying to find a misplaced object. (A prayer for this purpose is given at the end of the chapter.) Perhaps this is because things have a way of turning up for those who trust in God; and, in fact, Anthony discovered his own vocation almost by accident.

Early in the thirteenth century, when young Anthony saw the bodies of the first Franciscans who were martyred for the Faith, he conceived an intense desire to become a missionary himself and, he hoped, to die as a martyr. Anthony joined the Franciscans, and after Ordination, preached for a time to the Muslims of North Africa. A serious illness forced him to return to Europe, and while recuperating, he attended an Ordination ceremony. It turned out that, in all the preparations for the ceremony, it had been forgotten to assign someone to preach the homily. At the last minute, Anthony was asked to preach. Although hesitant, he humbly obeyed, and something wonderful happened. The saint's years of prayer, Scripture study, and poverty allowed the Holy Spirit to speak through him in a powerful and compelling way. Anthony's unprepared sermon was a sensation, and in this manner his true calling was discerned; he spent the remaining nine years of his short life preaching and upholding the teachings of the Church (and in so doing, he was no doubt aided by his own powerful memory).

Another renowned Franciscan preacher was Bl. Bernardino of Feltre — although his initial attempt at preaching unfolded in a different manner from St. Anthony's. Bernardino carefully prepared for his first sermon, but when he went to the pulpit, he panicked and forgot everything he was going to say. He did, however, remember events from the life of his namesake, St. Bernardine of Siena (whose feast it was), and he began speaking very naturally and effectively. Bernardino's first sermon was a success (and from that time on, he prepared himself for preaching, not with preparation and memory, but with prayer).

Other saints were also known for having excellent memories, including the seventeenth-century priest St. Peter Fourier, and the nineteenth-century virgin and religious St. Mary di Rosa — both of whom found the ability to memorize facts easily to be of major assistance in their extensive educations.

Bl. John Dominici, however, was notably lacking in his education, but his unusually good memory helped him overcome this handicap in his successful attempt to join the Dominican Order. Perhaps this is why he felt sorry for the fifteen-year-old St. Antoninus, who in 1404 asked his permission to join the order. John believed the youth was too frail for the Dominican lifestyle, but not wanting to refuse him outright, told Antoninus his request would be considered once he had memorized the *Decretal of Gratian* (the earliest compilation of canon law). To John's surprise, young Antoninus returned in less than a year, having memorized the entire work. The impressed Dominican promptly accepted the youth into the order.

In the sixteenth century, the Jesuit missionary priest Bl. Joseph de Anchieta was held hostage by a South American Indian tribe. To occupy his mind during his captivity, he composed a poem of five thousand verses, committing it to memory for several months until he was able to write it down after his release.

When it comes to vast knowledge and learning, however, few saints can compare with St. Albert the Great, the thirteenth-century bishop, scholar, and instructor of St. Thomas Aquinas. Known as the "Universal Teacher," Albert was an expert in theology, biblical studies, logic, rhetoric, ethics, mathematics, physics, astronomy, chemistry, biology, geography, geology, and botany. (One would need a good memory just to recall all the subjects in which the saint was proficient.) Albert resigned from his office as Bishop of Regensburg after two years, for he felt he had more to offer the Church as a teacher. He went to the University of Cologne as an instructor; however, during a lecture in 1278, when he was seventy-two years old, Albert's memory suddenly failed him, and this condition only worsened over the last two years of his life. Not even saints are immune to the problems of old age.

While we can feel sorry for a brilliant scholar like St. Albert who eventually lost his memory, we can probably relate more easily to those saints who never had great memories to begin with. Among them are St. Thomas of Villanova, a sixteenth-century Spanish bishop who suffered from a bad case of absentmindedness, and the fifth-century bishop St. Vincent of Lerins, who wrote a famous summary of the teachings of the Church Fathers called the *Commonitorium* — not so much for scholarly purposes, but to help himself remember important things he had learned in his reading, lest they fall prey to his own bad memory. The seventeenth-century priest St. Joseph of Cupertino suffered from a particularly bad case of absentmindedness; as a young man, he often failed to eat his meals, and when this was pointed out to him, he explained, "I forgot."

An Irish abbot named St. Colman once suffered from memory loss for a very specific reason: legend states that God caused him to lose his memory temporarily as punishment for excessive pride in his intellectual abilities (thus, in this case, "pride goeth before forgetfulness"). The Franciscan friar St. Peter of Alcantara was also known to be absentminded.

Perhaps the most extreme example of forgetfulness, however, comes from the life of the fifth-century Egyptian monk St. John, nicknamed "The Dwarf." He was so absentminded that he frequently forgot what he was doing. On one occasion, someone came to the door to borrow some tools. John went to get them, but on the way, he forgot what he was going to do and had to return to the door to ask the man for a reminder. That might not strike us as unusual, but John had to go through this process three times before he managed to complete the errand.

There's at least one recorded case of a saint suffering unpleasant consequences as a result of someone else's bad memory. The English priest and martyr St. Henry Morse was ministering in secret to the persecuted Catholics of England in the mid-seventeenth century. He was eventually arrested, imprisoned, and sentenced to death, and the cause of his capture by the authorities was a loss of memory on the part of a guide who was taking him to a safe house.

More fortunate was the experience of the abbot and missionary St. Columba over a thousand years earlier. Someone asked him to bless a sword, and the saint absentmindedly did so. Then, realizing what he had done, Columba amended his blessing, placing a restriction upon the sword: it would be useful, the saint declared, only for cutting bread and cheese, and so long as it was used for such peaceable purposes, it would never grow dull.

Sometimes forgetfulness actually serves its purpose in our relationship with God. In general, we might say that we should always remember the Lord's blessings; we should remember our sins until they're forgiven by God, and then forget them; and we should always strive to forget the sins committed against us.

This last point is illustrated by a story involving not a saint (indeed, not even a Catholic), but someone who is rightly esteemed by many people, Americans in particular: Clara Barton, who founded the American Red Cross and was famed for her nursing efforts during the U.S. Civil War. She made a point of not holding grudges against people. A friend of hers, who evidently forgot this fact, spoke of someone who had cruelly hurt Clara some years earlier, but Clara seemed to have forgotten the incident. When the friend asked in surprise, "Don't you remember the wrong that was done to you?" the great humanitarian answered calmly but firmly, "No, I distinctly remember forgetting that." There are indeed times when a "poor memory" is a blessing, for we can please God by choosing to forget certain things.

For Further Reflection

"Indeed, I have been amazed and continue to be amazed at the lack of perception and the callousness of those who were once connected with me, both my friends and my relatives. They have all completely forgotten about my unhappy state, and do not care to know where I am, whether I am alive or dead." — *St. Martin I (It's always an act of Christian charity to remember our loved ones, especially in their times of need.)*

The eighteenth-century former slave trader John Newton, who wrote the famous hymn "Amazing Grace" after his conversion to Christianity, suffered from a bad memory throughout his life. In his final years, a friend asked him whether he still had this problem. "Yes, I do," Newton replied, "but I remember two things: I am a great sinner, and I have a great Savior; and I don't suppose an old slave trader needs to remember much more than that."

"A retentive memory may be a good thing, but the ability to forget is the true token of greatness." — *Elbert Hubbard*

Something You Might Try

♦ When it comes to remembering, prayer is always helpful, especially when you're about to memorize something or learn something new ("Dear Lord, please help me to learn this material to the best of my ability"; "Dear Mother Mary, please help me recall what I need to know at the right moment"). Not only does prayer draw God's blessing upon your mental endeavors; a secondary bonus is that the act of praying can help calm your spirit and focus your mind (allowing it to act that much more effectively). For instance, if you're in a situation where you can't write a note to yourself as a reminder to do something later on, you can entrust the situation to your guardian angel through a simple prayer (e.g., "Dear angel of God, please remind me to make this phone call before four o'clock"). You might also pray for the assistance of saints known for their great memories — or even of those known for their forgetfulness. (Not only will the latter group understand and sympathize with you in a special way; their state of perfection in Heaven means there's no chance of their forgetting to respond.)

◆ When asked the secret of his great memory, Abraham Lincoln answered, "When I read aloud, two senses catch the idea: first I see what I read; second I hear it, and therefore I can remember it better." Lincoln's idea is a good one. Try it the next time you need to memorize something (and if possible, put the words to music or make mental pictures of what you're trying to remember); the more triggers, or associations, we give our brains, the easier it will be for them to recall the desired information.

Further Reading

Scripture: Proverbs 10:7; Isaiah 49:15; Luke 2:51; James 1:22-25.

Receive, Lord,
all my liberty, my memory,
my understanding, and my whole will.
You have given me all that I have, all that I am,
and I surrender all to Your divine will,
that You may dispose of me.
Give only Your love and Your grace.
With this I am rich enough,
and I have no more to ask.

St. Ignatius of Loyola

A Prayer to St. Anthony of Padua
(for the restoration of things lost or stolen)

Blessed St. Anthony,
the grace of God has made you a powerful
advocate in all necessities and the patron
for the restoration of things lost or stolen.

*To you I turn today with childlike
love and heartfelt confidence.
How many people you have miraculously
aided in the recovery of what was lost!
You were the counselor of the erring,
the comforter of the afflicted, the healer of the sick,
the raiser of the dead, the deliverer of the captive,
the refuge of the afflicted.
To you I hasten, blessed St. Anthony.
Help me in my present concern
(mention your request).*

*I commend what I have lost to your care
in the secure hope that you will restore it to me
if this be to the greater glory of God
and to my own spiritual benefit.
Obtain also for me an active faith,
peace of mind, sincere love for others,
and an ardent desire for eternal life. Amen.*

Gambling

The lot is cast into the lap,
but the decision is wholly from the Lord.
Proverbs 16:33

One day a family was driving past a dog-racing track, and the young son asked what it was. The father answered him, "That's where people go to race dogs." The boy thought about it for a moment, then said, "I bet the dogs always win."

Although, in one sense, the boy misunderstood the situation, in another way he understood it very well. It's hard for gamblers to win; most individuals end up farther behind than when they started. Certainly society as a whole seems to lose from gambling; money and time that could be spent or used for more valuable things disappears very easily — usually with little to show for it. It's estimated that well over four hundred billion dollars is gambled each year in the United States on dog races, on horse races, on lotteries, in casinos, and in other legal forms of betting (and this doesn't count the many billions of dollars involved in *illegal* gambling).

By contrast, money given to churches and religious organizations is but a small fraction of this amount. What does this say about our values as a society?

It's certainly true that gambling can have a legitimate aspect (for indeed, Catholic churches are famous for conducting Bingo and Vegas Nights); a responsible degree of wagering can be a worthwhile fundraiser and an acceptable form of entertainment. The problem, of course, arises when people let gambling — or any other legitimate pleasure or entertainment — interfere with their duties or come to play too great a role in their lives. As with the use of alcohol, gambling can soon get out of hand and even become addictive, and this type of problem definitely has moral and religious overtones. An English proverb says, "The best throw of the dice is to throw them away" — and in light of the harm gambling can cause to one's career, family life, and other relationships, such an approach is often the wisest one.

There aren't many examples from the lives of the saints that address this issue, although enough exist to suggest a need for great prudence and restraint when gambling is involved. St. Augustine stated very simply and bluntly, "The Devil invented gambling," and in one of his homilies, St. Basil the Great told his people, "If I let you go, and if I dismiss this assembly, some will run to the dice, where they will find bad language, sad quarrels, and the pangs of avarice. There stands the Devil, inflaming the fury of the players with the dotted bones, transporting the same sums of money from one side of the table to the other, now exalting one with victory and throwing the other to despair, now swelling the first with boasting and covering his rival with confusion."

The sixteenth-century priest St. Cajetan took the unusual step of opening several pawnshops in the city of Naples — not to facilitate gambling, however, but to assist persons in temporary financial trouble. This approach to Christian charity was also followed more than a hundred years later by another Italian priest, St. Francis di Girolamo.

Pawnshops evidently have their place, but few of the saints approved of gambling itself. The great French king St. Louis IX was strenuously opposed to wagering; when he heard that his brother and a member of his court were playing a game of chance, Louis climbed out of his sickbed and, with faltering steps, went to their apartment. The king rebuked the two gamblers sharply and threw their dice and part of their money out the window.

Only a few stories are recorded of saints who, before their conversion, were involved in gambling, none of them edifying. St. John of God was a Portuguese mercenary soldier, and like many soldiers throughout history, he spent his off-duty hours drinking and wagering. This continued until his conversion at the age of forty. Once he gave his life to God and devoted himself to the care of the poor and the ill, he had neither the time nor the inclination for his earlier activities.

A similar story can be told of St. Camillus de Lellis. He was also a mercenary soldier, and he had an even greater addiction to gambling. In 1574, he managed to lose everything — his savings, his military arms and equipment, and even most of his clothing. Being reduced to poverty caused him to remember a vow he had once made to join the Franciscans. He began working for them as a day laborer, and upon hearing one of them give a moving exhortation, he resolved to change his life completely. Like St. John of God, Camillus spent the remainder of his life caring for the sick. (Perhaps the two former gamblers realized that Christ's promise in Matthew 25:40 — "Whatever you did for one of the least of these brothers of mine, you did for me" — provided them, for the first time in their lives, with a can't-miss proposition of immense value.)

Another reformed gambler was the thirteenth-century hermit Bl. Torello. After his father's death, Torello fell in with the wrong crowd and gave himself up to a dissolute lifestyle. He was wagering with some friends one day when a cock flew out of a hen roost, perched on his arm, and crowed three times. Amazed (and perhaps reminded of the cock that crowed three times after St. Peter's denial of Jesus), Torello was convinced he had received a warning from God. He repented, gave up gambling, and thereafter lived as a hermit.

To turn from the ways of the world to the ways of God always guarantees spiritual happiness — and occasionally even material success. When St. Bernardine of Siena preached against games of chance, a maker of playing cards suffered a serious decline in business. He complained to the saint, who suggested that he instead manufacture medallions with the symbol *IHS* (the first three letters of the Name of Christ in Greek). When the man did so, he experienced much greater financial success than before.

Similar results today, of course, cannot be guaranteed, but Jesus does promise that all who forsake the values of this world by placing their trust in Him will never have cause to regret their choice.

For Further Reflection

"Games of chance (card games, etc.) or wagers are not in themselves contrary to justice. They become morally unacceptable when they deprive someone of what is necessary to provide for his needs and those of others. The passion for gambling risks becoming an enslavement. Unfair wagers and cheating at games constitute grave matter, unless the damage inflicted is so slight that the one who suffers it cannot reasonably consider it significant." — *Catechism of the Catholic Church, par. 2413*

"Dice, cards, and similar games, in which success depends mainly on chance, are not only dangerous amusements, like dancing, but actually and naturally bad and blamable. . . . Do you ask where the great harm is? The winner in such games does not win on his deserts, but according to chance and the luck that often falls to those who have exercised neither skill nor industry; and this is contrary to reason." — *St. Francis de Sales*

"Bets at the first were fool-traps where the wise / Like spiders, lay in ambush for the flies." — *John Dryden*

Something You Might Try

◆ St. Francis de Sales notes that gamblers are often disturbed, edgy, and melancholy — and these are hardly desirable traits. If you enjoy frequent gambling, ask yourself whether it makes you more relaxed or more irritable or depressed. An honest answer would seem to point to the latter state, at least much of the time. Shouldn't that tell you something? The Lord doesn't want you to devote time and money to things such as gambling, which keep you from fulfilling your duties to Him and to your family. In prayer, ask God to take away your desire to gamble, or to replace it with an even stronger desire (perhaps involving an activity you can share with your family).

◆ Consider contacting Gamblers Anonymous if you need help with this problem. Also, Gam-Anon is an organization for family members of problem gamblers.

Further Reading

Scripture: Proverbs 1:10-15; John 19:23-24.

Classics: St. Francis de Sales, *An Introduction to the Devout Life*.

Contemporary Works: Thomas M. Santa, *The Addiction of Gambling*.

⌒

Father of all,
please help me to overcome
my problems with gambling.
I thought the odds were with me,
but I begin to see now that there is

never any future in acting irresponsibly
and in a way that contradicts Your will.
Forgive me, and help all those whom
I've hurt or disappointed to forgive me.
Keep me from losing the things that matter:
faith, love, joy, health, dignity,
friendship, self-worth, life, and grace.
May the allurements of this world never
again ensnare me, and may I never again
be deceived by the desire for false
excitement and easy and instant wealth.
Let me trust only in Your promise of eternal life,
so that all my choices and actions
may be pleasing to You.

Greed

Do not lay up for yourselves treasures on earth, where moth
and rust consume and where thieves break in and steal, but
lay up for yourselves treasures in Heaven, where neither moth
nor rust consumes and where thieves do not break in and steal.
For where your treasure is, there will your heart be also.

Matthew 6:19-21

Some of the unsung heroes of Church history aren't the saints themselves, but those who lived and worked with them, and assisted them in their efforts to become holy — even if they didn't fully understand what holiness required. Saints, of course, live by values quite different from those of the world, and at times this can cause considerable frustration or bewilderment for their associates. A good example of this comes to us from the life of St. Robert Bellarmine and his faithful but anxious servant Peter Guidotti.

In 1599, St. Robert was appointed a cardinal, a position involving (then as now) a great deal of influence and prestige. Many ambitious churchmen have desired such an honor. Robert, who hadn't nursed such a desire for personal gain, viewed this advancement as a further opportunity to serve God and His people. Because cardinals frequently handled great sums of money in responding to the many requests they received for assistance, Robert put Peter in charge of his finances — which, as Peter soon discovered, meant almost exclusively giving away money to the needy.

Robert wasn't concerned where the money came from, but insisted that it be used in a charitable way. Peter, although he agreed in principle that the poor should be rendered aid, was constantly worried that the financial well might run dry. The master thought his servant needed to be more trusting in God's providence; the servant thought his master was far too careless with money and much too quick to believe every sad story he heard.

On one occasion, a deserter from the army appealed to St. Robert, mentioning the sum of money needed to release him from his military obligation. The saint quickly agreed, but Peter complained about the cost involved. In response, the holy cardinal told him, as Peter himself later recalled, "I ought not to be so terribly cautious and strict about the merits of a case; that if we gave freely and generously, God would see that we would not become bankrupt; that if I did not have the money at the moment, I could pawn something and get it that way."

Many similar instances occurred during St. Robert's time in Rome — so many that Peter claimed he could write a book just about his experiences concerning "his Lordship's instructions and doings" in the matter of almsgiving. For instance, many of the cardinal's possessions were pawned at one time or another to raise money for needy persons, including his ring, his silver candlesticks, and other gifts that he had received when raised to the cardinalate. Twice St. Robert gave away the mattress from his own bed (the second time carefully instructing a different servant to make sure Peter didn't find out). When the saint's parents died, Robert said of the memorial for their graves, "Let it be a simple memorial, for poor living men have greater need of my money than dead men have of rich tombs."

St. Robert was quick to think of the needs of others, even at the expense of his own comfort and convenience. For example, he always suffered greatly from the cold, but for most of his life, he never wore gloves (as the expense would deprive him of money to give away as alms), and he frequently made do with old, worn-out clothing rather than spend money on himself. One day Robert gave away some drapes from his apartments. When "Peter of little faith" (as the saint called him) complained that he had gone too far, Robert simply replied, "The walls won't catch cold." Peter was always worrying that the saint would one day finally become too generous for his own good (and presumably for Peter's as well), especially when up to three hundred people would be waiting to see his master and present their requests for help. St. Robert always reassured his fretful servant, "These are the people who will get us to Heaven."

Jesus did indeed announce that those who meet the physical needs of their neighbor will be welcomed into His kingdom.[24] Moreover, our Lord had a lot to say about the proper use of money: in the Gospels, He talked more about money than about Heaven or the Church, and sixteen of His thirty-eight parables are concerned with how to handle money and possessions. It's not surprising that Jesus was so insistent in warning us against greed and envy, for as Scripture says, "The love of money is the root of all evils."[25] Our Lord also called His followers to practice generosity, promising that the measure we use in giving to others will also be used in measuring what we receive,[26] and the saints give us a wonderful example of understanding and acting upon His words.

Besides St. Robert Bellarmine, there were many other holy Church leaders who, although for the most part limited in material wealth, freely shared with those in need. St. Vincent de Paul, for instance, once wrote to a former benefactor who later

[24] Matt. 25:31-46.
[25] 1 Tim. 6:10.
[26] Luke 6:38.

experienced a financial setback, "I beseech you to make use of our property as if it were your own; we are ready to sell everything we have for you, even our very chalices; by doing so, we shall only be carrying out what is laid down by the holy canons, and that is to return to our founder in his hour of need what he gave us in his days of prosperity. I am telling you this, sir, not out of politeness but before God, and I feel it in the depth of my heart."

Years before he became the Bishop of Philadelphia, St. John Neumann had taken a personal vow of poverty, for he worried that handling parish funds might make him greedy; therefore, he promised God that he would always live as simply as possible. John kept this vow to such an extent that his parishioners wondered if he was getting enough to eat. Even as bishop, his lifestyle was very austere. Once the saint arrived home with wet feet, and someone suggested that he change his shoes. John replied that he owned no others (although he did facetiously state that he could change them by putting the left shoe on his right foot and vice-versa). On another occasion, one of his priests told him frankly that he was dressed a bit too shabbily for a bishop and really should change his clothes. The humble bishop answered quietly that he owned no others. Indeed, when St. John died and his body was prepared for the funeral, it was the first time he wore new clothes in many years.

For many centuries in Rome, it was the custom, whenever a new pope was installed, to throw large sums of money to the crowds of people lining the streets as part of the official celebration. When St. Pius V was elected pope in 1566, however, he ordered that the money instead be given directly and specifically to those in greatest need, for he feared that those who were weak or infirm would be shoved aside should the coins be flung into the crowds in the customary manner. Also, Pius ordered the money normally spent on a banquet for cardinals and ambassadors to the papal court to be sent instead as alms to the city's hospitals and poorest convents. He said, "I know that God will not call me to account for suppressing a feast for the wealthy, but He may punish me severely if I neglect His poor."

Another saint who combined generosity with prudence was the fifteenth-century bishop St. Lawrence Giustiniani. He, too, lived a very austere lifestyle, in part to make more resources available for the poor. This assistance, however, usually took the form of food or clothing, for the saint knew that freely giving away money could lead to fraud or greed on the part of the recipients.

St. Alphonsus Liguori, however, wasn't as concerned about this possibility. When told that he was giving away money to undeserving persons, he answered, "It is more than likely, but what does it matter after all? It is better to be cheated into giving too much than to lose one's soul by giving too little."

All the saints were generous by nature. St. Dominic, for instance, once sold his valuable parchments to buy food for the poor when his town suffered from famine; as the saint said, "I will not study on dead skins, when living skins are dying of hunger."

In the religious community established by St. Bridget of Sweden, the rule was firmly enforced that at the end of the year, all excess money and possessions had to be given to the poor (although the saint, not facing the situation confronting St. Dominic, did make one exception: the members of her order could own as many books as they wanted).

St. Stephen, King of Hungary, not only made the assistance of the poor a royal policy; he personally went about in disguise and gave alms to the needy (and continued this practice even after being mugged by some lawless beggars).

A number of saints renounced their inheritances in order to follow Christ, including St. Norbert, St. Anthony Zaccaria, St. Stanislaus, St. Fidelis, St. Philip Neri, and, of course, St. Francis of Assisi. It was generosity of this sort that led to the martyrdom of the youthful St. Pancras in the fourth century: his countercultural

act of giving away all his possessions to the needy attracted the attention of the Roman authorities, who then arrested him upon suspicion of being a Christian. Other victims of the same persecution included Sts. Cosmas and Damian, Christian physicians who charged no fees of the patients they healed or treated, and who were known as "the holy moneyless ones."

As a rule, the saints were quite aware of their responsibility to share their material resources with the needy. In the United States, St. Katherine Drexel used her substantial inheritance to help finance her ministry to native Americans and blacks; during her lifetime, she gave away more than $12 million.

The holy fifteenth-century priest St. John Kanty was known for his great love of the poor. He kept only what he himself needed to live on and gave away the rest to those in need.

Similar acts of generosity are recorded about St. Ambrose, who, upon being chosen as Bishop of Milan, immediately gave away almost all his personal property to the needy, and Pope St. Pius X, who sold the jewels in his papal cross and ring and had them replaced with fake ones made of paste, so as to use the money for charity. As a parish priest, the future Pope gave away almost everything when someone in need requested his help: his coat, socks, the rectory firewood, and even a stew that his housekeeper was cooking for him. The Italian cardinal Bl. Benedetto Dusmet was so generous in responding to the needs of others that when he died in 1894, there were no good linens left in his residence with which to wrap his body.

Generosity can be a powerful way of proclaiming the gospel. For instance, the fourth-century hermit St. Pachomius, when a soldier in the Roman army as a young man, was immensely grateful for and impressed by the generosity shown him by some Christians in Egypt — so much so that when he was discharged from military service, he became a Christian and gave himself completely to God.

Far more famous is the immense influence exercised by St. Francis of Assisi. After publicly stripping himself of all his possessions — including his garments — in the presence of his father and the town leaders, Francis forever renounced ownership of all worldly things. His freely chosen lifestyle of utter simplicity and indigence (which he referred to as "Lady Poverty") gave him the freedom to live out the gospel in a powerful and joyful way. As a result, he attracted many followers and gave rise to a spirituality that continues to be a major influence in the Church today.

The radical spiritual freedom represented by Francis of Assisi, and many other saints known for being poor in spirit, contrasts vividly with the far-more-common human motivations of greed and envy; and one would rightly conclude from the example of the saints that these motivations can be a grave spiritual danger. St. Catherine of Siena warns us, "We go on always forming new attachments; if God cuts off one branch, we make another. We fear to lose perishing creatures much more than to lose God. And so, keeping them and possessing them against the will of God, we taste even in this life the foretaste of Hell: for God so permits that a soul which loves itself with irregular love should become insupportable to itself. It suffers from everything that it possesses because it fears to lose it; and to preserve what it possesses, there is anxiety and fatigue day and night."

Earthly wealth can be both a burden and a danger — one of the reasons St. Robert Bellarmine was so devoted to giving it away. The holy cardinal tells us, "Experience indeed teaches that possessions heaped up by greedy rich men go to their prodigal heirs, who quickly run through what their greedy parents gathered. Meanwhile, the sin of avarice remains and will remain forever, and the worm of conscience will not die, nor will the fire of Hell be extinguished." Wealth can be detrimental to our eternal salvation. St. Augustine uses this graphic image: "The love of worldly possessions is a sort of birdlime [bird droppings] which entangles the soul and prevents it from flying to God." St. Maximus of Turin warns, "Whoever craves money loses the Faith; whoever collects money squanders the Faith."

An inordinate love of money is wrong not only because it poisons our faith, but also because it leads to injustice against our neighbor. St. Maximus further tells us, "The person who is avaricious always takes advantage of someone else; he feasts himself on others' downfall." Those who rejoice in the fall of others will themselves be brought low. After noting that greed is restricted not only to money, but also to a desire for honor and status, St. Anthony of Padua tells us, "The more a greedy person possesses, the more does he strive to ascend. And so it happens that when a greedy, ambitious person falls, his fall is disastrous."

Greed and envy frequently go hand in hand. The danger represented by the envy is eloquently described by St. Peter Chrysologus: "Envy is an ancient evil, the first sin, an old venom, the poison of the ages, a cause of death. In the beginning, this vice expelled the Devil from Heaven and cast him down. This vice shut the first parent of our race out of Paradise. It kept this elder brother [of the prodigal son] out of his father's house. It armed the children of Abraham, the holy people, to work the murder of their Creator, the death of their Savior. Envy is an interior foe. It does not batter the walls of the flesh or break down the encompassing armor of the members, but it plies its blows against the very citadel of the heart. Before the organs are aware, like a pirate it captures the soul, the master of the body, and leads it off as a prisoner."

No one suffering from envy is truly free; according to St. Symeon, such a one "has the Devil within himself and cannot be said to be of Christ because he has no love for his neighbor." Furthermore, St. John Climacus states that, in a certain sense, envy is even more deadly than greed: "A greedy person is happy when he gets something. An envious person is happy, not when he gets something, but when someone else does not. He sees his personal profit, not in the good that comes his way, but in the evil that happens to someone else."

St. Gregory the Great calls envy "the rottenness of the bones" (meaning that it destroys a person from within), and St. John Vianney asserts that "envy is a public plague which spares no one." This spiritual disease causes people, out of spite, to act in ways against their own best interest; as St. Thomas More says, "Such is the wretched appetite of this cursed envy: ready to run into the fire, so that he may draw his neighbor with him!" Envy is very destructive; for this reason, St. Cyprian challenges us, "Why do you pile up the burden of your patrimony, that the richer you have been in the sight of the world, the poorer you may become in the sight of God? Divide your possessions with your God; share your gains with Christ; make Christ a partner in your earthly possessions that He also may make you co-heir of His heavenly kingdom."

According to Ven. Charles de Foucald, "The more we lack in this world, the more surely we discover the best thing the earth has to offer us: the cross." Jesus tells us that we must each take up our cross if we wish to travel the path to salvation,[27] and an important part of this process is developing the virtue of generosity. Giving to others is a form of self-denial, and acting in this sacrificial spirit allows God's grace much more room to work in our lives. In addition, sharing with those in need is an important form of stewardship and a matter of justice. According to Charles de Foucald, "If God allows some people to pile up riches instead of making themselves poor as Jesus did, it is so that they may use what He has entrusted to them as loyal servants, in accordance with the Master's will, to do spiritual and temporal good to others."

God has been generous to us as a sign of His immeasurable love, and if we truly love Him, it's only natural that we will be

[27] Mark 8:34-35.

generous in His Name to others. Practicing this virtue requires a certain amount of prudence, of course, especially in regard to our financial obligations (i.e., giving money to the poor is no excuse for ignoring our legitimate debts). Also, forming a habit of regular giving to charity and our church may involve some feelings of anxiousness at first, but, as the saying goes, we'll soon discover that "the Lord is never outdone in generosity."

Greed and envy imprison us; generosity sets us free. Moreover, the joy that comes from living in this spirit can't be purchased or even measured in monetary terms. As all true followers of Jesus know, the road marker on the path to salvation isn't the dollar sign, but the Cross. When we see this truth clearly, we also begin to see God; and when we see God, we also recognize His presence in the people around us. St. Edith Stein reminds us, "For the Christian there is no such thing as a 'stranger.' There is only the neighbor . . . the person near us and needing us." The saints bear witness that wisdom lies in accepting this truth, and happiness comes from acting upon it.

For Further Reflection

"The tenth commandment forbids greed and the desire to amass earthly goods without limit. It forbids avarice arising from a passion for riches and their attendant power. It also forbids the desire to commit injustice by harming our neighbor in his temporal goods: When the law says, 'You shall not covet,' these words mean that we should banish our desires for whatever does not belong to us. Our thirst for another's goods is immense, infinite, never quenched. Thus it is written: 'He who loves money never has enough money.'" — *Catechism of the Catholic Church, par. 2536*

"People will employ a hundred and one devices to conceal their envy from others. If someone speaks well of another in our presence, we keep silence: we are upset and annoyed. If we must say something, we do so in the coldest and most unenthusiastic fashion. No, my dear brethren, there is not a particle of charity in the envious heart." — St. John Vianney (*In other words, we must guard against being greedy for honor or praise.*)

"Cupidity never knows how to be satisfied. The greedy man is always in need; the more he acquires, the more he seeks, and he is tortured not only by the desire of gaining, but by the fear of losing. . . . We are born poor into this life, and shall leave it poor. If we believe the goods of this life are perishable, why do we want them with so much love?" — *St. Isidore of Seville*

Something You Might Try

◆ St. Thomas More says, "If we were to . . . esteem everything according to its true nature, rather than according to men's false opinion, then we would never see any reason to envy any man, but rather we would pity every man — and pity those most who have the most to be envied for, since they are the ones who will shortly lose the most." Thus, we're advised to keep everything in perspective: earthly wealth is transient, and those who enjoy this temporary benefit have no advantage over us (and, indeed, labor under a great disadvantage) when it comes to storing up treasure in Heaven. When we've learned the lesson (through spiritual insight, observation, and experience) that material things have no lasting value and can't bring us happiness, it becomes easier to practice generosity and to detach ourselves from worldly possessions. If necessary, pray for this perspective; ask the Lord to show you that "a man's life does not consist in the abundance of his possessions."[28]

◆ It's said that being rich isn't a case of having all you want, but of wanting all you have. In a similar vein, St. Josemaría Escrivá

---

[28] Luke 12:15.

tells us, "Don't forget it: he has much who needs least. Don't create necessities for yourself." A conscious decision to live a simple lifestyle, making do with less and giving up expensive hobbies and entertainment, can free us of much of the worry over money that afflicts so many Americans today. Perhaps the best way to tap into this joyful and generous spirit is to begin practicing the biblical standard of tithing: giving away ten percent of your income to charity or to the support of your church, or both. Invariably, those who tithe discover that finances become less of a problem than ever before. The more they give away, the more they experience the Lord's blessing. If setting aside ten percent of your income (after taxes) for charity seems too big a step to take at first, try easing into it: tithe for just one week or one month. Evaluate the results, and if they're favorable, experiment a little further. If you give tithing a try, chances are you'll happily choose to make it a way of life.

Further Reading

Scripture: Proverbs 3:27-28; Proverbs 22:9; Proverbs 28:27; Ecclesiastes 5:10-16; Wisdom 7:7-9; Sirach 3:29-30; Matthew 6:31-33; 16:23-24; Mark 12:41-44; Luke 12:15-21; Luke 16:9; Luke 16:19-31; 2 Corinthians 9:6-8; 1 Timothy 6:9-10; James 5:1-5.

Classics: St. Thérèse of Lisieux, *The Story of a Soul*; St. Francis de Sales, *An Introduction to the Devout Life*; St. Alphonsus Liguori, *The Practice of the Love of Jesus Christ*.

Contemporary Works: Randy Alcorn, *Money, Possessions, and Eternity*.

Not the goods of the world, but God.
Not riches, but God.

Not honors, but God.
Not distinction, but God.
Not dignities, but God.
Not advancement, but God.
God always and in everything.

St. Vincent Pallotti

Grief

You will weep and lament, but the world will rejoice;
you will be sorrowful, but your sorrow will turn into joy. . . .
I will see you again and your hearts will rejoice,
and no one will take your joy from you.

John 16:20, 22

A talented painter once gave an unforgettable performance in front of an admiring audience. With rapid strokes of his brush, he quickly and skillfully painted a beautiful country scene, replete with green meadows, golden fields of grain, farm buildings in the distance, peaceful trees, and a friendly blue sky punctuated with soft, white clouds. As he stepped back from his easel, the audience burst into appreciative applause — only to be silenced by the artist, who announced, "The picture is not complete."

He turned and began rapidly covering the canvas with dark, somber paints. The peaceful country scene was replaced with blotches of morose, unappealing colors, all seemingly thrown on the canvas in random disorder; only a patch of the blue sky and the peaceful countryside remained. "Now," he asserted, "the picture is finished, and it is perfect." The stunned audience looked on in disbelief; no one understood what had just happened. Then the painter turned the canvas on its side, and the onlookers let out a collective gasp of amazement, for now there appeared before their eyes a stunningly beautiful, dark waterfall, cascading over moss-covered rocks and creating a rich symphony of color.

The artist intended his amazing and unexpected demonstration to be a commentary or reflection on the reality of sorrow: one beautiful scene of life was transformed into another, even as observers wrongly believed something wonderful was forever lost. The meaning of this story is simple: God is the Artist who created our lives, and who desires to make them into something permanent and glorious; and sorrow and loss are often His instruments in bringing about this change. From our limited perspective, we believe that the original picture is fine as it is, and that any change, especially a painful one, can only be for the worse. The Lord, however, sees and understands the possibilities of life and eternity far more completely than we ever will, and if we allow it, He is able to use all the events and experiences of our lives — even the dark and somber ones — to bring about something of lasting and unequaled beauty.

Grief over any serious loss — especially the death of a loved one — is a very heavy cross to bear, and we're certainly not expected to see right away how the dark colors of our mourning can be transformed into the joyous hues of eternity. The Lord doesn't ask that we understand, only that we trust. This, too, can be quite difficult. Even some of the saints found their grief to be nearly overwhelming, but they persevered in their faith and eventually found peace and even joy in their sorrow. This is a hope that Jesus offers to us as well.

St. Francis de Sales came from a large family, and although he was often somewhat melancholy, he experienced great happiness in spending time with those he loved. This was especially true in regard to his youngest sister, Jeanne, who was born three days before his Ordination to the priesthood. Hers was the first Baptism St. Francis performed, and he always had a special fondness for her, so it was a terrible blow when she died suddenly and unexpectedly at the age of fifteen, while visiting the home of St. Jane Frances de Chantal and her family. Francis, by then a bishop, expressed his profound grief in these words: "I am nothing if not a man. My heart has been broken in a way that I could not have believed possible."

St. Jane, who understandably felt very guilty over the girl's death (even though it was in no way her fault), had herself drunk deeply from the cup of sorrow some years earlier. Her beloved husband, Christophe, was shot by a friend in a hunting accident. He was carried home, but there was nothing the doctors could do for him, and after nine painful days, he died. During this novena of suffering, Christophe resigned himself to the will of God and freely forgave his friend. Jane, however, was unable to react in such a holy manner. In her desperation she bargained with God: "Take everything I have, my relatives, my belongings, my children, but leave me my husband!" This prayer, of course, was not answered, and it was many years before the future saint (under the influence of St. Francis de Sales) was able to forgive her husband's hunting partner from her heart.

The grief St. Jane experienced made it possible for her years later to write this advice to her own daughter, who was herself grieving over the death of a husband: "My greatest wish is that you live like a true Christian widow, unpretentious in your dress and actions, and especially reserved in your relationships. . . . I know very well, darling, of course, that we can't live in the world without enjoying some of its pleasures, but take my word for it, dearest, you won't find any really lasting joys except in God, in living virtuously, in raising your children well, in looking after their affairs, and in managing your household. If you seek happiness elsewhere, you will experience much anguish, as I well know."

Another saint well acquainted with grief and loss, one we would rightly call a "man of sorrows," was Alphonsus Rodriguez. He was fourteen when he lost his father; when he was twenty-six, his wife died in childbirth. A few years later, his mother and his young son died, and shortly after this, his business failed. The grieving saint wrote, "I put myself in spirit before our crucified Lord, looking at Him full of sorrow, shedding His Blood and bearing great bodily hardships for me. As love is paid for in love, I must imitate Him, sharing in spirit all His sufferings. I must consider how much I owe Him and what He has done for me. Putting these sufferings between God and my soul, I must say, 'What does it matter, my God, that I should endure for Your love these small hardships? For You, Lord, endured so many great hardships for me.' Amid the hardship and trial itself, I stimulate my heart with this exercise. Thus, I encourage myself to endure for love of the Lord, who is before me, until I make what is bitter sweet."

This heroic act of resignation helped St. Alphonsus Rodriguez bear a very heavy cross of grief, although later in life, as a Jesuit lay brother, he still had much to suffer (including spiritual aridity, violent temptations, and even demonic assaults).

A somewhat similar approach was used by St. Teresa of Avila, who was only thirteen when her mother died. Teresa consoled herself by thinking each night of our Lord's agony in the Garden of Gethsemani. In her grief, she also turned to the Virgin Mary. She later wrote, "When I began to realize what I had lost, I went in my distress to an image of our Lady and with many tears besought her to be mother to me. Although I did this in my simplicity, I believe it was of some avail to me; for whenever I have commended myself to this sovereign Virgin, I have been conscious of her aid; and eventually she brought me back to myself."

Sorrow is often unavoidable in this life, but our response of faith and hope in eternal life can bring us a measure of peace. God knows everything we feel; no tear is unnoticed, and none need be wasted, for as St. Pio once said to a grieving person, "Your tears were collected by the angels and were placed in a gold chalice, and you will find them when you present yourself before God."

Nothing of value is permanently lost — especially not our loved ones, and the love we share with them — if we have faith in God. As St. Paulinus of Nola writes, "Granted our love may weep for a time, but our faith must ever rejoice. We should long for those who have been sent before us, but we should not lose hope of gaining them back."

Our Christian Faith teaches us that the separations from our loved ones caused by death are temporary; we're also taught that humbly bearing our burdens — including the burden of grief — is a valuable and even heroic way of growing in God's grace. As St. Teresa of Avila notes, "We always find that those who walked closest to Christ, our Lord, were those who had to bear the greatest trials." Our suffering and grief can lead us to everlasting joy, for as St. John Vianney tells us, "You must accept your cross; if you carry it courageously, it will carry you to Heaven."

As much as we'd like to when we're grieving, we cannot undo the past, but the saints assure us that turning to the Lord in our sorrows and placing our hopes in Him can give us strength here and now, and help prepare us for a future of new life and joy.

For Further Reflection

"It is a loving act to show sadness when our dear ones are torn from us, but it is a holy act to be joyful through hope and trust in the promises of God. . . . Thankful joy is more acceptable to God than long and querulous grief." — *St. Paulinus of Nola*

"No picture can be drawn with only the brightest colors, nor harmony created only from treble notes. . . . Our whole life is tempered between sweet and sour, and we must look for a mixture of both." — *Bl. Robert Southwell*

"The more we are afflicted in this world, the greater is our assurance in the next; the more we sorrow in the present, the greater will be our joy in the future." — *St. Isidore of Seville*

Something You Might Try

♦ Bl. Elizabeth of the Trinity advises, "During painful times, when you feel a terrible void, think how God is enlarging the capacity of your soul so that it can receive Him — making it, as it were, infinite as He is infinite. Look upon each pain as a love-token coming directly from God in order to unite you to Him." We needn't believe that God *causes* our grief, but we can be sure that, if we allow it, He *uses* our sorrow, thereby giving us a greater capacity for the future happiness that awaits us. The Lord doesn't ask that you stop grieving; He asks only that you trust in Him and believe that the day will come when you will once again rejoice.

♦ When her husband died after a long illness, leaving her with five young children, a grieving St. Elizabeth Ann Seton prayed, "I know that these contradictory events are permitted by Your wisdom, which solely is light. We are in darkness and must be thankful that our knowledge is not wanted to perfect Your work." As your grief begins to pass, look for opportunities to allow God's light to shine in your life. Consider joining a support group — people with whom you can share tears and laughter. Look for an organization or group (perhaps in your parish) that needs volunteers; activities of this sort can be a way of finding new meaning and making new friends. Cultivate a deeper relationship with Jesus and with Mary, who knew what it was to grieve, and to remain faithful in spite of grief. Being open to God's grace in these ways can slowly begin to replace darkness and mourning with light and peace.

Further Reading

Scripture: Psalm 126:5-6; Lamentations 3:17-25; John 16:20.

Classics: St. Augustine, *Confessions*; St. Francis de Sales, *An Introduction to the Devout Life*.

Contemporary Works: Joseph F. Nassal, *Faith Walkers: Passages of Suffering and Hope*; Pierre Wolf, *May I Hate God?*; Barbara Schiff Brisson, *Such Is the Way of the World: A Journey Through Grief*; Ann Dawson, *A Season of Grief*; Joan Guntzelman, *God Knows You're Grieving*.

Dear Virgin Mary,
in your role as Our Lady of Sorrows,
you know and understand my grief
and the full extent of my loss.
Please console me, embrace me in your love,
and obtain for me from your Son
the grace and strength I need
to bear this terrible cross.
Be my mother, my confidant,
and my grief-friend;
obtain the gift of eternal life from
your Son for my loved ones,
and help me find the path to holy
resignation, healing, and inner peace.

Household Duties

*Stand by your covenant and attend
to it, and grow old in your work.*

Sirach 11:20

The old saying "A man works from sun to sun, but a woman's work is never done" might need to be updated as we begin the twenty-first century, for we now live in an age of two-income families and single-parent households, with teenagers and children involved in sports and other extracurricular activities, with everyone — single persons included — having access to a wide range of leisure and recreational possibilities (such as surfing the Internet) that didn't even exist fifty years ago. Someone has to clean up after us and keep everything more or less in order at home. There's always cleaning, cooking, vacuuming, shopping, and laundry to do.

This ongoing cycle of household work keeps repeating itself, and it can be very tiring and depressing — especially when our efforts (particularly on behalf of a family) seem to be taken for granted. Whether we're male or female, young or old, rich or poor, there's a good chance we sometimes find our household chores to be rather tedious, but, if we choose, they can be part of our offering to God. He gives us the opportunity to offer our work, especially the part we don't like, as a sacrifice for His glory, and when we use this opportunity, our household duties can help us advance along the way of grace.

The things of God must always come first. This is the clear message of the Gospel story of Jesus' visit to the home of Martha and Mary.[29] Martha, ever the dutiful hostess, scurried about the kitchen and the dining room, making sure everything was in order (even though she had probably already spent many hours preparing for our Lord's visit). Mary, the more sensitive of the two sisters — and, in this case, the more sensible — sat with Jesus and listened to His teaching. When Martha complained and suggested that Mary's place was in the kitchen helping with the work, Jesus turned the tables on her: Mary's place was with Him — and, He implied, so was Martha's.

The Lord isn't seeking to be invited into spotless homes, but into attentive hearts. Yes, household duties have their place, and due diligence in meeting them can be a virtue, but not at the expense of our relationship with God. Should He wish to do so, God could render a filthy home utterly spotless with a simple word of command. What He can't do is compel our devotion or make us turn our hearts to Him; that's something we must do ourselves. Once Martha learned this lesson, she, like her sister Mary, began traveling the path toward sainthood. (St. Martha's feast day is July 29 — one week after her sister's. Maybe this means that Mary, having a head start in understanding what truly mattered, reached her goal first.)

If cleanliness is next to godliness, it must be that cleaning and other household activities can, if performed in the proper spirit, bring us closer to God. Being neat and tidy is certainly not a requirement for sanctity. John the Baptist, for instance, wore clothing made out of camel's hair[30] — a material that was presumably

---

[29] Luke 10:38-42.
[30] Mark 1:6.

difficult to launder — and many of the desert fathers and other hermits, unlike the typical Roman citizen of the time, had little desire (or peer pressure) to bathe or keep clean.

Today, however, we more closely identify with someone like St. Teresa of Avila, who by nature tended to be very fastidious; she preferred everything to be neat and orderly. On one occasion, she and another sister of her order arrived at the University of Salamanca, whose officials had several students vacate their room to make it available for the nuns. Observing all the books and personal belongings strewn about haphazardly, Teresa remarked, "Students are not very neat persons." (She would likely be able to make the same observation about many university dormitories today; academic responsibilities obviously have a higher priority than household duties.) St. Teresa, although she often fasted, also appreciated a good meal, and valued those who prepared it; her many letters to her friends and colleagues were just as likely to give recipes as spiritual counsel.

"Domestic engineers" (as stay-at-home wives and mothers are sometimes called) are just as much loved by God, and — as St. Francis de Sales so often stressed — just as much called to holiness, as members of any other profession.

St. Nicholas of Flue observed, "Each state of life has its special duties; by accomplishing them, one may find happiness." Moreover, every vocation is important in the Lord's eyes, and as Ven. Solanus Casey, a twentieth-century Capuchin priest, said, "We should be grateful for and love the vocation to which God has called us. This applies to every vocation, because after all, what a privilege it is to serve God even in the least capacity."

God always provides opportunities for spiritual growth for those who wish to come closer to Him. According to St. Mary Joseph Rossello, "You will become a saint by complying exactly with your daily duties," and St. Stanislaus Kostka was able to assert, "I find a heaven in the midst of saucepans and brooms."

Meeting the demands and responsibilities of daily life still leaves us plenty of opportunities to experience God's goodness. It's said that St. Teresa of Avila once had an ecstacy while frying fish. We shouldn't necessarily expect that sort of experience, of course, but we can certainly spend time with the Lord while performing our chores. Padre Pio advises us, "Remember that the mind can quite well be elevated to God while the body attends to material matters. Therefore, don't distress yourself if you are unable to carry out your usual spiritual exercises due to a great deal of work. Endeavor, without wearying yourself, to do what you can, and Jesus, who looks into the depths of the heart, will be pleased with you."

In the fifteenth century, St. Frances of Rome proved that housework and holiness can go hand in hand. Although she wished to enter a convent, she obeyed her parents and was instead, at age thirteen, given in marriage to a young nobleman. Frances lived as a loving wife and mother of three children, while managing the household with grace and efficiency, but in time she felt the need to expand her activities. She and her sister-in-law desired to grow spiritually and to spend time in service to the poor, so, with their husbands' permission, the two women combined household duties with various acts of faith and charity outside the home — including caring for victims of epidemics and wars. After her husband's death, St. Frances went on to establish a society of Roman women who desired to practice charity and service in the poorer areas of the city (and the skills she had developed in the service of her family undoubtedly proved useful in her new vocation).

Family servants, or those who do household work for pay, also have an example to imitate: that of St. Zita, who lived in the thirteenth century. She became a domestic servant for a well-to-do family at the age of twelve, fulfilling her duties at a nearby home after first attending Mass early each morning, while practicing various forms of penance, and, with the family's permission, distributing food to the poor. As Zita became older, the family children were placed under her supervision. Later, as housekeeper, she became almost a member of the family, serving as friend, advisor, and counselor (and she was the only one who could cope with the master when he went into a rage). As her holiness came to be recognized, Zita's workload was lessened so that she might increase her ministry among the poor, the sick, and prisoners.

St. Zita, who served this family for forty-eight years, shows that household duties and spiritual growth go together. Indeed, everything we do — no matter how mundane — can be offered as a sacrifice to God's glory. This doesn't release us from our duty to set aside time specifically for prayer, however, preferably in church. St. Alphonsus Liguori used to ask, "Do you not know that you may obtain more by a quarter of an hour's prayer before the altar than by all the other devotions of the day put together?" St. John Vianney advised, "When you think of going to Mass on working days, it is an impulse of the grace that God wills to grant you. Follow it."

If you can't make time to pray in church, however, God understands. Bl. Herman Joseph, as a young monk in the thirteenth century, was assigned to work in the kitchen and was upset when his duties left him little time for prayer. Our Lady appeared to him and reassured him that serving others in charity was more pleasing to God than anything else.

With so much to do, finding time is often a problem for us. Yet, if we set aside part of our day for God, the rest of our hours have a way of going more smoothly. Upon being asked if he ever felt overworked, the sixteenth-century priest St. Peter Canisius responded, "If you have too much to do, with God's help you will find time to do it all." As long as God is with us in our daily routines, everything that absolutely needs to be done will somehow be accomplished.

For Further Reflection

"To be perfect in our vocation is nothing else than to fulfill the duties which our state of life obliges us to perform, and to accomplish them well, and only for the honor and love of God." — *St. Francis de Sales*

"Be completely recollected and abandoned on the bosom of the heavenly Father, adoring Him in spirit and truth. Such recollection will not interfere with the attention you must give to domestic affairs. Rather will you take better care of them since all will be filled with divine love." — *St. Paul of the Cross*

"In reading the life of St. Catherine of Siena of all her visions and raptures, her sacred wisdom and her discourses, I should not doubt that with the eye of contemplation she had ravished the heart of her heavenly Bridegroom. But at the same time I delighted to find her attending to the lowly household cares in her father's house, turning the spit, lighting the fire, cooking and baking, with a heart full of love and yearning toward God. Nor do I value the humble meditations which occupied her whilst engaged in such lowly offices less than the ecstasies and raptures which she so often enjoyed, and which were perhaps granted as the reward of her humility and self-abnegation." — *St. Francis de Sales (Not only are our daily duties no impediment to a deep spiritual life; it's quite possible that they may be a means of strengthening our relationship with God.)*

Something You Might Try

◆ Prayer and work can go together. St. Francis de Sales advises us, "Remember, then, frequently to retire into the solitude of your heart, even whilst you are externally occupied in business or society. This mental solitude need not be hindered though many persons are around you, for they do but surround your body, not your heart, which should remain alone in the presence of God." Achieving this recollected state while working may take some time and practice on your part, but if you have this desire, God is happy to help you achieve it. Perhaps it would be helpful to begin each task or activity with a silent prayer: "Dear Jesus, please bless my work," or "Lord, may this labor I now perform give You glory."

◆ Mother Cabrini, the first American to be canonized, once wrote, "Our great patron, St. Francis Xavier, said, 'He who goes holy to the missions will find many occasions to sanctify himself more, but he who goes poorly provided with holiness, runs the risk of losing what he has and of falling away.' I become more convinced of this truth every day, and as experience is a great master, let us take advantage of the lessons it teaches and never let a day pass without examining our conscience and making serious resolutions to acquire the other virtues we need." Even though we're not missionaries, we're called to grow in grace, and reflecting on the state of our souls, perhaps even while we work, is an important part of this process.

Further Reading

Scripture: Luke 17:7-10; Luke 12:42-44.

Classics: St. Francis de Sales, *An Introduction to the Devout Life*.

Contemporary Works: Gunilla Norris, *Being Home: Discovering the Spiritual in the Everyday*; Hubert van Zeller, *Holiness for Housewives*.

☞

Lord Jesus,
You chose to come to earth
and share our human condition,
and You lived as the Son of

a simple, humble carpenter.
You knew what it was like to work,
assisting Joseph in the carpenter shop
and helping Mary in the home.
Grant me, I beg You,
the grace and humility,
perseverance and fidelity
I need to fulfill my daily duties.
Remind me, as often as necessary,
that there are no small jobs,
but only small and mistaken attitudes,
and show me how everything I do
can bring me closer to Your kingdom.
I offer You all the chores and duties,
labor and efforts,
and successes and failures of this day.
Please make them holy,
that they may be a source of glory for You
and a source of grace for me.

Imprisonment

*If you continue in my word, you are truly
my disciples, and you will know the truth,
and the truth will make you free.*

John 8:31-32

The prisoner's cell was crude and uncomfortable; it measured six feet by ten, and the only light came from a tiny window set high in the wall — so high that, in order for the inmate to read, he had to stand on a bench and hold his book out in his hands when the angle of the sun was just right. Otherwise, the room was one of shadows and darkness, bitterly cold in the winter and oppressively hot in the summer. Sleep was difficult: the poor sufferer's bed was only two old rugs covering a board laid on the floor. Meals consisted of barely enough food to maintain his strength — usually some scraps of bread and a sardine or two, along with water.

These harsh conditions didn't break the prisoner's spirit or addle his mind, however, and although he was willing to suffer for his principles, he wasn't going to await his fate passively. Each night, while his guards slept, the man furtively loosened the hinges on the door of his cell, a little at a time. Finally, his task finished, he seized his opportunity. Around two in the morning, the long-suffering inmate carefully lifted the door off its hinges and stepped softly into the hallway. Carrying a rope he had made from strips of a blanket and from his own clothing, he slipped by the sleeping guards. He crawled onto a balcony and, making sure no one was looking, jumped to the top of a wall surrounding the compound. After pausing to reassure himself that no one had heard him, he tied the end of the rope to a fixture, then lowered himself down the side of the wall and found himself in a large courtyard. Staying in the shadows, he went to the opposite corner, scaled another wall, and was free.

A scene from *The Count of Monte Cristo* or from a similar historical novel? The plot of a popular movie from the 1950s or of a contemporary stage play? No, the incident described above really happened, and the desperate but determined prisoner who made good his escape was the sixteenth-century Spanish mystic St. John of the Cross. Perhaps even more surprising is that his jailers were some of his fellow Carmelite friars.

John, a close friend of St. Teresa of Avila, imitated her efforts to restore the Carmelite Order (both the nuns and the male religious) to its original holiness and simplicity. Not everyone appreciated this crusade. John encountered great opposition, and in 1577, he was imprisoned by the Carmelite prior general. Considered a sinner and someone disrespectful to authority and to the established order, John was treated harshly. In an effort to make him confess his "sins," he suffered what was called the "circular discipline": his bare shoulders were struck with a cane or stick by each friar in turn, while the rest of the assembled monks chanted the penitential psalm known as the *Miserere* (Psalm 51[31]).

John bore these scourgings silently and patiently, winning the admiration of the younger monks ("Say what they like; he is a saint") and the anger of the older ones ("Look at him pretending to be submissive, when all the while he resists us; he is like a

---

[31] Douay-Rheims = Ps. 50.

snake in the grass"). During his long hours of solitude over a period of nine months, John experienced what he called his Dark Night of the Soul: a time of intense interior struggle, desolation, and doubt that drained his inner resources, but in the end left him spiritually purified and enlightened. It was during this period that he composed some of his most beautiful poetry, and immediately after his escape — for which he always credited the Virgin Mary — John dictated these poems so that they might be set down in writing. During the remaining fourteen years of his life, John never again suffered imprisonment, but he had many other crosses to bear.

It seems unfair that good people sometimes experience captivity — whether as prisoners of war, persons unjustly arrested, or convicted criminals paying for one isolated mistake or bad choice even as the perpetrators of far worse crimes remain free. It's also a tragedy when people remain imprisoned in their souls: afraid or forbidden to be themselves, not given the opportunity to develop their gifts or to share them and have them appreciated, victimized by misunderstanding and prejudice. Even worse is that imprisonment we impose on ourselves when we cling to our sins and refuse to seek God's mercy and reject His help in overcoming our faults. God created us to be free, but, through our sinfulness, captivity has become one of the defining experiences of human existence.

All the saints have wrestled with the need to overcome the bonds of sin. A number of them have physically ministered to prisoners, or have experienced actual imprisonment themselves. The patron saint of prisoners is St. Dismas, the "Good Thief" who, according to legend, had once heard Jesus preach but rejected His words. After being arrested, imprisoned, and sentenced to death by crucifixion, however, he turned to Jesus and sought and received forgiveness.[32]

---

[32] Luke 23:40-43.

Jesus didn't free Himself from His captors, although He could easily have called upon twelve legions of angels to do so.[33] There were later several instances, however, when His apostles were set free by the angel of the Lord.[34] St. Peter, for one, was miraculously released from his cell one night,[35] although the experience was so unreal that at first he thought it was only a dream. Sts. Paul and Silas, arrested for creating a public disturbance, prayed aloud in prison at night while the other inmates listened, and a sudden earthquake released them from their chains. When the jailer discovered to his relief that they hadn't escaped, he took them home and tended to their wounds; then he and his whole family were baptized.[36] Paul, in fact, was frequently imprisoned, but he bore this trial patiently, seeing in it an opportunity to suffer in the Name of the Lord Jesus and to share the Good News of salvation with his captors and his fellow inmates.

Other imprisoned saints include St. Patrick, who, as a youth, was captured by Irish pirates and enslaved until he escaped after six years; St. Francis of Assisi and a later Franciscan, St. John of Capistrano, who were both prisoners of war before they gave their lives to God; St. Ignatius of Loyola, who was detained and questioned no fewer than eight times by the Inquisition; St. Vincent de Paul, who was captured by pirates and sold as a slave (and who later wrote, "God always wrought in me a firm conviction that I should one day escape through the constant prayers I offered up to Him and the Blessed Virgin Mary, to whose sole intercession I firmly believe I owe my deliverance"); and the eleventh-century abbot St. Walter of Pontoise, whose reward for preaching against the sins of the local clergy was to be beaten and thrown into jail.

[33] Matt. 26:53.
[34] For instance, Acts 5:19-20.
[35] Acts 12:6-10.
[36] Acts 16:19-34.

Imprisonment can, for those who choose, serve as a time of spiritual awakening or growth. In the fourteenth century, Bl. Charles of Blois, a French prince, was captured in battle by the English and imprisoned in the Tower of London for nine years before money was raised for his ransom. During this period, Charles patiently devoted himself to prayer and meditation (winning the admiration of his captors in the process).

The Croatian priest St. Leopold Castronovo was captured by the Austrians during World War I and spent his one year in a POW camp ministering to his fellow prisoners.

In 1864, the Polish patriot St. Raphael Kalinowski took part in an uprising against the Russians. He was arrested and sentenced to ten years of hard labor in a camp in Siberia. During this time, he developed a strong religious vocation and, after his release, became a Carmelite priest.

A number of saints, besides St. John of the Cross and the apostles mentioned above, managed to escape from their captors. The third-century priest St. Felix of Nola was arrested during the persecution of the Emperor Decius in 250. He was treated brutally and imprisoned, but was then miraculously set free (and, according to a pious legend, when the authorities tried to arrest him a second time, a spider helped to hide him by spinning a web over the doorway to a ruined building where he had taken refuge).

A story about the Irish abbot St. Columban relates how he visited a city jail and asked the prisoners there to repent. When they did so, he told them to free themselves by pulling away their chains from the walls; and when the men obeyed him, the chains gave way. Columban and the men he had liberated fled to a nearby cathedral, with troops in pursuit; the barred doors miraculously opened in response to the saint's prayers and then firmly closed themselves in the face of the pursuing soldiers.

Somewhat better documented is an incident from the life of St. Jerome Emiliani at the beginning of the sixteenth century. As a prisoner of war, he was chained in the dungeon of a mountain fortress, but, through divine assistance, managed to escape. Jerome had led a dissolute life until that point, but he took his miraculous liberation as a calling from God to enter the religious life. (Needless to say, inmates today who are incarcerated by the proper authorities for legitimate reasons are expected by God to serve their terms with due cooperation and obedience, and it would be morally wrong for them to try to escape.)

As a young man, St. Peter of Mount Athos, after being captured by the Saracens in the eighth century, prayed to St. Nicholas and St. Simeon. According to legend, St. Simeon miraculously freed Peter from prison, and St. Nicholas guided him to Rome, where he received a monastic habit from the Pope.

In the twelfth century, St. John of Matera was accused of theft and was imprisoned, but managed to escape — supposedly with the help of an angel. The vast majority of prisoners, of course, never escape — saints included. St. Joan of Arc made an unsuccessful attempt to do so, before suffering martyrdom at the hands of the English, and the fifth-century bishop St. Flavian died in prison, as did the fourteenth-century layman St. Roch. Roch was the son of a French governor. At the age of twenty, he went to Rome and cared for victims of a plague. He himself contracted the disease, and when he recovered, he returned to France, where he was arrested as a spy! It wasn't until after his death in prison that his true identity was discovered. We're thus reminded that true justice can be expected only in the life to come.

Jesus will say to the just on Judgment Day, "I was in prison and you came to me,"[37] and many of the saints devoted themselves to this form of ministry, including St. John Leonardi, who visited the imprisoned, while also tending to the poor and the sick; St. Peter Armengol and St. Peter Nolasco, both of whom — like St. John of

---

[37] Matt. 25:36.

Matha — sought to ransom Christians enslaved by the Muslims; and St. Peter Claver, a missionary priest who spent his life working among the black slaves imported from Africa to the Spanish colony of Colombia. Peter Claver made a point of boarding each ship as it arrived in port, ministering to the needs of its miserable passengers. As the slaves were being auctioned, he went among them, distributing food and medicine. Even after they were taken to the plantations, he continued to visit them, always sleeping with them in their crude huts, rather than accepting the hospitality of the slave owners.

All during this time, although he cared for their physical needs as best he could, St. Peter Claver placed priority on their souls; he gave the slaves basic instructions in Christianity and baptized some three hundred thousand persons over a period of thirty-eight years.

As Peter Claver realized, physical imprisonment, although often a terrible ordeal, pales in comparison with the spiritual lack of freedom caused by our sins. No one can chain the spirits of those who, through divine grace, are at peace with themselves; no one can release those who, even if the whole world is theirs, will not turn to God and admit their guilt. Even if we're literally behind bars, Jesus offers us the only freedom that matters; in His Name alone will we find our peace.

For Further Reflection

"I rejoice, and thank God more for the patience He gave me in the time of my imprisonment [when captured by the Muslims during a Crusade] than if I had acquired all the earth." — *St. Louis IX of France*

"He who is kind is free, even if he is a slave; he who is evil is a slave, even if he is a king." — *St. Augustine*

"No man is free who is not master of himself." — *Epictetus*

Something You Might Try

◆ The founder of the Jesuit Order, St. Ignatius of Loyola, was imprisoned for a time. When someone asked whether this trial was difficult, he responded, "Do you think that prison is such a great hardship? Well, let me tell you that for the love of God, I would suffer much worse, if that was possible!" If you (or someone you love) are in prison, try to offer up the experience as a sign of your love for God. This spiritual offering may not necessarily advance your release date, but it will give value to what you're undergoing.

◆ The most important type of freedom is liberation from sin, and one who experienced this in a dramatic way was Bl. Bartolo Longo. He was a former satanic priest, and after his return to the Church, he was still spiritually imprisoned, for he worried that his consecration as a priest of Satan might be permanent in nature. When he learned, however, of our Lady's promise that "one who propagates the Rosary shall be saved," Bartolo dedicated the remainder of his life to honoring Mary and promoting the Rosary. In the same way, a devotion to Mary will surely help us achieve freedom from sin and guilt, for Jesus is pleased to answer every prayer we offer through the intercession of His Mother.

Further Reading

Scripture: Psalm 102:19-20; Luke 4:18-19; Romans 6:22-23; Galatians 5:1.

Contemporary Works: Ann Ball and Maximilian, S.F.O., *Prayers for Prisoners*.

☞

O God,
let the sighing of the prisoners
come before You,

and mercifully grant unto us
that we may be delivered
by Your almighty power
from all bonds and chains of sin,
whether in our bodies or in our souls,
through Jesus Christ our Lord.

Roman Breviary

Insomnia

In peace I will both lie down and sleep;
for Thou alone, O Lord makest me dwell in safety.

Psalm 4:8

Bl. John XXIII, elected as Bishop of Rome in 1958, was known for his down-to-earth style and gentle humor. One day a newly appointed bishop, in his first private audience with the Holy Father, admitted that he was having trouble sleeping because of the burdens of his new office. John commiserated with him, saying, "Oh, the very same thing happened to me in the first few weeks of my pontificate, but then one day my guardian angel appeared to me and whispered, 'Giovanni, don't take yourself so seriously.' And ever since then I've been able to sleep."

Sometimes insomnia, especially when it's a regular occurrence, can have a physical or psychological cause, and professional care is appropriate. Many times, however, it's due to something more mundane: indigestion, a poorly timed nap during the day, excitement over recent or upcoming events, worry, or — as Pope John XXIII suggested — taking ourselves too seriously. There are non-prescription medications available for occasional use (and these can be helpful, as long as they're not overdone); there are also traditional remedies or suggestions, such as counting sheep, reading, eating a slice of bread or drinking a glass of warm milk, and so on. If none of these work, however, we can recognize sleeplessness for what it sometimes is: an added opportunity to talk to the Lord.

Some saints had difficulty sleeping (such as St. Peter Julian Eymard, who suffered from insomnia during the last four years of his life), and some deliberately chose to deprive themselves of sleep in order to do penance and to pray; all of them recognized that the hours of night are often a special time of grace.

The Scriptures record that sometimes Jesus spent the night in prayer,[38] and St. Paul spoke of spending many sleepless nights because of his ministry.[39] Other saints sometimes sacrificed rest periods so as to praise God. For instance, the eighteenth-century lay brother St. Ignatius of Laconi would frequently spend the entire night in prayer. The same was true of the fourteenth-century monk Bl. Alvarez of Cordova and the fourth-century hermit St. Pachomius. St. Peter Damian, a Benedictine priest and later bishop in the eleventh century, would sometimes do penance by going for long periods without food or sleep. The seventeenth-century virgin St. Mariana of Quito managed to get by on just three hours of sleep a night, and St. Rose of Lima limited herself to only two. (Rose spent ten hours a day working, and the other twelve in prayer — a schedule to be admired and wondered at, but not to be imitated.) Surely the unenviable record in this regard belongs to St. Lydwina, whose paralysis resulting from a skating accident at age sixteen left her an invalid for the rest of her life. It's said that (presumably due in large part to the almost constant pain she suffered) she had the equivalent of only one full night's sleep over a thirty-five-year period.

As a missionary in the Philippines, Bl. Francis de Capillas slept only a few hours a night, lying on a wooden cross. St. Peter of

[38] Luke 6:12.
[39] 2 Cor. 11:27.

Alcantara generally slept only ninety minutes a night, and spent part of each night kneeling and part of it sitting (making him the patron saint of night-watchmen). The hermit Bl. John Buoni alternated among three beds in his cell; the first was uncomfortable, the second more uncomfortable, and the third most uncomfortable.

Other saints known to have spent very little time sleeping each night are St. Margaret of Cortona, St. Lawrence O'Toole, and St. Anthony Claret, who, as a young priest in Spain, heard confessions for up to fifteen hours a day. (In a letter, Anthony admitted, "I was never much for sleep.")

Another holy priest famous for his long hours in the confessional was St. John Vianney, the Curé d'Ars, and he, too, made do with minimal amounts of sleep. Part of the reason was that he was performing penance and praying for his parish, but there was another cause of many sleepless nights: diabolic harassment. For more than thirty years, evil spirits attacked the saint during the nighttime hours, disturbing his rest by talking and howling, and by cursing and threatening him. They also physically threw him from his bed and on one occasion set his bed on fire. Taking all this as a sign that his ministry was bearing fruit, John bore these nocturnal assaults patiently.

A twentieth-century victim of similar demonic attacks was St. Pio of Pietrelcina, who frequently experienced physical beatings in the middle of the night.

Sleep-related suffering of a different sort was inflicted upon the seventeenth-century English priest and martyr St. John Oglivie. In an attempt to break his spirit, his captors forcibly kept him awake over a period of eight days and nights. This cruel torture failed: St. John Oglivie didn't betray his comrades or renounce his Catholic Faith; and he went on to win the martyrs' crown of glory.

Few of us would ever willingly undergo the torture forced upon St. John Oglivie, but almost everyone would appreciate having a talent possessed by St. Anselm: the ability to fall asleep anywhere at a moment's notice. As an abbot, he sometimes presided over hearings involving matters of Church and civil law, and on occasion, he was known to nap while the various parties advanced their claims. However, Anselm had the knack of entering back into the discussion at just the right moment, and in a way that convinced those present he had actually heard every word. (Those tempted to imitate Anselm by napping during meetings or classes should do so only if they can also imitate his amazing presence of mind.)

Most of us dislike being awakened from a restful sleep for anything but a true emergency, but the saints learned to make the best of such interruptions. For instance, the English monk St. Cuthbert remarked, "If anyone wakes me in the middle of the night, I am never in the least annoyed. Instead I get up straight away and begin to think of something useful."

Throughout the ages, many holy men and women have made a point of arising quite early, so as to have ample time for prayer. While a duchess, St. Elizabeth of Hungary would have her servant silently come into her room and awaken her by grabbing her foot; this allowed her to rise early without disturbing Louis, her husband. On one occasion, however, the servant mistakenly grabbed, not Elizabeth's foot, but Louis's. The duke, realizing what had happened and appreciating his wife's pious practices (although without imitating them in this instance), lay down again and returned to sleep without complaining about the interruption.

We don't necessarily have to cut short our sleep or regularly perform special prayers in the middle of the night, but we can offer God our patient endurance of those nighttime annoyances and problems that inevitably arise from time to time. St. Thérèse of Lisieux, who is closer to us both in history (dying in 1897) and in similarity of experience, is famous for her "Little Way": becoming a saint not by doing great or heroic deeds, but by offering the little events and activities of life to God with great love. Thus, it's no surprise that her nighttime difficulty was a "little" one: she never really felt warm the entire time she was in the convent, and often had trouble sleeping because of the cold. Characteristically, Thérèse never mentioned this inconvenience to anyone.

The other famous Teresa — St. Teresa of Avila — usually had no difficulty sleeping (perhaps because she tended to be very lively and active during the day). On one occasion, she was sharing a room with a nervous Carmelite sister, who awakened her and asked in all seriousness, "Mother, if I were to die tonight and you found yourself alone here, what would you do?" Teresa responded in a drowsy voice, "When that happens, Sister, I will consider the problem. Now let us have some sleep." As the saint knew, unnecessary worrying interferes with our rest, and the Lord wants us to remain in Him, not fearing anything.

There's a legend that St. Ulphia was kept awake one night by the croaking of frogs, causing her to oversleep in the morning. Therefore, she forbade them to croak anymore at night — and they were silent from that time on. Even if the story is genuine, her approach is unfortunately not one we can imitate; disturbances are usually beyond our ability to control.

Moreover, there are nights when we're worried or distracted, or when our minds seem unwilling to turn themselves off. What of those times when we simply can't fall asleep and nothing seems to work? Aside from offering our restlessness to God, is there anything else we should do?

There's a story about a devout older woman who had experienced much heartache, yet remained faithful to the Lord. Someone once asked her, "What do you do when you have trouble falling asleep at night? Do you count sheep?" The saint-in-training answered, "No, I used to do that when I was younger, but now I just close my eyes and talk to the Shepherd." That's good advice for all of us.

For Further Reflection

"Do not think that this blessing of sound sleep which God gives you is an unimportant one. I assure you, it is very precious. And I tell you once more, you must not try to do with less sleep: this is no time for you to do so. Remember that we middle-aged people need to treat our bodies well so as not to wreck the spirit, which is a terrible trial." — *St. Teresa of Avila*

"I worry until midnight, and from then on, I let God worry." — *Bl. Louis Guanella*

"Go to bed modestly and sleep with a good thought in your mind. This will be a useful means of remembering God when you awake and, in the morning, your mind will be better prepared for prayer." — *St. Vincent de Paul*

Something You Might Try

♦ Research has discovered an interesting point: we get much more of the restful and beneficial rapid-eye-movement (REM) sleep our bodies need when we go to bed grateful, whereas our REM sleep is reduced by going to bed in an anxious state. As St. Joseph Cafasso once said, "I have always preached that every Christian should, before retiring, leave his affairs settled as if it were the last night of his life." If our spiritual affairs are in order (in other words, if we're in a state of grace), we can rest securely in the experience of God's loving care. Thus, instead of counting sheep, we should count our blessings. As we're waiting to fall asleep, we should consciously remember and thank God for the blessings of the day.

♦ If your sleeplessness is caused by worry, do something about it: silently pray the Rosary while lying in bed. This will help take your mind off your troubles. It's even possible that repetitive praying of this type will lull you to sleep (and you can ask your guardian angel to finish the Rosary for you if that happens).

Further Reading

Scripture: Sirach 40:5-8; Job 7:4; Psalm 3:5; Proverbs 3:24.

Let my eyes take their sleep, Lord,
but may my heart always keep watch for You.
May Your right hand bless Your servants who love You.
May I be united with the praise that flows
from You, Lord Jesus, to all Your saints;
united with the gratitude drawn
from Your heart, good Jesus,
that causes Your saints to thank You;
united with your passion, good Jesus,
by which You took away our guilt;
united with the divine longing
that You had on earth for our salvation;
united with every prayer that welled from
Your divine Heart, good Jesus,
and flowed into the hearts of Your saints.

St. Peter Canisius

Irritations

Share in suffering for the gospel in the power of God.
2 Timothy 1:8

Some saints had a knack for getting along with animals. St. Francis of Assisi is, of course, the best-known example of this. Other saints, however, were quite out of place when it came to relating to this aspect of God's creation, as we see in a story about St. John Neumann.

After coming to the United States from Bohemia and being ordained a priest in 1836, John was made pastor of a large parish in rural New York State — "large" in this case meaning a territory of nine hundred square miles. Naturally, a horse was essential for all the traveling involved in parish ministry, but John had no particular aptitude for horse-riding. To make matters worse, the horse he was given was unfriendly and stubborn; for instance, it often stopped dead in its tracks and refused to go any further, no matter what John did. This was inconvenient and at times quite embarrassing. The saint and his horse usually didn't see eye to eye. On one occasion, John noticed some rare flowers growing alongside the road; he plucked them and carried them along, intending to send them to some botanist friends back in Bohemia — until his horse later snatched them from his hand and ate them before he could do anything. Instead of complaining, John later laughed about the incident, saying, "That was the sacrifice God wanted of me at that moment."

Life is full of surprises, and not all of them are pleasant (a lesson St. John Neumann literally learned straight from the horse's mouth). While we'll probably never have a horse or other pet inconveniently eat something of rare value ("my dog ate my homework" doesn't count), we all encounter numerous other irritations every day, and many of them have the potential to be quite upsetting. None of us can ultimately control what happens to us, but each of us is accountable for how we respond. This is a freedom and responsibility God gives to us, and also a wonderful opportunity to practice charity, patience, and humility. The Lord doesn't expect us to *enjoy* the things that annoy us, but He does ask us to let them become moments of grace.

The saints, being human, were just as capable of being irritated as the rest of us, but because they looked upon life from the perspective of eternity, they learned to respond in a holy way to the things that annoyed them. For instance, on her deathbed St. Thérèse of Lisieux admitted, "I've suffered from the cold in Carmel even to the point of dying from it." This astonished Mother Agnes (Thérèse's sister Pauline, who served as prioress at the convent), for as she later testified, "Not even in the coldest weather did I see her rub her hands together or walk more rapidly or bend over more than was her usual habit, as all of us do naturally when we are cold."

St. Thérèse also had her a unique way of giving thanks for each meal — including the ones she found unappealing: she imagined herself serving the food to the Holy Family while in their home at Nazareth. Describing this ritual, she wrote: "If, for instance, I am served salad, cold fish, wine, or anything pungent in taste, I offer it to the good St. Joseph. Hot portions, ripe fruits, and the like are for the Blessed Virgin. To the Infant Jesus goes our feast-day fare, in particular, puddings, rice, and preserves. Whenever there is a wretched dinner, however, I think to myself cheerfully, 'Today, my little one, it is all for you!' "

The Little Flower, as St. Thérèse is known today, looked upon every blessing in life as an expression of God's love for her, and upon every annoyance or irritation in life as an opportunity to express, by patient endurance, her love for Him. She writes, "True love grows by sacrifice and . . . the more thoroughly the soul rejects natural satisfaction, the stronger and more detached its tenderness becomes." In other words, our love for Christ grows deeper the more we offer sacrifices in His Name, and, as St. Thérèse tells us, "The food of real love is sacrifice."

As the saints truly understood, no one can grow in love and holiness without being willing to make sacrifices for God — although, according to St. John Bosco, this exchange is truly to our benefit. Commenting on all he endured for the conversion of sinners and for the spiritual well-being of the boys entrusted to his care, the holy priest said, "It's a form of trade, you see. I ask God for souls and pay Him by giving up everything else."

Feelings of irritation are rooted in our desire, or our perceived need, to be in control of our lives. When we surrender that control totally to God and renounce our own preferences, the need and motivation for being irritated disappears. This simple idea (although admittedly a very hard one to practice) helps us to remain even-tempered in the face of major setbacks and minor annoyances.

As an example of the former, Bl. Marie of the Incarnation worked for a long time in arranging for a convent to be constructed in rural Canada, only to see it burn down completely. Instead of giving up or giving in to anger or despair, she immediately made an act of faith and began arranging for it to be rebuilt.

A far more routine situation, and a response much easier to imitate, is described for us by St. John Vianney: "St. Francis de Sales, that great saint, would leave off writing with the letter of a word half-formed in order to reply to an interruption."

Interruptions, unkind words from others, unexpected problems or delays, aches and pains, inconvenient changes in plans, and other such irritations and annoyances are all of potentially great spiritual value. This is even truer of life's serious trials and burdens. St. Faustina Kowalska tells us, "Oh, if only the suffering soul knew how it is loved by God, it would die of joy and excess of happiness! Someday, we will know the value of suffering, but then we will no longer be able to suffer. The present moment is ours." Freely and un-complainingly accepting our sufferings, large and small, helps unite us to Christ; St. Faustina says, "Suffering is a great grace; through suffering the soul becomes like the Savior; in suffering, love be-comes crystallized; the greater the suffering, the purer the love."

The Lord doesn't ask us to seek out occasions for suffering, but He does want us to make good use of the trials and irritations that arise in the normal course of life. According to Ven. Solanus Casey, our crosses "are the best school wherein to learn apprecia-tion for the love of Jesus Crucified. . . . If we only try to show the dear Lord goodwill and ask Him for resignation to the crosses He sends or permits to come our way, we may be sure that sooner or later they will turn out to have been just so many blessings in dis-guise." The idea that these crosses truly are blessings is seconded by St. Pio, for he insists, "The angels envy us for one thing only: they cannot suffer for God."

It's also important to remember that our sacrifices, no matter how difficult they may seem, are inconsequential compared with what the Lord offers us. According to St. Teresa of Avila, "We should not attach much value to what we have given God, since we shall receive for the little we have bestowed upon Him much more in this life and in the next."

Sacrifice is meant to be a regular and ongoing part of every Christian life, for Jesus speaks of the importance of taking up our cross each day and following Him.[40] Certain sacrifices are required of us by the Church — for instance, attending Sunday Mass even when we'd rather sleep in or go to the beach, and abstaining from meat on the Fridays of Lent. Other freely chosen sacrifices can be quite pleasing to God, such as fasting one day a week for world peace, or not turning on the television in the evening in order to make time for prayer and spiritual reading. Along with these important forms of self-denial, the effort to control our natural irritation when things go wrong can be a very practical way of showing our love for God, and as St. Josemaría Escrivá tells us, "If there is sacrifice when you sow love, you will also reap love." According to St. Ambrose, patient endurance is a sign that our love for God and neighbor is genuine, and St. Peter Damian suggests, "Let your understanding strengthen your patience. In serenity, look forward to the joy that follows sadness."

When we find it difficult to control our tempers or to respond calmly when irritations arise, the saints advise us to look to Christ. As Bl. Angela of Foligno reminds us, "He submitted Himself to the elements, unto cold and heat, hunger and thirst . . . concealing His power and despoiling Himself thereof in the likeness of man, in order that He might teach us weak and wretched mortals with what patience we ought to bear tribulations."

In particular, we should look to the Cross of Jesus. St. John of the Cross suggests, "Whenever anything disagreeable or displeasing happens to you, remember Christ crucified and be silent." A similar idea is expressed by St. Elizabeth Ann Seton, who challenges us, "You think you make sacrifices. Look at the sacrifice of Calvary, and compare yours with it." St. John Vianney takes this point a step further by advising, "When we must do something we dislike, let us say to God, 'My God, I offer You this in honor of the moment when You died for me.' "

---

[40] Luke 14:27.

Many of our irritations are centered in other people. At times their bad habits, ungracious manners, deliberate insults, unintentionally offensive words or actions, and disturbing personality quirks can be very annoying. St. Robert Bellarmine tells us, "As this matter is one of such great consequence, try to look upon the defects of your companions as a kind of special medicine and cross prepared for you by God. There are many people who willingly practice penances which they have chosen for themselves, but who refuse to put up with their neighbors' faults, although that is the penance which God wants them to bear. . . ."

As a wife and mother, a daughter-in-law of a cranky old man, and a cofoundress and mother superior of a religious order, St. Jane Frances de Chantal certainly knew a lot about irritations from firsthand experience, so her reflections have great value for us. She writes, "Suppose you have a little pain in your head or stomach, or you've made a great blunder, or you've been upset. Don't stop at all that. Pass on and go to God without scrutinizing your trouble. 'But I want to look at it so I can offer it to God.' That's good. But when you offer it to Him, don't look on your trouble so much that you magnify it and confirm that you have good reason to complain. Oh, indeed, we must be more courageous and abandon ourselves totally to God, wishing for Him only and being satisfied with Him alone."

St. Jane further advises, "Be very faithful about responding to occasions for putting virtues into practice. For instance, is there something about your clothing or your bed that inconveniences and annoys you — something that doesn't fit well or that isn't to your liking? Accept it heartily, kiss it, if you can, and be very glad to have it. Perhaps the soup given to you at dinner is too thin or too thick; or it's unsalted or watery; there isn't enough oil on your salad or the vinegar isn't strong enough. Rejoice at these opportunities to discipline your sense of taste. Embrace them with love and cheerfulness. . . . Something you don't like is given to you;

something has been forgotten, but you can do without it — love all situations like this. Adapt yourself to God's providence, which allows them. If you know how to take them in the right way, you can benefit by them and grow in the perfection of divine love."

As St. Jane's examples illustrate, we have a wealth of daily opportunities to practice discipline and self-denial, thereby growing in grace and conforming ourselves more completely to Christ. Rather than wasting such precious gifts, the saints urge us to recognize, to accept, and to use them for God's glory and our own sanctification.

For Further Reflection

"We do well to remember how short, after all, it is till our suffering and our time of merit will be over. Let us offer everything, therefore, to the divine Spouse of souls, that we may accept it as helping Him to save immortal souls, our own included." — *Ven. Solanus Casey*

"All our life is sown with tiny thorns that produce in our hearts a thousand involuntary movements of hatred, envy, fear, impatience, a thousand little fleeting disappointments, a thousand slight worries, a thousand disturbances that momentarily alter our peace of soul. For example, a word escapes that should not have been spoken. Or someone utters another that offends us. A child inconveniences you. A bore stops you. You don't like the weather. Your plan is not going to work. A piece of furniture is broken. A dress is torn. I know these are not occasions for practicing very heroic virtue. But they would definitely be enough to acquire it if we really wished to." — *St. Claude de la Colombière*

"Complete serenity of mind is a gift from God; but this serenity is not given without our own intense effort. You will achieve nothing by your own efforts alone; yet God will not give you anything, unless you work with all your strength. This is an unbreakable law." — *St. Theophan the Recluse*

Something You Might Try

♦ As she became increasingly famous throughout the world, Bl. Teresa of Calcutta was constantly being photographed — an experience she heartily disliked. Finally she made a bargain with God: every time she had her picture taken, He had to welcome one of her poor, suffering clients into Heaven. There's every reason to believe the Lord graciously agreed to this arrangement, and no reason we can't propose a similar agreement with the Lord. For instance, we might pray, "Dear God, I greatly dislike this situation [or experience]. I will endure it without complaint, but in return, I ask You to release one soul from Purgatory [or to grant the grace of repentance to one hardened sinner, or to bestow one special blessing upon this particular person]." God doesn't owe us anything, but He's happy to respond generously to our freely given sacrifices (especially when our prayer is intended to benefit someone else, and not primarily ourselves).

♦ St. Louis de Montfort advises, "Do as the storekeeper does with his merchandise: make a profit on every article. Suffer not the loss of the tiniest fragment of the true cross. It may only be the sting of a fly or the point of a pin that annoys you; it may be the little eccentricities of a neighbor, some unintentional slight, the insignificant loss of a penny, some little restlessness of soul, a light pain in your limbs. Make a profit on every article as the grocer does, and you will soon be wealthy in God." Additionally, we might "take inventory" at the end of each day, asking ourselves: What irritations and problems did I experience today? How did I respond to them? Did I obtain the greatest possible spiritual value from each of them? If not, what can I do differently the next time they arise?

Further Reading

Scripture: Mark 11:25; Romans 5:3-5; Ephesians 4:24; Colossians 3:13.

Classics: St. Thérèse of Lisieux, *The Story of a Soul*; Thomas à Kempis, *Imitation of Christ*; St. Francis de Sales, *An Introduction to the Devout Life*.

Contemporary Works: Charles J. Keating, *Dealing with Difficult People*.

⌒

*It amazes me, Lord Jesus, how You managed to put up
with so much without losing Your cool or venting Your frustration.
People doubted You, opposed You, twisted Your words, and
eventually tortured You and nailed You to the Cross — yet You
said, "Father, forgive them, for they know not what they do."*

*I couldn't have done that; I would have made them pay,
right then and there. Even with the Apostles, I would have
been very strict and demanding; I wouldn't have put up
with their many words and acts of foolishness. Yet You,
O Lord, were forgiving and understanding and accepting;
and I know You want me to follow Your example.*

*Help me, Lord; give me patience and holy resignation,
and remind me that whenever something goes wrong,
it's an opportunity for me to do something right — namely,
to offer up that situation as a small but worthy sacrifice,
a sacrifice for Your glory and my growth in holiness.*

Legal Problems

There is one Lawgiver and Judge,
He who is able to save and to destroy.

James 4:12

Abraham Lincoln, although he was a lawyer and a politician, is very highly regarded by most Americans (and was respected by many, but by no means all, of his contemporaries). Lincoln once told this joke about his profession: A minister and attorney were riding together, and the clergyman asked, "Sir, do you ever make mistakes while in court?" "Very rarely," the lawyer answered haughtily, "but on occasion, I must admit that I do." "And what do you do when you make a mistake?" the minister asked. The attorney responded, "Why, if they are large mistakes, I mend them. If they are small, I let them go. Tell me, don't you ever make mistakes while preaching?" "Of course," answered the preacher. "And I dispose of them in the same way that you do. Not long ago, I meant to tell the congregation that the Devil is the father of liars, but I made a mistake and said the father of lawyers. The mistake was so small that I let it go."

Why are there so many jokes about lawyers? Why are lawyers (and perhaps the judicial system as a whole) held in such low esteem? Part of the reason seems to be that they have a reputation for being dishonest and for using the law for their own purposes. Obviously, this isn't entirely true. There are vast numbers of honest attorneys who do their very best on behalf of their clients, but there are enough recorded cases of greed and underhanded tactics to justify a certain amount of suspicion or mistrust on the part of the rest of us.

Moreover, legal judgments rendered by fallible human beings are often influenced by powerful persons or groups, and thus anything but impartial. As St. Thomas Aquinas noted, there are "two main reasons why men fall short of justice: deference to magnates, and deference to the mobs."

Another reason for disliking lawyers might be that the law has become so complicated and involved — and, in many cases, downright illogical or perverse — that the average, reasonable person has difficulty interpreting or comprehending it. (For instance, just try reading and explaining all the fine print on a legal contract.) Indeed, the complexity of the law sometimes seems to be a tool used by the wealthy and powerful in preserving their privileged position. In this regard, Bl. Placid Riccardi noted, "It is little use expecting anything from the mighty ones of this world; for the most part, they leave the poor in their poverty and, mean and ungenerous as they are, turn a deaf ear to the cry of those who are weak and helpless."

A third reason the legal profession may be held in low esteem is a simple one: many honest people fear getting in trouble with the law — not because of any direct criminal actions on their part, but because of circumstances largely beyond their knowledge or control. This fear is not unfounded; as a basic rule of thumb, it's often said that, in our litigious society, anyone can be sued by anyone else for anything at almost any time. This is something of an exaggeration, of course — but not as much as most of us would like. We fear being sued and losing valuable time and money defending ourselves — not to mention the possible loss of our reputation and liberty — and so we take out our frustrations on lawyers as a group (even though we quite rightly seek the services of an attorney in certain situations).

If you're having legal difficulties, you need a good, honest lawyer (and yes, they do exist). You can also benefit from the prayers and intercession of the saints. A number of them were lawyers, and several of them had legal difficulties of their own.

If we were to consider illegal trials, of course, we must begin with the one involving Jesus Himself: He was condemned although innocent, as shown by Pontius Pilate's willingness to release Him after an examination of the facts.[41] Jesus, the Son of God and the One who will judge the world, placed Himself under human authority and was unjustly handed over to death. If this could happen to Him, it shouldn't surprise us that we might be similarly abused, for as Jesus remarked to His disciples, "If the world hates you, know that it has hated me before it hated you."[42] It was our Lord's mission to go to His death like a lamb, not opening His mouth,[43] but this isn't necessarily expected of us. It's quite legitimate for us to defend ourselves (so long as we trust not primarily in ourselves or our attorneys, but in God).

St. Paul, after being placed on trial before the Jewish Sanhedrin and the Roman governor, exercised his rights as a Roman citizen by appealing to the emperor.[44] We may legitimately stand upon our legal rights as American citizens, so long as we recognize that, as Christians, we're subject to a higher law, and that all our choices and actions will ultimately be judged by God.

Several saints have been the victims of illegal trials, just as Jesus was — and, like Him, died as martyrs. A famous example, of

[41] John 18:38; 19:4.
[42] John 15:18.
[43] Isa. 53:7; Matt. 26:63.
[44] Acts 25:11.

course, is St. Joan of Arc, the great leader of the French army during the Hundred Years' War. Betrayed to her enemies, Joan was condemned in a mock trial for allegedly practicing sorcery and was burned at the stake.

Less well known is the story of the seventeenth-century Irish martyr St. Oliver Plunkett, the Archbishop of Armagh during a time of severe persecution of Catholics by the English. After ministering to his flock in secret for a number of years, Oliver was betrayed to the English authorities, accused of treason, and taken to London for his trial. There he wasn't allowed sufficient time to gather witnesses or documents needed for his defense, nor was he allowed a defense counsel, any challenges to unfriendly jurors, or a specific statement of charges. The witnesses against him had been coached by the prosecutors regarding what to say (and when they forgot, one of the court attorneys or justices helped them along), and these witnesses resorted to half-truths or outright lies. Oliver's cross-examination was often cut short by the judges, and only one witness appeared in his defense. Although the odds were stacked completely against him, the archbishop defended himself with dignity and grace — but the outcome was predetermined. After only fifteen minutes, the jury declared him guilty of treason — to which the saint responded, *"Deo gratias"* ("Thanks be to God"). A few weeks later, St. Oliver Plunkett was hanged, his final words being, "Lord Jesus, receive my soul."

This would be a tragic and upsetting story, were it not for the fact that God, as the Divine Judge, always has the final word. Heavenly justice, although often long-delayed, is certain and unassailable. In the meantime, Christians involved in legal difficulties are entitled to defend themselves. In choosing an attorney, and in using legal means to mount a defense, one might well seek intercession from the following saints: St. Raymond of Penafort, a great canon lawyer (that is, an expert on Church law); St. Francis de Sales, who received a doctorate in law (primarily at his father's insistence); St. Ambrose, an attorney in fourth-century Rome who later became the great bishop of Milan; St. Thomas More, a lawyer who used every legal means to defend himself against a false charge of treason and, when these failed, was willing to die for his principles; St. Alphonsus Liguori, a talented young lawyer whose loss of an important case prompted him to enter religious life; St. Andrew Avellino, who, after telling a lie in court to win a case, repented and entered religious life after reading the words of Scripture, "The lying mouth destroys the soul";[45] St. Turibius of Mongrovejo, a professor of law at the University of Salamanca in sixteenth-century Spain; St. Cajetan, a lawyer-turned-priest who played a major role in reforming the Church following the rise of Protestantism; the thirteenth-century priest and attorney St. Ives, who was known as "an attorney who was an honest man"; and St. Fidelis of Sigmaringen, who, in his legal career before becoming a priest, dedicated himself to defending the rights of the oppressed, thus receiving the nickname "the poor man's lawyer."

Centuries ago, St. Ambrose stated, "The rule of justice is plain: namely, that a good man ought not to swerve from the truth, nor inflict any unjust loss on anyone, nor act in any way deceitfully or fraudulently."

All of us who follow Jesus certainly agree with Ambrose's words; but experience and observation have taught us that many people today pay no heed to the obligations of justice, and we're certainly within our rights to defend ourselves against them, legally and otherwise.

Even as you take any necessary legal steps to protect yourself from actual or potential opponents, also prepare yourself spiritually: admit your sins to God and seek His forgiveness, remain honest in all your dealings, ask the Lord for His guidance, pray to the saints (especially those listed above) for their intercession, and

[45] Wisd. 1:11.

trust that whatever happens can be used by God for His glory and your spiritual and moral growth.

For Further Reflection

"Do not forget that, at the side of the Son of God, you have a tireless lawyer, an invincible litigant for the most hardened sinners: Mary, the Mother of God." — *St. Seraphim of Sarov (Mary is willing to intercede for us in all our problems, including legal difficulties.)*

"What was it that I loved in that theft? Was it the pleasure of acting against the law, in order that I, a prisoner under rules, might have a maimed counterfeit of freedom by doing what was forbidden, with a dim similitude of omnipotence? The desire to steal was awakened simply by the prohibition of stealing." — *St. Augustine (In reflecting on his youthful act of stealing apples from an orchard, Augustine came to realize that his misdeed was primarily an act of rebellion. If we're having trouble with authority, we must honestly ask ourselves why. Is it possible we're acting out of misplaced anger or pride? Is our legal dispute with an opponent truly a matter of principle, or might it be a contest of wills or of stubborn egos? We can and should defend our legal rights, but we should also examine our motives to see whether there might be another, less honorable dynamic at work.)*

"Once charity begins, justice begins; as charity increases, justice increases; when charity is perfect, justice is perfect." — *St. Robert Bellarmine (Thus, it may be possible to minimize or even forestall certain legal difficulties by reaching out to a potential opponent in a friendly and charitable way; and even if this fails from a legal perspective, it's still the Christian thing to do.)*

Something You Might Try

♦ In Matthew 18:15-17, Jesus advises, "If your brother sins against you, go and tell him his fault, between you and him alone.

If he listens to you, you have gained your brother. But if he does not listen, take one or two others along with you, that every word may be confirmed by the evidence of two or three witnesses. If he refuses to listen to them, tell it to the Church; and if he refuses to listen even to the Church, let him be to you as a Gentile and a tax collector." Our Lord recommends a gradually escalating attempt to resolve serious disputes, including the use of mediation. Thus, instead of immediately resorting to lawsuits, we should explore all other possible options, such as third-party mediators, binding arbitration, and so forth. Not only might this be less stressful and expensive, but it would also seem to be more consistent with the gospel.

♦ Consider this reflection by St. Augustine: "You say the times are troublesome, the times are burdensome, the times are miserable. Live rightly, and you will change the times. The times have never hurt anyone. Those who are hurt are human beings; those by whom they are hurt are also human beings. So, change human beings, and the times will be changed." Lawsuits and legal problems are certainly a sign of our times, but this shouldn't discourage us from living out our Faith; and if enough of us do this, the times will change.

Further Reading

Scripture: Proverbs 13:23; Sirach 33:2-3; Luke 12:58; 1 Corinthians 6:1-4.

Contemporary Works: Joseph G. Allegretti, *The Lawyer's Calling: Christian Faith and Legal Practice.*

☞

Lord, my opponent and the attorneys are out to get me —
or so it seems. I fear the law will be used against me;

More Saintly Solutions

I worry that all my honest efforts to do what's right
and to correct my mistakes won't count in my favor;
I dread the possible cost to me and my family
in terms of money, time, and reputation.

It isn't fair, O Lord — and this reminds me
that there really isn't anyone I can turn to except You.
I call upon You, O Lord of justice and truth,
and beg You to protect my rights and to defend my cause.

I do not ask that my opponent be crushed or shamed,
but only prevented from doing me harm; and if his heart
be touched by the grace of repentance,
I will even more rejoice and give thanks.

I turn to You, O Lord, and ask for Your assistance.
Grant me vindication and a sense of inner peace;
help me to forgive those who are harming me,
and let me remember that, no matter what the
outcome may be, You love me and
are with me every step of the way.

Lust

*It is these who have not defiled themselves with women, for they
are chaste; it is these who follow the Lamb wherever He goes;
these have been redeemed from mankind as first-fruits for God and
the Lamb, and in their mouth no lie was found, for they are spotless.*
Revelation 14:4-5

St. Thomas Aquinas came from a noble Italian background, and
as a young man, he desired to enter the priesthood. His family was
not averse to the idea, but they strongly opposed his intention to
enter the relatively new and politically uninfluential Dominican Order. Being related to the royal houses of several European
nations, they felt it important that Thomas join a religious order
whose prestige would make possible a rapid advancement to high
ecclesiastic office. Thomas, however, followed through on his intention to join the Dominicans and then asked his superiors to
send him far away from his family's meddling. Accordingly, they
decided he would go to Paris for his formation, but they failed to
take into account the determination of Thomas's mother, the
Countess Theodora.

While he was on his way to Paris, two of Thomas's brothers —
the knights Landolf and Reginald — kidnaped him, acting on
their mother's orders, and forcibly took him to the family estate,

holding him as a virtual prisoner. Thomas's family endeavored, over a long period, to get him to change his mind, but the youth remained unwavering in his determination to become a Dominican. Finally his brothers took a radical step: they arranged for a beautiful, naked young woman of loose morals to enter Thomas's room, hoping lust would subvert his good intentions. Acting decisively, the saint took an iron from the fire and used it to chase the temptress from the room; then he fell to his knees in prayer, begging the Lord's deliverance.

According to legend, at that moment two angels appeared and, in answer to his prayer and as a reward for his fidelity, wrapped Thomas with a cord of chastity, saying, "On God's behalf we gird thee with the girdle of chastity, a girdle that no attack will destroy." As a result, St. Thomas was never troubled by temptations against purity for the remainder of his life. (It still took over a year for his mother to bow to the inevitable and accept his vocation — a surrender prompted in part by Thomas's success in convincing his sisters, who had come to debate him at Theodora's bidding, to join him in entering the religious life.)

St. Thomas Aquinas may have been completely freed from all temptations of the flesh, but this is certainly a rare experience. The vast majority of Christians, including saints, have had to struggle against lust to one degree or another. According to St. Thomas, "It belongs to the perfection of the moral or human good that the passions be governed by reason"; but the flesh wars against the spirit, most especially in the area of sexual feelings and desires. Before Original Sin, man's physical desires were in harmony with his will; as St. Thomas writes in his *Summa Theologica*, "Moral perfection consists in man's being moved to the good not by his will alone, but also by his sensitive appetite, as in the words of the psalm: 'My heart and flesh sing for joy to the living God.' "[46]

---

[46] *Summa Theologica*, I-II, Q. 24, art. 3; Ps. 84:2.

This restored perfection, however, is the struggle of a lifetime and requires constant vigilance against lust. The saints triumphed in this battle — sometimes in spite of great difficulties — and their victory holds out hope for us all.

St. Cyril of Jerusalem advises us, "Let us not for a short pleasure defile so great, so noble a body: for short and momentary is the sin, but the shame for many years and forever. Angels walking upon earth are they who practice chastity; the virgins have their portion with Mary the Virgin. Let all vain ornament be banished, and every hurtful glance, and all wanton gait, and every flowing robe, and perfume enticing to pleasure. But in all, for perfume let there be the prayer of sweet odor, and the practice of good works and the sanctification of our bodies."

This is wonderful advice, but as most of us would agree, it's very difficult to put into practice, for lust is a powerful lure and an ever-present danger to our souls. As St. Thomas Aquinas notes (not from experience, but through his powers of intellect and observation), "In the realm of evil thoughts, none induces to sin as much as do thoughts that concern the pleasure of the flesh." St. Augustine would have agreed quite readily with these words, as for many years he was the slave of his passions. After his conversion, he wrote, "My God, my Mercy, how much gall did You mingle in my lustfulness. I secretly entered the prison of pleasure and was sorrowfully bound with its chains." Even after he was baptized, Augustine needed to learn to rely on God's strength, not on his own: "I thought that continence arose from one's own powers, which I did not recognize in myself. I was foolish enough not to know . . . that no one can be continent unless You grant it. For You would surely have granted it if my inner groaning had reached Your ears and I with firm faith had cast my cares on You."

Because human sexuality can be a very powerful force, sins and temptations of the flesh can be conquered only with the help of divine grace. Augustine's contemporary St. Jerome had to learn this lesson. In a letter to the virgin St. Eustochium, he wrote, "How often when I was living in the desert, in the vast solitude which gives to hermits a savage dwelling place, parched by a burning sun, how often did I fancy myself among the pleasures of Rome! . . . Now, although in my fear of Hell I had consigned myself to this prison, where I had no companions but scorpions and wild beasts, I often found myself amid bevies of girls. My face was pale and my frame chilled with fasting; yet my mind was burning with desire, and the fires of lust kept bubbling up before me when my flesh was as good as dead. Helpless, I cast myself at the feet of Jesus; I watered them with my tears; I wiped them with my hair; and then I subdued my rebellious body with weeks of abstinence. . . ."

Jerome also admitted, "When I have been angry, or have had evil thoughts in my mind, or some phantom of the night has beguiled me, I do not dare to enter the basilicas of the martyrs; I shudder all over in body and soul." Knowing that one of the best ways to rid oneself of sinful thoughts is to replace them with holy or morally acceptable ideas, Jerome attempted to distract himself from sexual temptations by learning Hebrew (a project that also helped him become a great scholar).

The saints were capable of a very holy and chaste love, as demonstrated most perfectly by the Virgin Mary and her husband, St. Joseph. Other married couples, such as St. Isidore the Farmer and his wife, St. Maria de la Cabeza, observed continence for all or part of their lives together. It was also possible for saints to fall in love and not marry, but to remain completely celibate. This may have been true, for instance, of St. Francis of Assisi and St. Clare, and even more so for Bl. Diana d'Andalo and Bl. Jordan of Saxony.

More often than not, however, chastity was a struggle for the saints. There's the famous story about St. Francis of Assisi, who finally conquered lust only after throwing himself naked into a briar patch (a radical step deserving admiration, but not necessarily imitation).

A somewhat similar event in the life of St. Francis occurred before his final triumph over lust. Reacting decisively to a sexual temptation one winter day, he ran out of his cell and into the garden, and there rolled naked in the snow. Then he made seven small snow figures, saying to himself, "Look, this larger one is your wife; these four are your two sons and two daughters; the other two are a servant and a man whom you should have to serve you. Hurry, then, and clothe them since they are dying of cold. But if it is too much for you to care for so many, then take care to serve one Master!"

As Francis reminded himself, a momentary desire for pleasure can have lifelong consequences. Occasionally, however, great figures in the Church's history have converted after a lifetime of illegitimate pleasures. This was the case with St. Cyprian, who, until his conversion at age forty-six, was well known in Carthage as both a successful lawyer and a ladies' man. When he took a vow of chastity, someone who knew his past exclaimed in shock, "Whoever saw such a miracle!"

Perhaps an even more miraculous conversion was experienced by Ven. Charles de Foucald, who, as a young man, crudely warned each of his new mistresses: "I rent by the day, not by the month." The grace of God finally touched his heart, prompting him to live a life of prayer and penance, and he later wrote, "Chastity became a blessing and inner necessity to me."

Most of the saints, of course, didn't have immoral lifestyles in their past that required repentance and conversion, but many of them had ongoing struggles with impure thoughts. As a young woman in the thirteenth century, St. Aldobrandesca decided to dedicate herself to prayer after her husband died, but she was immediately afflicted with sexual temptations, triggered by memories of the legitimate pleasures she and her husband enjoyed. The holy widow overcame them to a certain degree by wearing a hairshirt and undertaking other forms of penance.

Another saint afflicted with erotic thoughts and dreams was the widower St. Alphonsus Rodriguez, who, even after becoming a Jesuit lay brother in his fifties, continued to struggle in this area for the rest of his life.

A somewhat happier and more amusing story regards the Irish monk St. Columban, who went to a female hermit for advice after being tempted by the young women of the area. She suggested he leave Ireland and go somewhere else — it didn't matter where — because the women would be less beautiful than Irish girls, thus lessening the power of the temptation. (Columban thereupon went to continental Europe, where he did indeed find it easier to overcome this difficulty.)

Our efforts to remain chaste are important not only for our own sanctification, but also because of the influence our example — and sometime our words — can have on others. St. Afra was a prostitute and the owner of a brothel. During a persecution early in the fourth century, a bishop named St. Narcissus took refuge at her establishment — and soon succeeded in converting not only Afra, but also all her employees. Someone (perhaps a regular client, angry that the women would no longer cater to his vices) informed the authorities, who arrested the bishop and his new converts and had them executed.

Another saint who ministered to sinful women was the sixth-century hermit St. Vitalis of Gaza. At the age of sixty, he felt God was calling him to seek out lost members of the flock of Christ, so he went to the great city of Alexandria and there found a job as a day laborer. Using the money he earned, each night he purchased the companionship of one of the local prostitutes — and spent the entire night kneeling in her room and praying for her conversion. His ministry bore considerable fruit, but it also caused a great deal of scandal, especially as he remained silent about his reasons for frequenting the company of loose women. As Vitalis was leaving a house of ill repute one morning, an angry but misguided

Christian struck him a blow on the head, killing him; and as a crowd gathered, one newly converted prostitute rushed to the scene and, amid her tears, explained to the amazed crowd what the saint had actually been doing.

Even as reformed sinners are very dear to Christ, the Church has always celebrated in a special way those who have preserved their virginal purity and innocence — particularly the young. Legend states that at the end of the third century, when St. Philomena was thirteen, she and her parents were summoned to an audience with the fiercely anti-Christian emperor Diocletian. Taken with her beauty, the emperor promised her and her family many benefits if she'd agree to marry him, but the girl responded, "What! Do you wish that for the love of man I should break the promise I made to Jesus Christ?" Philomena stood firm against the entreaties of her parents and the threats of the emperor and was thereupon tortured severely before being beheaded.

In a talk to young people, St. John Vianney, who had a strong devotion to Philomena, said, "St. Philomena has great power with God. Her virginity and generosity in embracing her heroic martyrdom have made her so agreeable to God that He will never refuse her anything that she asks for." The holy French priest then urged his hearers to pray for Philomena's help in overcoming all their temptations, sexual or otherwise.

Another hero of youthful virtue is St. Maria Goretti, who, at the age of twelve, withstood the impure advances of a young man named Alessandro Serenelli, whose family lived next door to Maria's. Alessandro began reading pornographic materials as a teenager, and these stirred up feelings of lust, which he frequently expressed to Maria. As a result, she made a point of never being alone with him, but on one occasion, this situation couldn't be avoided. Alessandro gave her an ultimatum: "I will not take no for an answer! Give in, or I will kill you!" The young saint responded, "No, I will not. It's a sin!" The enraged youth stabbed her fourteen times, and it was some time before her parents returned home and rushed her to a hospital. As she lay dying, Maria said, "It was Alessandro, Mama. He wanted me to do a terrible sin, but I would not." (After his arrest and conviction, Alessandro Serenelli was an angry and embittered prisoner, until he had a dream of Maria gathering flowers and presenting them to him as a sign of forgiveness. This prompted his conversion, and after his release years later, he not only apologized to Mrs. Goretti, but actually accompanied her to Rome for Maria's canonization.)

On the twenty-fifth anniversary of the canonization of St. Dominic Savio, another youthful role model of purity, Pope John Paul II said in an address to young people, "Dominic Savio, on the occasion of the proclamation of the Immaculate Conception, December 8, 1854, before the altar of Mary — as St. John Bosco testifies — renewed the promises of his First Communion, saying over and over again, 'Mary, I give you my heart. Always keep it yours. Jesus, Mary, always be my friends. I beg you, let me die rather than be so unfortunate as to commit a single sin.' Beloved sons, here is where to get strength for your programs of renewal: Jesus and Mary. They are not only role models; they are friends; even more, they are part of your life. You belong to them; they belong to you. It is a question of knowing it and believing it."

As St. Dominic Savio knew, a firm devotion to our Lord and our Lady is a powerful defense against sin and temptation. The saints also offer us additional advice when it comes to maintaining purity. For instance, St. Philip Neri tells us, "Humility is the safeguard of chastity. In the matter of purity, there is no greater danger than not fearing danger." Just because we've never given in to sexual temptations doesn't mean we can become complacent, for doing so may be a form of pride, and pride — being one of Satan's most useful tools — can easily lead to other offenses, including sins of the flesh. St. Philip also instructs us, "In all other temptations, he who fights overcomes. But against lust, he overcomes who runs away." In other words, as soon as an immodest thought presents itself, we must turn away completely and allow it no foothold in our consciousness.

St. Clement Hofbauer suggests, "When impure thoughts come into our minds, we should think of them as little as we do of the leaves that fall from trees. We must not dwell on them for a moment and, without heeding such suggestions from the enemy of souls, go quietly on our way."

Spiritual masters have long recognized that indulging the body in one area may stimulate other physical appetites, and by the same token, carefully disciplining our bodies may have a range of benefits. This, of course, is the reason vigorous physical exercise is often recommended. Not only is exercise a remedy against laziness, but it can also lead to a lessening of sexual urges.

The same thing has been found true of fasting. The hermit St. Hilarion used to eat only one small meal each day at sunset; and when subject to sexual temptations, he ate even less, claiming, "A lustful horse and an unchaste body should have their feed reduced." A similar warning is given by St. Jerome, who claimed, "The stuffing of the stomach is the hotbed of lust."

Carefully guarding our thoughts, practicing humility, and disciplining our bodies (by avoiding laziness and gluttony) are all important weapons against lust. Scripture asserts that those who persist in sexual immorality will have no part in the kingdom of God,[47] and even though this divinely inspired teaching is largely ignored or rejected in contemporary society, it remains just as true today as it was two thousand years ago. Chastity has always been a difficult standard to achieve, but never an impossible one; and as the saints demonstrate and assure us, those who persevere in this struggle will, with the help of God's grace, be victorious.

[47] 1 Cor. 6:9.

For Further Reflection

"Purity of heart requires the modesty which is patience, decency, and discretion. Modesty protects the intimate center of the person. . . . It encourages patience and moderation in loving relationships; it requires that the conditions for the definitive giving and commitment of man and woman to one another be fulfilled. Modesty is decency. It inspires one's choice of clothing. It keeps silence or reserve when there is evident risk of unhealthy curiosity. It is discreet." — *Catechism of the Catholic Church, pars. 2533, 2522*

"By lust the Devil triumphs over the entire man, over his body and over his soul; over his memory, filling it with that remembrance of unchaste delights, in order to make him take complacency in them; over his intellect, to make him desire occasions of committing sin; over the will, by making it love impurities as his last end, and as if there were no God." — *St. Alphonsus Liguori*

"Our relentless enemy, the teacher of fornication, whispers that God is lenient and particularly merciful to this passion, since it is so very natural. Yet if we watch the wiles of the demons, we will observe that after we have actually sinned, they will affirm that God is a just and inexorable Judge. They say one thing to lead us into sin, another thing to overwhelm us in despair." — *St. John Climacus (Therefore, we must always maintain a proper perspective: sexual sins are serious in nature, but our loving Father will always forgive every sin for which we're truly sorry, including those against chastity.)*

Something You Might Try

♦ The great Franciscan preacher St. Anthony of Padua once fell ill while visiting a Benedictine monastery. The monk who cared for the saint during his illness confessed that he experienced strong temptations against purity, which persisted in spite of much prayer and fasting on his part. Anthony told the Benedictine to put on his (that is, Anthony's) habit for a moment; and after doing so, the monk was freed from his difficulty. In a somewhat analogous way, in times of temptation we might imagine ourselves "putting on" the identity or outlook of our favorite saint — for example, seeing ourselves visiting the Holy Family in Nazareth and observing their perfect love for one another, pretending we're accompanying St. Paul on one of his missionary journeys and asking for his advice on this matter, interviewing St. Mary Magdalene on how meeting Jesus allowed her to change her life completely, and so on. It's not possible or necessary to wear the actual robes of a saint, but we can let ourselves be filled with the same gifts of divine grace that motivated and strengthened them.

◆ According to St. Clement of Alexandria, "Filthy talk makes us feel comfortable with filthy action. But the one who knows how to control the tongue is prepared to resist the attacks of lust." Thus, certain behaviors and settings must be avoided if we are to overcome sexual temptations. These include not only unclean conversations, but also sinful companions and many forms of entertainment, such as certain movies, television shows, magazines, books, and Internet websites and chat rooms. Society sees all these things as fun, but spiritually mature people recognize them as frequently being the bait Satan uses to draw us into much more serious sins and enslaving addictions.

Further Reading

Scripture: Sirach 9:8; Matthew 5:27-28; 1 Corinthians 6:18-20; 1 Peter 3:1-7.

Classics: St. Augustine, *Confessions*; St. Francis de Sales, *An Introduction to the Devout Life*; Dom Lorenzo Scupoli, *Spiritual Combat*.

More Saintly Solutions

Contemporary Works: Rev. H. Vernon Sattler, *Challenging Children to Chastity*; Fr. Richard Rego, *No! No! It Is a Sin!*

⌐

Dearest Jesus!
I know well that every perfect gift,
and above all others that of chastity,
depends upon the most powerful
assistance of Your Providence,
and that without You a creature can do nothing.
Therefore, I pray You to defend with Your grace,
chastity and purity in my soul as well as in my body.
And if I have ever received the impression
of anything sensible that can
stain my chastity and purity,
take it from me,
Supreme Lord of all my powers,
that I may with a pure heart advance
in Your love and service,
offering myself chaste all the days of my life
on the most pure altar of Your divinity.

St. Thomas Aquinas

Marital Problems

Love is patient and kind; love is not jealous or boastful;
it is not arrogant or rude. Love does not insist on its own way;
it is not irritable or resentful; it does not rejoice at wrong,
but rejoices in the right. Love bears all things, believes
all things, hopes all things, endures all things.

1 Corinthians 13:4-7

A couple was celebrating their fiftieth wedding anniversary, and because the husband was known to be somewhat moody and eccentric, the wife was asked — out of earshot of her spouse — how she managed to put up with his behavior. "It's simple," she replied. "On my wedding day, I decided I would choose ten of my husband's faults and promised myself I would overlook them for the sake of our marriage." The well-wisher remarked, "That was a wonderful idea. Say, if you don't mind my asking, what were some of the faults you chose?" "To tell the truth," the woman replied, "I never got around to listing them. But every time my husband did something that really upset me, I used to say to myself, 'Lucky for him that's one of the ten!'"

God intended marriage to be a blessing, but it's often hard work, and many times it involves misunderstandings, hurt feelings, and even serious injustices. One or both spouses may be selfish, insensitive, critical, disengaged, unsupportive, or even un-faithful. Husbands and wives may magnify each other's faults while overlooking their own failings, and their children, if any, may be deprived of a critically important sense of emotional secu-rity and affection while learning the wrong lessons about relation-ships. Unhappy marriages can cause great suffering and distress, especially for a faithful husband or wife who wants to make every-thing work, but who receives little cooperation from his or her spouse. This isn't God's plan, but our Faith teaches us that God is able to bring some good out of every situation; and this truth can be a source of hope for those enduring marital problems.

Persons involved in troubled marriages have powerful spiritual allies in Heaven, whose example can be instructive and inspira-tional, and whose prayers and intercession can be a source of re-newed strength and hope.

Any discussion of saintly marriage must begin, of course, with Mary and Joseph, the Mother and foster-father of Jesus. Theirs was a perfect love, with each holy spouse seeking to outdo the other in expressions of appreciation, deference, and support. Joseph knew that his wife was the sinless Mother of God, and he treated her with the greatest possible love and respect, never thinking of his own needs, but concerning himself only with the care and protec-tion of Mary, and later, also of Jesus.

Mary, for her part, humbly accepted the leadership of her husband, deferring to his judgment, supporting his decisions, and seeing to all his needs. They prayed and worshiped God together, and together taught the child Jesus all the mysteries and beauty of their Jewish faith. Mary and Joseph understood one another's hearts and joyfully encouraged each other's ongoing growth in holiness.

When Joseph experienced his final illness, Mary and Jesus were at his side, loving him and supporting him. The three mem-bers of the Holy Family experienced sorrow at their separation, but no regret, as their life together lacked nothing in terms of grace and love.

Similar marriages that were "made in Heaven" were experienced by St. Isidore the Farmer and his wife, St. Maria de la Cabeza, who were both known for their piety and concern for the poor, and by St. Henry and his wife, St. Cunegund, who, as emperor and empress, promoted religion and defended the rights of the Church. St. Frances of Rome was very happily married to her husband, Lorenzo, and it's said that they never quarreled during their forty years of married life.

St. Margaret of Scotland married King Malcolm III, a good but uncultured man; Margaret softened the rough edges of his personality and helped him grow in holiness. This same vital service was performed by St. Louis IX, king of France. When he was nineteen, he married Marguerite of Provence, who was only twelve. Marguerite was something of a spoiled child, restless and arrogant by nature, but she was charmed by Louis's love and piety, and his good influence aided her growth in wisdom and maturity. They and their ten children had a very happy family life.

God blesses those who seek to be a blessing to others, especially within marriage. As a widower, St. Thomas More desired to remarry for the sake of his young children. He was attracted to the younger daughter of a particular family, but didn't want to embarrass her older sister Jane (for in sixteenth-century England, it was considered shameful if the older siblings didn't marry first). So, in an unusual act of Christian charity, he took Jane as his wife. Thomas's generosity was rewarded: he and Jane had a happy life together, and their home was known as a place of laughter and merriment.

Marriage is meant to assist the mutual sanctification of the spouses, and this was dramatically true of a young Christian couple in Egypt near the end of the third century. Sts. Timothy and Maura were devout Christians with a deep love for God; they also fell deeply in love with each other and were married. After only twenty days of wedded bliss, however, Timothy was arrested and taken before the Roman governor, who ordered him to turn over his books of sacred Scripture to be burned. Timothy refused, even after enduring brutal tortures, and so Maura was arrested in the expectation that this would cause the young man to submit. Maura, however, urged Timothy to remain unyielding and declared that she was ready to die with her husband. This holy couple was thereupon put to death in an exceedingly painful way, being nailed to a wall and remaining alive for nine agonizing days before finally dying. It can be said that Sts. Timothy and Maura loved God together, died together, and entered Heaven together.

Unfortunately, not all marriages are as happy or holy as those described above; and here, too, we see that the saints are able to understand and sympathize over our difficulties. In the fourth century, a Christian and future saint named Fabiola was born of a noble Roman family and for a time was a follower of St. Jerome. She had a difficult marriage, however; she fell away from the Church and then divorced her husband because of his immorality. Fabiola remarried; when her second husband died, she returned to the Church with Jerome's encouragement.

The death of a spouse also proved to be a release for Bl. Albert of Bergamo. He was known for patiently and silently enduring his wife's earnest attempts to make his life miserable, and her death freed him to enter the Dominican Order (which surely seemed like Heaven on earth compared with his earlier state of life).

One of the worst imaginable experiences of marriage occurred to St. Godelive in the eleventh century: she was abandoned by her new husband and terribly mistreated by her mother-in-law. Later her husband returned, but only pretended to seek reconciliation. He actually desired to be rid of his wife, and so had Godelive murdered by strangling and drowning.

Another unfortunate spouse was the medieval knight St. Gengulf, who heard rumors that his beautiful wife had been cheating on him. When she brazenly denied this, Gengulf challenged her to plunge her arm into the cool water of a well, thereby proving her innocence. The lying wife confidently agreed, but when she did so, the water suddenly began to boil, scalding her arm. Rather than slaying the adulteress, as many a knight would have done, the saddened Gengulf responded in a truly noble way: he moved to another castle and devoted himself to a life of charity and penance (presumably praying, among other things, for his wife's repentance). Rather than responding with shame and remorse, however, the unfaithful wife acted out of rage; she sent her lover to Gengulf's castle, where he murdered the saint in his bed.

The saints sometimes suffered grave injustice as a result of their marital commitments. On other occasions, though, they were able to prevent an injustice from being done. In 1069, St. Peter Damian was sent by the Pope to Henry IV, the Holy Roman Emperor, a man of great ambition but limited morals. Peter's task was to convince the emperor not to divorce his wife, as he was planning to do. The saint succeeded in his mission — so much so that Henry was from that time on an ideal husband. When later asked why he was so convincing, Peter explained, "I seek the favor of no one; I fear no one."

In regard to marriage, husbands and wives shouldn't fear one another, but they certainly should seek each other's favor. Spouses should strive to please each other, while living together in mutual harmony and respect. According to St. John Chrysostom, "There is no relationship between human beings so close as that of husband and wife, if they are united as they ought to be."

Close and happy marriages are an important priority for the Church. This is one reason why most dioceses and parishes require some type of marriage-preparation process for engaged couples. Along with these, there are also various marriage-encounter or enrichment programs for married couples designed to make good marriages even better.

In addition, several of the saints have certain important things to say about the relationship between husband and wife. St. John Chrysostom, writing in an age when women had little freedom and generally weren't considered the equal of men, had much advice for husbands. He wrote, for instance, that love should be the force binding a wife to her spouse: "One's partner for life, the mother of one's children, the source of one's every joy, should never be fettered with fear and threats, but with love and patience. What kind of marriage can there be when the wife is afraid of her husband? What sort of satisfaction could a husband himself have, if he lives with his wife as if she were a slave, and not with a woman by her own free will?" The saint also insists, "Your wife is God's creation. If you reproach her, you are not condemning her, but Him who made her."

Divorce is widespread today, but it was also known (although much less common) in the ancient world; and divorced women had far fewer legal safeguards, and much less social acceptance, than they do today. That's part of the reason St. John Chrysostom, defending the Church's teaching on the sanctity of marriage, delivered this rather blunt message to the men of his day: "If you take a bad wife, you must endure the annoyance." The saint also noted, "When there is an infection in our bodies, we do not cut off the limb, but try to expel the disease. We must do the same with a wife. If there is some wickedness in her, do not reject your wife, but expel the evil." John Chrysostom's emphasis on marital duties and authority wasn't completely one-sided; he also had this message for women: "A wife should never nag her husband: 'You lazy coward, you have no ambition! Look at our relatives and neighbors; they have plenty of money. Their wives have far more than I do.' Let no wife say any such thing; she is her husband's body, and it is not for her to dictate to her head, but to submit and obey."

Today such a message would be unwelcome or even offensive to many ears, but St. John Chrysostom's underlying point is surely a valid one: husbands and wives each have mutual responsibilities toward one another, and each must help make Christ present in their home.

Sexual fidelity is one obvious example of this. As John Chrysostom says, "Husband and wife are equally responsible for the honor of their marriage bed" (a very even-handed approach when one considers that, throughout much of history, women have often suffered a greater penalty for adultery than men). Spouses are also supposed to respect each other's spiritual and emotional needs, and be supportive in their efforts to live out their particular vocations.

St. Robert Bellarmine warns, "Everyone has faults. If they are patiently endured, peace will reign happily, but if each little peccadillo is going to arouse friction and put the other out of temper, it will be impossible to live in harmony." Marriage partners aren't supposed to be a source of irritation to each other; they must be willing to compromise and, if necessary, give up certain quirks or habits, or even change their behavior, for the sake of their spouses. It's very easy for husbands and wives to take one another for granted, but God requires more of them than this. St. Robert states, "The wife must love her husband as if there were no other man in the world, in much the same way as the husband should love her as if no other woman existed."

Christian couples have the duty of living in a way that witnesses to the gospel. According to St. John Vianney, "Husbands and wives should live peacefully in their union of marriage; they should be mutually edifying to each other, pray for one another, bear patiently with one another's faults, encourage virtue in one another by good example, and follow the holy and sacred rules of their state, remembering that they are the children of the saints and that, consequently, they ought not to behave like pagans, who have not the happiness of knowing the one true God."

Our experience of the mercy of God should make us forgiving toward one another. This truth applies in a special way within marriage. St. Elisabeth of Schönau tells us, "With patience and compassion let the man support the frailties of the woman, and the woman support the frailties of the man. Do not disdain each other; instead, vie in showing the greater honor to each other. Bitter and contentious words should never arise between you; rather, reprove each other's excesses in the spirit of gentleness and good severity." Because of human weakness, there will almost certainly be differences in opinion, and disagreements of a more serious nature, but because each human being is a valuable part of God's creation, there's never an excuse for one spouse to speak or act disrespectfully toward the other (nor for parents and children to speak or act in such a manner).

Sadly, not all married couples are closely united in the way God intends, and this sometimes calls for heroic courage and self-denial on the part of one of the spouses. Infidelity, hostility, unreasonable demands or expectations, self-absorption, or indifference on the part of one's husband or wife can be a very heavy cross to bear. In such cases, God asks the suffering spouse to remain faithful, to pray for the conversion and spiritual well-being of the other party, and to seek consolation from the Church and emotional support from family and friends. In many instances, marriage counseling, or individual counseling for the suffering spouse, can be helpful. There are also programs for troubled marriages, such as Retrouvaille, which have been quite successful in restoring and renewing troubled relationships.

In the book of Revelation, St. John describes how he was told by an angel, "Blessed are those who are invited to the marriage supper of the Lamb." The angel also assured him, "These are true words of God."[48] Jesus, the Lamb of God, invites each of us to the heavenly celebration of His marriage to His own bride, the Church; and this invitation includes all who faithfully try to serve Him,

[48] Rev. 19:9.

even if their own marriages on earth are far from perfect. Let us persevere here and now, that we may rejoice in the age to come.

For Further Reflection

"As a break with God, the first sin had for its first consequence the rupture of the original communion between man and woman. . . . Nevertheless, the order of creation persists, though seriously disturbed. To heal the wounds of sin, man and woman need the help of the grace that God in His infinite mercy never refuses them. Without His help man and woman cannot achieve the union of their lives for which God created them in the beginning." — *Catechism of the Catholic Church, pars. 1607, 1608*

"A wife should respect her husband even when he shows her no love, and a husband should love his wife even when she shows him no respect. Then they will both be found to lack nothing, since each has fulfilled the commandment given to him." — *St. John Chrysostom*

"Let there be one home, one table, a shared wealth, one bed, and one soul for you, and make room for the fear of the Lord in your midst. Fear of the Lord is the ornament of the marriage bed; the marriage bed that is devoid of it will be judged cursed and unclean by the Lord." — *St. Elisabeth of Schönau*

Something You Might Try

◆ St. Théophane Vénard writes, "Happiness is to be found only in the home where God is loved and honored, where each one loves, and helps, and cares for the others." Without God, there is no lasting happiness, and without God, unhappiness can't be borne successfully or given a deeper meaning. If there are problems in your marriage, you might do well to look also at your relationship with God. Is it everything it should be? Is the Lord asking something more of you at this stage of your life? The more open you are to His grace, the more spiritual resources you'll have in coping with your problems.

♦ This advice to married persons comes from St. Bernadine of Siena: "Even as you seek a virtuous, fair, and good spouse . . . it is fitting that you should be the same." One of the results of Original Sin is that each of us is sometimes quicker to see the faults of others than to see our own, and this can be especially true within marriage. Spouses must honestly ask themselves, "How am I contributing to the difficulties between us? Which of my faults or habits annoy my husband or wife? What can I do to make things better between us?" Quite often the best way to improve one's spouse is to begin improving oneself. An indirect approach, marked by sensitivity, compassion, and acceptance, has sometimes been known to work wonders.

Further Reading

Scripture: Mark 10:9; Ephesians 5:21; Hebrews 13:4.

Classics: St. Francis de Sales, *An Introduction to the Devout Life*.

Contemporary Works: Kathleen Fischer and Thomas Hart, *Promises to Keep: Developing the Skills of Marriage*; James Greteman, *Creating a Marriage*; Beverly and Tom Rodgers, *Soul-Healing Love: Ten Practical, Easy-to-Learn Techniques for Couples in Crisis*; Gerald Foley, *Courage to Love . . . When Your Marriage Hurts*.

Dear Virgin Mary,
I ask you and your spouse, St. Joseph,
to intercede with your Son
on behalf of my marriage.
My spouse and I are having difficulties;

we don't always see eye to eye,
and we find it hard to communicate.
I pray that our mutual respect can be restored,
that we can learn to love one another
wholeheartedly once again,
and that our marital commitment to each other
can be renewed and enriched.
Please obtain for us, from your Son,
the special graces we need,
and help us to remain faithful
to our sacred calling.

Mental Illness

And as he thus made his defense, Festus said with a loud voice, "Paul,
you are mad; your great learning is turning you mad." But Paul said,
"I am not mad, most excellent Festus, but I am speaking the sober truth."

Acts 26:24-25

The experience of mental illness is a difficult one for many people; it's estimated that one in every four American families is affected by it, with millions of Americans actually experiencing it in one form or another. The National Alliance for the Mentally Ill defines mental illness as "a group of disorders causing severe disturbances in thinking, feeling, and relating" — disorders that greatly diminish the sufferer's ability to cope with the normal demands of life. Some forms of mental illness include dementia, obsessive-compulsive disorder, schizophrenia, Alzheimer's disease, panic disorder, psychosis, phobia, and severe depression (not the mild form that most people experience from time to time).

Quite often mental illness has a physiological cause (for instance, a chemical imbalance), and thus, it's not something the person can just "snap out of." Sufferers require compassion and understanding (although often they experience just the opposite).

If you (or a loved one) suffer from mental illness in any form, it's important to realize that God always loves and cherishes you;

and the lives of many of the saints bear witness to this truth. Some of them are especially known for their compassion toward those who suffered this cross, and several of them were themselves considered insane or unbalanced by their contemporaries.

For instance, one of the most-loved figures of history, St. Francis of Assisi, had a very difficult start to his ministry; his disheveled appearance after several days of prayer and fasting caused the townspeople to accuse him of being mad and to pelt him with stones. (Francis's angry father took him home, beat him, and chained his feet — a fate often suffered by the mentally ill and other misunderstood people throughout the ages.)

Living out the Gospel in a dramatic way has always struck the world as somewhat insane, as many holy people have discovered. St. Michelina of Pesano, on being widowed at an early age, underwent a dramatic conversion, and after giving away her possessions, begged in the streets on behalf of the poor. Her relatives, believing her to have lost her mind, temporarily had her confined to an asylum. (Her gentleness and patience eventually led to her release, as her family concluded that she was deluded but harmless.)

In earlier centuries, there were saints known as "fools for Christ" because of their eccentric behavior; some of them deliberately sought mistreatment and humiliation as a way of growing in sanctity. In the sixth century, for instance, St. Simon Salus (the word *salus* means "crazy") cared for the poor and other outcasts of society, including reformed prostitutes. Wanting to understand and share in their sufferings, he acted outrageously and gained a reputation as — depending on one's point of view — either a madman or a saint. One who followed his example about a thousand years later was St. Basil the Blessed, a holy man who lived in Moscow and devoted himself to caring for the poor. (On one occasion, he actually rebuked Czar Ivan the Terrible. Basil's reputation for insanity may have caused Ivan to overlook the offense and spare his life.)

Sometimes the saints have had reason to doubt their own sanity. The great Spanish mystic St. Teresa of Avila was blessed by many spiritual experiences, including hearing heavenly voices and seeing visions. When these first began, they caused her great concern, until the assistance of her spiritual director, St. Peter of Alcantara, helped her discern their authenticity. (Teresa's friend and fellow mystic, St. John of the Cross, instructs us to be very suspicious of such mysterious sights and voices: quite often, he suggests, if we're not actually imagining these things, they have a demonic origin.) The need to discern one's own calling from God is often a challenging one, and people of a more energetic or excitable temperament can sometimes behave in ways that cause concern in their neighbors.

One saint whose spiritual conversion at first raised questions about his sanity was John of God, a mercenary soldier given to drinking and gambling. At the age of forty, he was profoundly moved by the preaching of St. John of Avila — so much so that he spent a day publicly tearing his hair, beating his breast, and crying aloud for divine mercy. The authorities, quite understandably for the time, confined him to a lunatic asylum. There he was visited by St. John, who rejoiced in his moral conversion, but urged him to express it in a more acceptable manner — such as actively caring for the needs of the poor. (Even then John tended to go overboard, at least in the eyes of many people. He was summoned by the Archbishop of Granada in response to a complaint that John's hospital accepted even prostitutes and other undesirables. John answered, "The Son of Man came for sinners, but I confess that I know of no bad person in my hospital except myself alone, who am indeed unworthy to eat the bread of the poor." Greatly touched by John's humility, the archbishop became one of his most fervent supporters.)

Holiness has often been mistaken for insanity — especially in some of its more extreme manifestations. After the death of her husband, Bl. Clare of Rimini enrolled in the Third Order of St. Francis (a branch of the Franciscans intended for lay associates) and inflicted severe penances upon herself. During Lent she slept among ruins and was exposed to the weather, and she made a point of eating the most revolting food available. On Good Friday, she had her hands bound behind her and let herself be pulled through the streets by a rope around her neck, in imitation of Christ. Members of the Poor Clares, considering their sister in Christ unbalanced, locked her up to prevent her from returning to her "home" among the ruins of an old city wall.

In the sixteenth century, Bl. Julian of St. Augustine twice sought entry into the Franciscans, but he, too, was considered mentally unstable because of his severe penances (although he did eventually succeed in becoming a Franciscan brother). The nineteenth-century Italian widow Bl. Paula Cerioli founded a religious order (the Institute of the Holy Family of Bergamo) after her husband's death. Because of her unorthodox methods, some critics considered her strange or "cracked." "So I am," Paula replied, "by the lunacy of the Cross."

Another religious foundress, St. Raphaela Maria Porras, who established the Handmaids of the Sacred Heart of Jesus, was falsely accused of mental incompetence by other members of her order (including her own sister) so as to further their own ambitions. The saint responded in a manner the world would certainly consider crazy: she humbly practiced obedience and resignation to the will of God, spending the rest of her life as a simple sister in one of her order's convents.

Those who truly love God show this by their compassion toward others — including persons suffering from mental illness and related diseases and conditions. For instance, in the sixteenth century, the Jesuit priest St. Francis Borgia proved to be of great assistance to the dowager queen Joanna (mother of Emperor Charles V). The death of her husband fifty years earlier had caused Joanna to go mad, and in particular she developed an irrational fear of the clergy; but the saint was able to calm her in her final days and help her prepare for a happy death. St. Thérèse of Lisieux had a first-hand experience of how mental illness can afflict a family; her beloved father experienced senility during his last few years of life — which Thérèse referred to as "the three years of my father's martyrdom."

An awareness of the sufferings of the mentally ill has sometimes been demonstrated by popular religious piety. For instance, the burial site of the Irish monk St. Fillan was, up to the nineteenth century, reputed to be a place where miraculous cures occurred. Persons afflicted with mental illness were taken there, dipped in the pool, and then tied up and left overnight in a corner of the ruined chapel that had belonged to the saint; those who were found loose in the morning were considered to be cured.

This, of course, is no longer practiced, nor would it be considered an effective or compassionate form of treatment today, but the Church is ever ready to affirm the value and dignity of the mentally ill. The martyr St. Dymphna is considered the patron saint of those suffering from mental illness, and all who faithfully bear this cross will certainly be made whole and glorious in God's kingdom.

For Further Reflection

"To be a saint, one must be beside onself. One must lose one's head." — *St. John Vianney*

"People should rejoice in their neurotic suffering, for this is a sign of the availability of energy to transform their characters." — *Rollo May (It should be added, of course, that only with God's help can such a transformation be lasting and of a positive character.)*

"The best way to be healthy is not to spend your life trying to be healthy. There is not only sound theology, but profound human psychology in the words: 'Seek ye therefore first the kingdom of God, and His justice, and all these things shall be added unto you.' In our modern language, aim at Heaven, and you will get earth thrown in!" — *Archbishop Fulton J. Sheen (Thus, our goal shouldn't be to make ourselves well — physically or mentally — but to serve God. If this is our aim, the Lord will give us whatever opportunities or assistance we need to find fulfillment while being of service to His kingdom. Living for His glory will help us find the balance we need in life.)*

Something You Might Try

♦ If you're trying to help someone who's mentally ill, you'll probably be more effective if you aim at getting the person to focus on symptoms and short-term goals ("Let's find someone to help you with the voices that are keeping you from sleeping at night"), instead of urging him or her to admit to having an illness. (Admitting the presence of unpleasant symptoms usually has fewer negative connotations for the person than admitting to the illness itself.) Try to remain low-key and nonjudgmental, and discover — for instance, through your parish, Catholic Charities, government agencies, or the Internet — what local resources are available.

Further Reading

Scripture: Luke 1:51; Matthew 4:23-24.

Contemporary Works: Xavier Amador, *"I Am Not Sick; I Don't Need Help" — Helping the Seriously Mentally Ill Accept Treatment;* E. Fuller Torrey, *Surviving Schizophrenia: A Manual for Families, Consumers, and Providers.*

O God,
we humbly beseech You

through Your servant, St. Dymphna,
who sealed with her blood
the love she bore you,
to grant relief to those who
suffer from mental afflictions
and nervous disorders (especially N.).
St. Dymphna,
helper of the mentally afflicted,
pray for us.

Glory be to the Father . . .

Traditional

Physical Deformities

Then shall the lame man leap like a hart,
and the tongue of the dumb sing for joy.

Isaiah 35:6

In the days of the Roman Republic — years before the coming of Christ — when a child was born deformed, the father, as head of the household, could legally decide to have the child abandoned somewhere outside the city, where the child would die from exposure or be killed by wild animals. As members of a highly advanced society, we like to think we're much more civilized than that — but our actions contradict us. Instead of allowing unwanted children to be born, we abort them in the womb — especially when prenatal testing suggests that a child might be "defective." We've lost sight of an important truth: every person sent into the world by God is here for a reason, including the retarded, the handicapped, and the deformed. The Lord has a plan for each of them, and when we reject this plan, we shortchange *ourselves* most of all.

Persons suffering from physical deformities are greatly valued by God, "for the Lord sees not as man sees; man looks on the outward appearance, but the Lord looks on the heart."[49] Weaknesses

---

[49] 1 Sam. 16:7.

211

in the human body do not detract from holiness. In a number of cases, they have greatly contributed to it.

A moving example of this is provided by Bl. Margaret of Castello, who was born in 1287. Her noble parents were horrified to discover that their daughter suffered from severe afflictions: she was so small that she would never attain a normal height, she was hunchbacked, she was very unattractive in appearance, and, because her right leg was much shorter than her left, she was lame. Moreover, young Margaret was also blind. The little girl's parents didn't welcome her; at best they tolerated her, while grudgingly caring for her needs. When Margaret was six, she was taken to a nearby chapel, where her parents had her walled up in an alcove. She couldn't leave, but could attend Mass and receive the sacraments. Fourteen years later, her ashamed but desperate parents took her to a religious shrine and prayed that she might be cured; when this didn't happen, they abandoned her. Margaret had much to suffer until her death at the age of thirty-three.

The behavior of Margaret's parents was shameful, and this story is a tragic one — but only from a human point of view. In God's kingdom, Bl. Margaret of Castello is beautiful, perfect, and whole; her terrible sufferings brought about a wonderful increase of grace within her soul.

Other saints have also grown in sanctity as a result of their physical burdens. The holy Jesuit priest St. Peter Canisius, who played a vital role in the Catholic Reformation in the sixteenth century, was crippled by an illness at age seventy, but with the help of a secretary, he continued his ministry of preaching and writing until he died six years later. Bl. Kateri Tekakwitha, a member of the Mohawk Indian tribe, contracted smallpox when she was four. The disease killed her parents and brother; she survived, but was left partially blind and with a pockmarked face. (Upon Kateri's death at age twenty-four, her face immediately became beautiful and radiant.)

The nineteenth-century religious brother St. Miguel Cordero suffered from a physical deformity as a child; it was not until age five, when he saw a vision of the Virgin Mary, that he was able to stand and walk. St. Joseph Cafasso, a priest of the same century, was slightly deformed due to a curvature of the spine, and the famous bishop St. Alphonsus Liguori suffered for the last twenty years of his life from rheumatism, which bent his head into his chest.

Sometimes deformities and other physical afflictions are miraculously healed, as in the case of a girl whose misshapen face was instantly made perfect after being covered with the cloak of St. Raymond of Penafort. More often, however, they remain as an ongoing condition — a challenge that, if accepted, can lead to great holiness.

This was the case for St. Joan of France (not to be confused with the holy maiden St. Joan of Arc). The daughter of King Louis XI, Joan was hunchbacked and had a pockmarked face. Her father, valuing physical beauty, disliked her, and looked for an opportunity to be rid of her. When Joan was twelve, she was married off to the Duke of Orleans, although against his will (royal marriages were often political affairs, necessitated by interests of state). The marriage was never consummated, allowing the duke to have it dissolved later on, after he had become king and desired to marry someone else. Joan didn't complain, but accepted the situation patiently, and spent the remainder of her life in charitable activity.

Another holy person who had much to suffer was St. Servulus, a layman who lived in the sixth century. He was afflicted with palsy as an infant and, as a result, was never able to stand, sit upright, or feed himself. His family would carry him to the Church of St. Clement, where he used to beg alms. Servulus would share the money he received with others in need. He also purchased books of Scripture, which he asked others to read to him (never having the opportunity for an education himself).

More Saintly Solutions

There have been a few instances of saints actually *seeking* a physical disfigurement so as to be left in peace to serve God as they wished. A legend states that a Portuguese princess named St. Wilgefortis had taken a vow of chastity; not knowing this, her father arranged for her marriage to the king of Sicily. Wilgefortis's prayer for deliverance was answered when she grew a beard over-night, causing her prospective husband to recoil in horror and reject the marriage. The legend states that her enraged father thereupon had her crucified.

More reliable is the story of St. Rose of Lima, a headstrong young woman who was determined, contrary to her family's wishes, to live her life solely for God. For ten years, her parents tried to ar-range a marriage for her, but Rose sabotaged their efforts by rub-bing her face with pepper, so as to produce ugly blotches on her skin.

A thousand years earlier in Ireland, a young St. Flannan over-heard his father request a blessing from the abbot St. Colman, who said in response, "From you shall seven kings spring." Fearing that he himself might receive a royal office, Flannan prayed that he would receive a physical deformity so as to prevent this from hap-pening. In response, his face was soon covered with repulsive scars and rashes.

In the fourth century, St. Syncletica cut off her hair in the presence of a priest as a sign of her renunciation of the world and as an act of consecration to God. A number of female saints down through the ages have followed her example, including St. Catherine of Siena. At least one instance is recorded of a dramatic gesture getting out of hand, however. In twentieth-century India, Bl. Alphonsa Muttathupandatu desired a religious vocation; to forestall an arranged marriage, she went to the local fire pit, in-tending to burn her feet so as to discourage potential suitors. Un-fortunately, Alphonsa accidentally fell into the pit and suffered severe burns over her entire body. Her initial aim was fulfilled, however; after her recovery, her family allowed her to enter the convent.

No one is expected to pray for (or even less, to attempt to bring about) physical deformities. God asks us only to bear whatever afflictions we already have (and even then, proper medical attention and therapy is legitimate and advisable). The Lord wants us to be beautiful in His sight. If we have physical deformities, we can grow in grace by offering everything we experience as a humble prayer and sacrifice, bearing our struggles with as much patience and trust as possible. If we're not so afflicted, we can be especially understanding and accepting toward those who do suffer in this way.

A wonderful example of this is given by Bl. Pier-Giorgio Frassati at the beginning of the twentieth century. A friend asked why he had visited a badly disfigured leper, and the saintly youth responded, "How rich we are to be in good health. The deformation of that young man will disappear in a few years when he enters Paradise. But we have the duty of putting our health at the service of those who haven't it. To act otherwise would be to betray the gift of God."

Holy resignation and trust on the part of those who suffer from physical deformities, and compassion and acceptance on the part of those who don't, are signs of a true Christian spirit. We can't always control the appearance of our bodies, but on the Day of Judgment, we will be responsible for the appearance of our souls. As the lives of the saints remind us, everyone is important to God. Learning this truth, and living by it, is an essential element of holiness.

For Further Reflection

"Our every breath yearns for Christ. He alone is the Desired One, the most beautiful of all. Christ loved us in our unloveliness, in order to make us beautiful like Himself." — *St. Augustine*

"Some parents have an aversion for a virtuous child on account of some bodily defect, whilst they show undue preference to one who is attractive and vicious. . . . Now, Holy Scripture says that deceitful lips speak with a double heart [Ps. 12:2], and that to have two weights [or standards of measurement] — the one heavy, for receiving, the other light, for giving — is an abomination to the Lord." — *St. Francis de Sales* (*Thus, it is unchristian to judge other people solely on their physical appearance.*)

"At present we have a human body, but in the future we will have a celestial one, because there are human bodies and celestial bodies. There is a human splendor and a celestial splendor. The splendor that can be attained on earth is temporary and limited, while that of Heaven lasts forever, which will be shown when the corruptible becomes incorruptible and the mortal immortal." — *St. Basil the Great*

Something You Might Try

♦ St. Alphonsus Liguori writes, "If we have any natural defect either in mind or body — a bad memory, slowness of comprehension, a crippled limb, or weak health — let us not complain. What were we entitled to? What obligation had God to give us a mind more richly endowed, or a body more perfectly made? Could He not have created us mere brute animals or have left us in our own nothingness? Whoever receives a gift and tries to make bargains about it? We should give Him thanks for what, through a pure act of His goodness, He has bestowed upon us; we should be content with the manner in which He has treated us. Who can tell, if God had given us more ability, better health, or more beauty and charm, whether we should not have used them to our destruction?" It may be of some consolation to reflect on the truth expressed here by St. Alphonsus; if necessary, you can make this idea more vivid by asking yourself this question: "Would I rather be beautiful in this life, and condemned to Hell, or unattractive in this world, with eternal joy and beauty reserved for me in Heaven?" Sometimes, unknown to ourselves, these may be the only alternatives available to us; and when that occurs, Jesus leaves us with no doubts as to the better choice.[50]

♦ The great French Impressionist Auguste Renoir produced many beautiful paintings alive with light and color, but few people realized how much his artistic efforts cost him. The artist was crippled with arthritis during the last twenty years of his life; his gnarled hands and twisted spine made painting an agony. When one of his students asked, "Why do you torture yourself to go on like this?" Renoir answered, "The pain passes; the beauty remains." If you're carrying the heavy cross of a physical deformity, your efforts to remain faithful to Jesus can be likened to painting, at great personal sacrifice, a valuable and glorious work of art — one whose beauty will last forever.

Further Reading

Scripture: Micah 4:6-7; Zephaniah 3:19; Luke 6:6, 10; Acts 14:8-10.

Classics: St. Alphonsus Liguori, *Conformity to the Will of God.*

Contemporary Works: Carl Koch and Joyce Heil, *God Knows You'd Like a New Body.*

⌒

Lord, I know that,
compared with that of many people,
my burden isn't so great —
but even so, it seems too much for me.

[50] Mark 9:43-48.

I dream of what life would be like
if I were physically whole,
I complain about how life has been unfair to me,
and, I admit, I even entertain the idea
that You have abandoned me,
or that I'm somehow being punished
for something I or someone else did.
I know this isn't true, but I can't help
but feel this way sometimes.
It's hard, Lord; it's very hard.
I get discouraged and depressed;
I get upset over the things I can't do
and angry at the people who don't understand or care,
who ignore me, stare at me, or make fun of me.
I wish things were different, very different —
and I suspect I'll never stop feeling that way.
Nonetheless, my God, I want to please You,
for I need to believe that all
I'm going through has a purpose,
a goal that You'll one day reveal to me.
I need You; I rely on Your help.
Without You, I know I wouldn't make it
through another day — nor would I care to.
This cross You've given me is a painful one, Lord,
but, because You know all about painful crosses,
I trust that You'll see me through this ongoing trial.
Give me courage and peace, strength and trust,
and a spirit of understanding and acceptance;
help me to offer my life —
my broken, disfigured, imperfect life —
to You, that it may be made
whole and complete in Your Kingdom.

Pride

For everyone who exalts himself will be humbled,
and he who humbles himself will be exalted.

Luke 14:11

At the end of the nineteenth century, a little-known but talented Russian author named Vladimir Soloviev, born Orthodox but a later convert to Catholicism, wrote a fascinating and insightful novel called *Tale of the Antichrist.* Describing the future arrival on the world scene of the figure St. Paul calls the "man of lawlessness,"[51] Soloviev writes, "There lived at the time a remarkable man — many called him superhuman — who was as far from being a child in heart as in intellect." The Russian author elaborates on this point by portraying the Antichrist in a way quite different from what we might expect; instead of being thoroughly evil, this counterfeit savior is shown to have many admirable qualities. He isn't subject to envy, lust, or self-indulgence, and he carefully controls his emotions and doesn't give in to anger. He has an almost unprecedented depth of spirit, and even regards his many talents and abilities as a sign of heavenly favor. However, Soloviev describes the future Antichrist as having one overriding moral flaw:

[51] 2 Thess. 2:3.

he will be completely lacking in humility. It is pride, therefore, that will make this most gifted of all men the perfect agent of Satan.

Soloviev's identification of pride as the underlying motivation of the future opponent of Christ and His Church is scripturally accurate, for St. Paul predicts that this most arrogant person in history will exalt himself above everyone and everything, declaring himself a god and demanding all humanity give him that worship and homage which is due to God alone.[52] All his other virtues and admirable qualities, no matter how genuine, will be spiritually meaningless, for as St. Bernard of Clairvaux warns us, "Pride is the greatest sin, because it taunts the people of God to a higher degree, and especially rises up against those who seem to have already conquered the other sins. Therefore, once the others have been subdued, pride challenges to single combat." Moreover, as St. John Climacus states, "Humility is the only virtue no devil can imitate."

Pride can provide an opening for Satan's entry into even the noblest soul, and so the vital importance of humility becomes readily apparent. Jesus warns us against the dangers of pride,[53] telling us that we shall not enter into the kingdom of Heaven unless we do so with the humility and trust of a little child. Furthermore, as St. Paul reminds us, our Lord Himself gave us the greatest example of One who humbled Himself, even to the point of dying a shameful death on the Cross;[54] and the apostle tells us that we must have this same attitude. This is a message the saints understood well, and their words and example have much to offer us in our ongoing efforts to become (and remain) humble.

As a young man of a noble family, Bl. Peter Gonzalez was educated by his uncle, the Bishop of Astorga in Spain; but the

[52] 2 Thess. 2:4.
[53] Cf. Matt. 18:1-5.
[54] Phil. 2:5-11.

churchman was more interested in his nephew's worldly success than in his spiritual growth and had him appointed a canon of his cathedral, even though he was underage. (Canons were clerics assigned to the cathedral and entitled to a share of its revenues.) Young Peter decided to make an impressive entry into the city on Christmas Day, in keeping with his new dignity, but as he proudly rode into Astorga, his horse stumbled and threw him into the mud, causing the onlookers to burst into laughter. Amid the jeering, Peter said, "If the world mocks at me, I will mock at the world," and this he proceeded to do in the best way imaginable — by setting aside the world's vain preoccupations with honor and success for the sake of eternal values. Peter resigned his office and entered the Dominican Order, and eventually became known as a powerful preacher and a humble servant of Christ.

Humility didn't come naturally to all the saints, and even some of those who had mastered this lesson needed a refresher course from time to time. St. Vincent de Paul, for instance, was once visited by a relative from the country, a poor young man lacking in education and social graces. At first the saint responded with a natural fear of embarrassment and had the porter take the youth to his room, where he might meet with him privately. Then, however, Vincent realized he had given in to the sin of pride, so he apologized to his relative, and took him to the rest of the community members and introduced him as a valued member of his family.

Satan tempts us to pride not only by fear of embarrassment or through worry over what others might think; he also slyly suggests that we attempt seemingly good things that in fact aren't God's will for us. In the fourth century, St. John Kolobos, also known as John the Dwarf (*Kolobos* meaning "small"), told a fellow hermit that he was going deeper into the desert to "live like an angel." He then set off completely naked to prove that, in his deep commitment to prayer and penance, he was above such mundane considerations as food and clothing. However, one week later, the other hermit heard a knock at the door of his hut, and asked, "Who is it?" "It's John," replied the now-humbler saint. "Let me in." His brother hermit, sensing the opportunity to make an important point, responded, "You can't be John; he's an angel now, not a man," and made John wait outside until the following morning before giving him food and shelter.

Pride can make us do foolish things that interfere with our spiritual growth; humility prompts us to act in a way that benefits ourselves and others, even though our behavior may appear foolish in the eyes of the world. Many of the saints humbled themselves by sacrificing their reputation, social status, and even legitimate rights, for the sake of following Jesus more closely. For instance, as queen of Portugal, St. Elizabeth didn't scorn or ignore the illegitimate children of her royal husband, let alone drive them away from court; rather, she ignored convention and loved and cared for them as if they were her own flesh and blood.

On one occasion, St. Edward of England was approached by a lame man named Michael, who claimed that St. Peter had appeared and told him that he would be cured if the king of England carried him to church. Setting aside any thoughts of royal dignity, Edward immediately answered, "Of course; climb on my back, and put your arms around my neck," and carried his lowly subject to church — where the promised cure promptly occurred.

Another example of royal humility was given by St. Louis IX of France, who was roundly scolded by a woman who thought he was neglecting his duties to the kingdom because of his many religious practices. Instead of responding with anger or defensiveness, Louis said, "My dear lady, what you say is true. I am not fit to be a king. But God made me king, and I try to do the best I can. Come to me at any time when I can help you, and I will attend to your problems as if they were my own."

There are a number of instances of saintly churchmen, motivated at least in part by humility, going out of their way to avoid appointment to higher office. In the thirteenth century, for instance, St. Philip Benizi was once regarded as a likely candidate for the papacy. To forestall this possibility, he hid in a cave for three months while a conclave took place. Of the thirty male Doctors of the Church, the only one never ordained a priest or bishop — by his own choice — was St. Ephrem. St. Basil the Great had ordained him a deacon, but Ephrem refused what he considered the higher honor of priestly Ordination. When Basil later summoned Ephrem to be consecrated as a bishop, Ephrem took a radical step to prevent this: he pretended to be mad. His performance was so convincing that the messengers assured Basil his choice for bishop was totally unsuitable, as he had lost his mind. Basil, knowing of his fellow saint's humility (and holy wiliness), responded, "O hidden pearl of great price whom the world knows not! You are the madmen and he the sane!"

The saints often practiced humility not only by declining worldly or ecclesiastical honors, but also by trying to hide marks of heavenly favor. St. Catherine of Siena, for instance, received the stigmata. This was a sign of her great intimacy with the Lord, but not wanting to attract attention to herself, she prayed that these wounds, while remaining, might become invisible; and her prayer was granted. Other stigmatics, such as St. Catherine de Ricci, also wanting to remain humble and desiring to appear unimportant in the eyes of the world, made similar requests of God.

One of the signs of a mature humility is the ability to rejoice in the great things God does through us, without seeking to appropriate any of the credit for ourselves. St. Bernard of Clairvaux was known for the many miracles he worked, sometimes curing people by blessing them, other times by merely allowing them to touch his clothing. Bernard was a miraculous agent of divine grace for the lame, the blind, the insane, and the possessed; and it's even claimed that he raised more than a hundred people from the dead. However, he never let himself be affected by the wild enthusiasm and praise of the crowds, saying that it always seemed to him that they were really honoring someone more worthy than himself.

A different but related type of humility was shown by St. Francis de Sales, who admitted to St. Vincent de Paul that sometimes he wept with joy while reading his own books — not with pride, but with gratitude, for he knew the great wisdom they contained came not from himself, but from the Lord.

As the saints knew, opportunities to grow in humility are to be treasured. Thus, St. Bonaventure was grateful for a friend's ongoing teasing about his preaching ("On former occasions you have preached without knowing precisely what you were talking about. I sincerely hope you are not going to do that now"); this playful criticism not only kept him humble, but also inspired him to make even greater efforts.

On one occasion St. Peter Canisius, as provincial of the Jesuit houses in Germany, traveled to Italy with a companion. The porter of the Jesuit house where they stopped wouldn't allow them to enter without a letter from their superior, and refused to believe that Peter himself was the superior. When the matter was straightened out an hour later, Peter refused to criticize the porter, but instead praised him for doing his duty.

A still greater act of humility was performed by St. Chad, who was consecrated bishop in the seventh century. When the Archbishop of Canterbury refused to recognize the validity of this consecration, the saint responded, "If you consider that I have not been properly ordained, I gladly resign. I never thought myself worthy of the office and agreed to undertake it, though unworthy, only under obedience." (The impressed archbishop thereupon had St. Chad reconsecrated as bishop for a different diocese.)

Quite often the passage of time can help us gain a more realistic perspective on life, and this can be an aid to our growth in humility. St. Teresa of Avila once noted, "When I was young, I was told that I was pretty, and I believed it; later on people found me intelligent, and I believed that too; they tell me today that I am a saint. But now I have no illusions." (We, of course, rightly venerate Teresa as a saint, but it was certainly to her own spiritual benefit not to think of herself in those terms.)

In a sense, virtue is indeed its own reward, as it offers us the joy of imitating our Lord and freely humbling ourselves in His service. Near the end of his life, St. John Berchmans recalled, "I resolved always to prefer labors to comforts, contempt to honors. And, in particular, if on one side a kingdom were offered and on the other the washing of dishes, I would refuse the kingdom and accept the dishwashing so as to be truly like Christ, who humbled Himself."

St. Thérèse of Lisieux is famous for her "Little Way": the recognition that holiness can be achieved by doing simple, everyday things with as much love as possible. Often overlooked in this simple spirituality is the important role that humility plays. Those who are proud seek to do great and important things (usually for their own glory first, then God's); those who are humble gladly accept whatever role is assigned to them, and even come to rejoice in being given the least important and appealing tasks, so as to follow more closely in the footsteps of Christ. As a postulant, St. Thérèse was frequently scolded for her apparent inattentiveness at prayer, and for working too slowly. On one occasion, the prioress said in a loud voice, "It's easy enough to see that our corridors are swept by a child of fifteen. Sweep away that cobweb, and be more careful in the future." A much larger opportunity to practice humility occurred when, after her year as a novice, it was time for Thérèse to make her profession as a Carmelite. To her intense disappointment, the saint was informed that this was to be delayed for eight months. Although hurt and confused, she humbly accepted this decision, reminding herself that it was God's will for her that mattered, not her own.

Again and again, the saints speak to us of the importance of humility. St. Melania the Younger, for instance, warns us that this virtue is essential if we are to avoid sharing in Satan's fate. The saint writes, "The Devil can imitate all the righteous acts that we appear to do, but he is splendidly defeated by love and humility. . . . We fast, but he eats absolutely nothing. We keep watch, but he does not sleep at all. Let us therefore hate pride because, through it, he fell from Heaven, and again, because, through it, he wants to drag us down with him."

Worldly allurements are among Satan's favorite weapons against us, and so, as St. Thomas Aquinas tells us, "The reason Christ especially recommended humility to us is because it most effectively removes the main obstacle to our spiritual welfare, the preoccupation with earthly greatness that holds us back from striving for spiritual and heavenly things." Even when we give ourselves to God, we're often tempted to do so on our own terms. Our willing obedience to those with legitimate authority over us can counteract this and aid our growth in humility; but, as St. Josemaría Escrivá notes, "If obedience does not give you peace, it is because you are proud."

Our society's emphasis on self-esteem can easily degenerate into an unhealthy form of self-absorption and pride — and regardless of what psychology might say, this can be spiritually dangerous. According to St. John Chrysostom, "Pride is a terrible rock where wild beasts lurk that would tear you to pieces every day." Moreover, pride underlies every other sin. This is why, for example, St. Aelred of Rievaulx warns, "The one who loses humility will not be able to preserve chastity of the flesh." St. Pio tells us we must hate our faults, but without allowing ourselves to become worried and upset over them; patience and humility will allow us to conquer them. The holy Capuchin also uses this instructive image: "It is equally true that God allows the master spies — venial sins and imperfections — to circulate freely in His kingdom, but this is merely to show us that, without Him, we should be a prey for our enemies."

Humility keeps us close to Jesus, and only by remaining rooted in Christ can we find true peace. St. Jane Frances de Chantal notes, "We want and seek so many things along with God that this hinders us from finding Him. We want to be loved and highly regarded, and we think that everything we do should be approved of. . . . This only serves to make us restless and troubled. If we sought God only, we would always be content and would find all things in Him."

We cannot *make* ourselves holy; we can only use the grace that God freely gives us. According to St. Mechthild of Magdeburg, "Those who would storm the heavenly heights by fierceness and ascetic practices deceive themselves badly. Such people carry grim hearts within themselves; they lack true humility, which alone leads the soul to God." Moreover, St. John of the Cross insists, "All heavenly visions, revelations, and feelings — or whatever else one may desire to think on — are not worth as much as the least act of humility."

Pride focuses our attention on ourselves; but St. Catherine of Siena reminds us that, as God's creatures, we have no real reason to praise or congratulate ourselves for anything we've accomplished, for without God, we can do nothing. St. Thomas More expresses a similar idea: "Just as men may call the one a fool who bears himself proudly because he struts about in a borrowed suit, so may all of us, too, be rightly called true fools if we take pride in anything that we have in this life. For nothing we have here is our own, not even our bodies. All that we ever have, we have received from God: riches, royalty, power, beauty, strength, learning, intelligence, body, soul, all."

Without God, we can do nothing worthwhile, and as a firm but loving Father, the Lord often finds it necessary to remind us of this. According to St. Francis de Sales, "It is a remarkable thing: God so loves humility that He sometimes tests us, not to make us do evil, but to teach us by our own experience what we really are, permitting us to say or do some foolish thing, giving us reason to humble ourselves." Such an experience allows us to grow in grace and to fulfill our role in the divine plan, for as St. Angela Merici says, "In order to become an instrument in God's hands, we must be of no account in our own eyes." Also, St. John Eudes notes, "The humbler we become, the more will God protect us and convert all things to our welfare."

We've all had the experience of disappointment, irritation, and failure — which means we've all had opportunities to practice humility. As St. Bernard once wrote to Pope Innocent II, "If things always went wrong, no one could endure it; if they always went well, anyone would become arrogant." A similar point is made by Ven. Solanus Casey, who states, "The weaknesses we experience are naturally providential guards against one of the very greatest dangers to our holiness: pride." This saintly twentieth-century Capuchin friar also reminds us, "God knows as no one else knows how we all and each need penance. God knows we need humiliations to foster humility. Hence, in His love, He never fails to provide occasions for each one to practice penance."

This idea echoes a point made four centuries earlier by St. Teresa of Avila, who wrote, "It constantly happens that the Lord permits a soul to fall so that it may grow humbler. When it is honest, and realizes what it has done, and returns, it makes ever-increasing progress in our Lord's service." Thus, if we allow, God mercifully uses our human weakness and sinfulness as a means of drawing us closer to Himself.

Humiliation is something few of us would naturally choose for ourselves, but all the saints discovered that this bitter medicine leads to lasting spiritual health. According to St. Faustina Kowalska, "Nothing is better for the soul than humiliations. . . . If there is a truly happy soul upon earth, it can only be a truly humble soul. . . . A humble soul does not trust itself, but places all its confidence in God." The holy Polish nun took this message seriously, even declaring, "Humiliation is my daily food." Such a sentiment goes against our natural human inclinations, and this fact prompted the saint to observe, "Now I understand why there are so few saints; it is because so few souls are deeply humble." St. Faustina also tells us, "The Lord Jesus gave me to know how very pleasing to Him is a soul who lives in accordance with the will of God. It thereby gives very great glory to God." This message was reinforced by the Blessed Virgin Mary, who told the saint, "I desire, my dearly beloved daughter, that you practice the three virtues that are dearest to me — and most pleasing to God. The first is humility, humility, and once again humility."

In some ways, this is the most important chapter in this book, for pride is the gravest spiritual threat we face — and humility is the only possible antidote. Jesus tells us that pride invalidates our prayers in God's eyes, while humility guarantees us a hearing.[55] St. Alphonsus Liguori comments on this truth by saying, "The cry of the humble man penetrates the heavens, and he will not depart till God hears his prayer." If we are able to pray in a spirit of genuine humility, our prayer will be answered, and this will give us the confidence to persevere in our spiritual journey. This is why St. Pio advises us, "Try more and more to hold firmly to humility and charity, which are the main supports of the whole vast building [of our spiritual lives] and on which all the rest depends. . . . If the heart is always striving to practice these two virtues, it will meet with no difficulty in practicing the others."

We must humbly trust in God's love for us, firmly believing that everything He allows to happen to us is truly for our benefit. As Ven. Solanus Casey tells us, "God's plans are always for the best, always wonderful. But most especially for the patient and the humble who trust in Him are His plans unfathomably holy and sublime." Fr. Solanus also urges us to reflect on this thought: "God condescends to use our powers, if we don't spoil His plans by ours." The more we surrender our own wills, the happier we'll become;

---

[55] Cf. Luke 18:9-14.

the more we let go of our egos, the sooner we'll discover our true selves; and the more we renounce our pride, the greater will be our growth in holiness and inner peace. We're involved in a constant struggle for our souls, and Satan seeks to use our pride against us, but as Fr. Solanus says, "If you can honestly humble yourself, your victory is won."

For Further Reflection

"I would wish that you place yourself with all your love under Christ, and that you pave no other way in order to reach and to attain the truth than has already been paved by Him who, as God, knows the weakness of our steps. This way is, in the first place, humility; in the second place, humility; in the third place, humility. . . . As often as you ask me about the Christian religion's norms of conduct, I choose to give no other answer than: humility." — *St. Augustine*

"Don't permit your miseries or defects to depress you. Rather, let them be steps by which you descend the deep mine where we find the precious gem of holy humility. Learn that it is our littleness that buys this unique and true treasure that alone renders the soul that possesses it blessed in time and in eternity." — *St. Paola Frassinetti*

"Avoid being bashful with God, as some people are, in the belief that they are being humble. It would not be humility on your part if the King were to do you a favor and you refused to accept it; but you would be showing humility by taking it, and being pleased with it, yet realizing how far you are from deserving it." — *St. Teresa of Avila*

Something You Might Try

♦ Our Lord once instructed St. Faustina Kowalska, "Write these words on a clean sheet of paper: 'From today on, my own will does not exist,' and then cross out the page. And on the other side, write these words: 'From today on, I do the will of God everywhere, always, and in everything.' " If you find it hard to be humble, consider performing this practice at the beginning of each day, for often the act of writing down an idea helps instill it in our own mind, and writing these words given by Jesus to St. Faustina may make it easier to form the habit of acting humbly and obediently.

♦ According to St. Bernard, "If you pass through a low doorway, you suffer no hurt, however much you bend. But if you raise your head higher than the doorway, even by a finger's breadth, you will dash it against the lintel and injure yourself. So also a man has no need to fear any humiliation, but he should quake with fear before rashly exalting himself even a little. So then, beware of comparing yourself with your betters or your inferiors, with a particular few or with even one." To the saint's advice, we might add this thought: if we feel we must make comparisons, let us compare ourselves only with the persons God wants us to be. Honestly making such a comparison will compel us to admit that our sins and weaknesses are holding us back, and keeping this truth firmly in mind will help us remain humble.

Further Reading

Scripture: Proverbs 11:2; Sirach 11:12-13; Matthew 11:29; Matthew 18:1-5; Luke 18:9-14; 1 Peter 5:5-6.

Classics: St. Bernard of Clairvaux, *On the Love of God*; St. Francis de Sales, *An Introduction to the Devout Life*; St. Alphonsus Liguori, *The Practice of the Love of Jesus Christ*.

⤳

Behold, O Lord, all my wretchedness!
See my proud intellect, my stony heart!

See my mind filled with worldly thoughts,
my will disposed to evil and my body
rebellious to every good work.
Help me, O my God, to correct myself.
This grace I beg through Your own
infinite goodness and mercy.
To obtain it, I offer You the merits of
Your Son, Jesus Christ, our Redeemer.
I have no merits of my own.
I am destitute of all good,
but His wounds are my hope.
Had I shed my blood for love of You,
like Your Son,
would You not grant me this favor?
How much more ought You to hear me now,
since He shed His blood for me.

St. Gabriel Possenti

Scrupulosity

The saying is sure and worthy of full acceptance,
that Christ Jesus came into the world to save sinners.

1 Timothy 1:15

St. Arnulf served as bishop of Metz in the seventh century. In spite of his holiness, at one point he became consumed with a need to know whether God had completely forgiven him and cleansed him of the sins he had committed as a youth, or whether he still needed to satisfy divine justice. This question filled him with on-going anxiety and made it difficult for him to concentrate on the fulfillment of his duties. One day Arnulf came to a bridge over the Moselle River. He suddenly stopped, removed his bishop's ring from his finger, and threw it into the river, saying, "If I find this ring again, I will believe that my sins are forgiven me." A number of years passed, and Arnulf sadly concluded his prayer hadn't been heard. Then, one day, he discovered his ring in the belly of a fish that was being served at dinner.

The holy bishop's prayer was answered, but we might argue that it never should have been uttered in the first place, for it seemed to represent an almost sinful doubting of God's mercy and fidelity. However, the problem of scrupulosity can bring people to such a point — even saints. By *scrupulosity*, we mean an irrational and disproportionate sense of guilt, and an anxious fear that, no matter what one does, divine mercy will always remain just out of reach. Some might refer to scrupulosity as a "religious obsessive-compulsive disorder," in which a person feels compelled to fulfill certain religious duties perfectly and exactly — overemphasizing their outward form, at the expense of their spiritual content.

Those who suffer from overly strong scruples can experience great emotional and spiritual difficulty; intellectually, they may know that God loves them, but it's very hard to translate this knowledge into a practical experience or to be at peace in God's presence. Worry and fear are often present in their lives, and the joy and trust that are the inheritance of God's children are frequently lacking. As the experience of St. Arnulf shows, saints are not immune to the trials associated with scrupulosity, and so it's possible for us to learn from their own struggles and hard-won wisdom regarding this problem.

The more we become aware of our sinfulness, the more important it is to believe in divine forgiveness, but sometimes this takes a great act of faith. St. Pio of Pietrelcina, the holy twentieth-century Capuchin priest, once underwent an attack of scruples that lasted for three years. In a letter written during this period, he stated, "I live in a perpetual night. . . . I find myself troubled by everything, and I do not know if I act well or ill. I can see that it is a scruple: but the doubt I feel about whether or not I am pleasing the Lord crushes me. And this anxiety recurs to me everywhere: at the altar, in the confessional, everywhere!"

Other famous saints suffered from scrupulosity at different points in their lives. For instance, soon after her twelfth birthday Thérèse of Lisieux began suffering in this way, and this spiritual affliction continued for over eight years. It helped her to discuss the matter with one of her older sisters, Marie, but when Marie entered the convent the following year, Thérèse felt she had lost the only person to whom she could open her soul. In desperation, she prayed to the four children of her family who had died in infancy, and as she later wrote, "The answer was not long in coming; soon my soul was flooded with the sweetest peace." Even after she entered the convent, however, the problem of scrupulosity would occasionally arise, clouding Thérèse's judgment, but she overcame this difficulty by discussing it with her confessor, to the point where she could say, "It is not because I have been preserved from mortal sin that I fly to God with loving confidence. I know I should still have this confidence even if my conscience were burdened with every possible crime."

Much as a virus affects a computer program and prevents it from operating properly, so does scrupulosity undermine the reliability of our moral judgment, making it difficult for us to perceive the workings of God's grace, even if we approach our problem in a rigorously logical way. This was the experience of St. Francis de Sales, who, at the age of seventeen, suddenly and illogically began to fear that he wasn't in a state of grace. Recognizing this as a temptation, he tried to face it head-on, but this led to a further disquieting thought: even if he was currently in a state of grace, he would nevertheless surely commit a mortal sin as soon as the opportunity arose. Francis reminded himself that God will never desert those who call upon Him in time of temptation, but his illogical fears persisted; moreover, the spiritual consolations he once experienced in prayer disappeared. Was this the result, he wondered, of some hidden sin on his part?

Then a new torment revealed itself: the concept of predestination. If it were true that only a small portion of humanity would be saved, then surely someone as unworthy as himself was damned to Hell, no matter what he did (and to assume otherwise would make him guilty of presumption).

Young St. Francis bravely struggled against his oppressive and unrelenting thoughts for six weeks, telling himself that even if he were to be damned, he still wanted to love God for as long as possible. He even prayed, "O my Savior, if I should go to Hell, never permit that I should curse Thee and blaspheme Thee." Soon after this, Francis entered a church and, before a statue of our Lady, prayed the *Memorare* with great devotion. Then, imploring Mary's intercession, he asked God to restore his emotional health, made a vow of chastity, and promised to pray the Rosary each day. Almost immediately a sense of peace flooded his soul, but Francis remembered this ordeal for the rest of his life, and this painful memory no doubt contributed to his great kindness and gentleness toward sinners, particularly the scrupulous.

Even the holiest people can find it nearly impossible at times to believe that the Lord is pleased with them; scrupulosity can induce a feeling of "spiritual weightlessness," in which one's "moral compass," while still delineating the difference between right and wrong, fails to function reliably when it comes to being at peace in God's sight. In some cases this can approximate the Dark Night of the Soul described by St. John of the Cross — a time of intense scruples, spiritual dryness, and severe temptations. When this situation occurs, it's often, in fact, a favorable sign: it can indicate the passage from one stage of spiritual growth to another, higher stage. This progress is not without cost; the time of desolation can be prolonged, but it eventually ends and is followed by a new experience of consolation.

St. John of the Cross and other spiritual writers agree that the Dark Night is not something to flee (were such a thing even possible), but to embrace, endure, and offer up as a sacrifice, consciously uniting it to Christ's cry of desolation from the Cross: "My God, my God, why hast Thou forsaken me?"[56] Indeed, this choice of offering it up — requiring a heroic act of the will — is sometimes the only form of prayer possible for the sufferer. Most people don't undergo such an intense experience, but many have at least

---

[56] Mark 15:34.

some fairly serious fears and doubts on occasion. A firm and continuing belief in God's love — even when every sign of it seems to be absent — is the highest form of praise a person can render to God, and the best "cure" (although a slow-acting one) for this type of spiritual difficulty.

At the beginning of the twentieth century, Bl. Assunta Pallotta wrote, "I have had some scruples since I entered the Institute [of the Franciscan Missionaries of Mary], but now it seems that I have even more. When I went to confession and Father asked me if I was sure that I had committed a certain fault, I did not know what to say. I was in doubt, and I answered that I did not think I had committed any fault voluntarily. He replied, 'Go to Holy Communion, and obey.' He sent me away without even letting me recite the Act of Contrition."

Most priests hearing the confessions of scrupulous persons learn not to let them obsess over possible but uncertain guilt, as this merely keeps them from focusing on God's mercy. Honest doubts must not be allowed to keep us from experiencing God's grace. That's why St. Joseph Cafasso once said, "You're troubled about your preparation for Communion? Don't make any. You should always be ready to receive Communion. Just see if you have any venial sins, make an Act of Contrition, kiss a crucifix, and receive without fear."

Scrupulosity is problematic not only because of the suffering it can cause to the one afflicted, but also because (when it's not part of the process associated with the Dark Night of the Soul, as described above) it can interfere with one's spiritual growth. According to St. Peter of Alcantara, "Scruples obstruct devotion for the same reason [making the soul restless, depressed, and weak]. They are like thorns that prick the conscience and prevent it from resting in God and enjoying true peace."

Padre Pio notes that excessive guilt over sin can be a form of demonic attack, and he advises, "Open up your heart to a holy and unbounded trust in Jesus. Believe that God is not the cruel task-master depicted for you by that perpetrator of iniquity, but the Lamb who takes away the sins of the world, interceding for our salvation with sighs too deep for words." To a woman who was terribly worried about falling into serious sin, the saint once said, "As long as you are afraid to fall, you will not sin. You should be afraid when you are *not* afraid anymore."

A healthy fear of sin is a good thing; we must avoid the extremes of an excessive fear of sin, or scrupulosity, and a total lack of fear, which indicates a foolish pride on our part. A balanced approach to sin and guilt is a sign of spiritual health, and a requirement for continued spiritual growth. According to St. Bernard of Clairvaux, "Sorrow for sin is indeed necessary, but it should not be an endless preoccupation. You must dwell also on the glad remembrance of God's loving kindness. Otherwise sadness will harden the heart and lead it more deeply into despair." St. Bernard also poses this question: "How can you entertain a doubt of Jesus pardoning your sins, when He has affixed them to the Cross, whereon He died for you, with the very nails by which His own hands were pierced?"

We're called to make an act of faith in God's boundless mercy, rejecting that anxious guilt which would keep us far from Him. As Padre Pio states, "Your every fear is useless and lying; it is imaginary. Live tranquilly in the presence of God, who has loved you for a long time now. . . . Your miseries and weaknesses should not frighten you, because God has seen more serious ones within you and did not reject you for this, due to His mercy. So even less can He reject you now that you work untiringly for your perfection. God does not reject sinners, but rather grants them His grace, erecting the throne of His glory on their vileness." Moreover, as Jesus promised St. Faustina Kowalska, "When you approach the confessional, know this: that I myself am waiting there for you. I am only hidden by the priest, but I myself act in your soul. Here the misery of the soul meets the God of mercy."

How are we to overcome a tendency toward scrupulosity? Speaking with an authority based on his deep insight into souls and on his own trying experiences as a young man, St. Francis de Sales instructs us, "Don't examine so anxiously whether you're being perfect or not. . . . This self-examination, when made with anxiety and perplexity, is just a waste of time. Those who engage in it are like soldiers who, in training for combat, have so many mock battles and drills among themselves that when it comes right down to the real thing, they find themselves tired and spent. Or they are like musicians who get hoarse with practicing to sing a motet. The mind wearies itself with such a searching and continual examination, and when it comes to the moment of action, it can do no more. . . . 'If your eye is simple, your whole body will be full of light,' says our Savior [Matthew 6:22]. Simplify your judgment; don't reflect and dwell so much on yourself, but walk simply and with confidence."

St. Philip Neri further advises us, "Let such as desire to advance in the way of God submit themselves to a learned confessor, and obey him in God's stead; let him who thus acts assure himself that he will have to render no account to God for his actions." In other words, those who prayerfully obey their confessor or spiritual director are entitled to be free of all anxiety.

It's also important not to expect perfection of ourselves. The Lord asks us to do our best, but no more than that, for His grace will make up what is lacking. In this regard, St. Clement Hofbauer tells us, "We should be like a little child who goes simply on his way and only cries out for his mother when he meets with some grave difficulty." The saint also advises us, "When we are conscious of having failed and done wrong, we must humble ourselves before God, implore His pardon, and then quietly move ahead. Our defects should make us humble, but never cowardly."

According to St. Alphonsus Liguori, "There is only one course of action: go ahead in blind obedience." Similarly, St. Francis de

Sales tells us, "The best thing is to walk on blindly through all the darkness and perplexity of this life, under the providence of God." This approach was of inestimable help to St. Ignatius of Loyola. Some time after his conversion, an attack of scruples, along with an accompanying depression, was so intense that he even seriously considered suicide (which, of course, is a grave sin against God). By holding out through an unyielding desire to please God, Ignatius was freed from this torment.

Most of us do not have to face spiritual trials nearly this severe, although if we do, God's grace is every bit as available to us as it was to Ignatius of Loyola, Francis de Sales, Padre Pio, and other saints afflicted in this manner. If necessary, we must continually remind ourselves that the Lord loves us and appreciates our efforts to be honest with Him. We may still feel guilty, dissatisfied with ourselves, or unworthy of divine blessings, but none of this matters, for one simple reason: God's grace doesn't depend on human feelings. As long as, through an act of the will, we choose to love God, His blessing will be upon us, regardless of what we feel or don't feel. St. Paul assures us that nothing can keep us from Christ's love[57] — not even our own feelings. Scrupulosity may make us think we're spiritually imprisoned by doubts and guilt, but if we trust in Jesus, He will set us free.

For Further Reflection

"You should not afflict yourselves too much; for if the soul once begins to grow timorous, it [has] a very bad disposition to all kinds of good, and sometimes she becomes scrupulous; and lo! here she is unserviceable, both for herself and others. And suppose she not fall into scrupulosity; it may be well for herself, but she will not bring many souls to God, when people see so much fear and anxiety." — *St. Teresa of Avila (Thus, we can construct*

---

[57] Rom. 8:31-39.

a simple syllogism: A. Jesus wants us to spread the gospel to all nations. B. People will not be attracted to the gospel if those who preach it are burdened with scrupulosity and guilt. C. Therefore, Jesus does not want us to be scrupulous.)

"Let scrupulous souls, then, suffer this cross of theirs with resignation, and not perplex themselves in the greatest distresses which God may send or permit. It is for their profit, to the end that they may be humbler, may guard better against such occasions as are beyond doubt and seriously dangerous, may commend themselves oftener to the Lord, and put a more entire trust in the divine goodness. Meanwhile let them often have recourse to the most holy Virgin Mary, who is called, and is in truth, the Mother of Mercy, and comforter of the afflicted." — *St. Alphonsus Liguori*

"We may conclude that persons who suffer from scruples are the most favored by divine love, and the most certain of reaching Heaven when they bear this trial in patience and humility. Scrupulous souls die continually, they suffer a perpetual purgatory, and so they leave the earth to fly to Heaven purified and free from sins to expiate." — *Bl. Henry Suso*

Something You Might Try

♦ A dying nun afraid of divine judgment sought assurance from St. Claude de la Colombière, who wrote to her, "Do you know what would stir up my confidence, if I were as near to giving account to God as you are? It would be the number and seriousness of my sins. Here is a confidence really worthy of God. Far from allowing us to be depressed at the sight of our faults, it strengthens us in the idea of the infinite goodness of our Creator. Confidence inspired by purity of life doesn't give very much glory to God. Is this all that God's mercy can achieve — saving a soul that has never offended Him? For surely the confidence of a notorious sinner honors God most of all. For he is so convinced of God's mercy that all his sins seem no more than an atom in its presence." Therefore, if you feel your sins are especially displeasing to God, this is reason to rejoice, for you have the glorious opportunity of paying Him the supreme compliment: asking Him to forgive you, in spite of your complete unworthiness. If you choose, you can turn every thought of your own sinfulness into an act of praise, simply by trusting in the Lord's mercy. Also remember that even when your love is weak, the Lord will never stop loving you, for, according to an anonymous saying, "Justice is God's middle name; Love is His first name."

◆ Padre Pio advises us, "Think no more of your past life, except in order to admire the heavenly Father's goodness, which . . . did not want to reject you, but rather, with great care, wished to overcome your hardness and, winning you over with His grace, wanted and wants to demonstrate His power over you." Therefore, when we think about the past, we should focus on the way God has always forgiven us, not on the sins which necessitated that forgiveness. When these useless memories and scrupulous thoughts arise, we shouldn't fight against them, but simply turn them over to God, perhaps by means of a simple prayer: "Lord, I'm feeling guilty [or scrupulous] right now, so I give these feelings to You. Jesus, I trust in You."

Further Reading

Scripture: Tobit 13:6; Wisdom 12:18-19; Nehemiah 9:17; Psalm 130:3-4; John 3:17; Romans 12:2.

Classics: St. Ignatius of Loyola, *Spiritual Exercises*; St. Teresa of Avila, *The Way of Perfection*; St. Alphonsus Liguori, *The Practice of the Love of Jesus Christ*.

Contemporary Works: Russell Abata, *Why Am I Scrupulous?*; Thomas N. Santa, *Understanding Scrupulosity*.

God Almighty,
eternal, righteous, and merciful,
give to us poor sinners [the desire]
to do for Thy sake
all that we know of Thy will,
and to will always what pleases Thee,
so that inwardly purified, enlightened,
and kindled by the fire of the Holy Spirit,
we may follow in the footsteps
of Thy well-beloved Son,
our Lord Jesus Christ.

St. Francis of Assisi

Self-Indulgence

Put on the Lord Jesus Christ,
and make no provision for the flesh.

Romans 13:14

In the year 503, a hermit known as St. John the Silent, accompanied by his disciple Roubâ, left the monastery of Mar Saba in Palestine to spend the penitential season of Lent farther in the desert. Toward the end of Holy Week, Roubâ, hoping for an Easter feast, wanted to return to the monastery for the celebration, but John reminded him that the God who fed the Israelites in the desert would also provide sufficient food for them, and then warned, "Self-indulgence in this world begets eternal punishment, while present mortification is a preparation for the enjoyment of good things." The disciple was unconvinced and set off on his own for the monastery.

Soon after his departure, an unknown man came to John, bringing an ass loaded with loaves of bread, bottles of wine, cheese, oil, eggs, and honey, and presented these gifts to the saint. In the meantime, Roubâ had lost his way, and after three days returned to his master, starving and exhausted. Seeing the unexpected feast, the disciple humbly confessed his own stubbornness and lack of faith, and begged John's forgiveness. The saint responded, "Recognize precisely that God is able to prepare a table in the desert,"[58] and then invited his chastened disciple to dine with him.

God is able to provide us with all we need, and He wants us to enjoy the blessings of His creation, but we must do so in a balanced and reasonable way. Food and drink, clothing, shelter, and rest are all necessary things, and seeking various other comforts and enjoyments can be quite legitimate. The failing of self-indulgence, however, occurs when we give these things a higher priority than we give the will of God. Roubâ wasn't wrong in hoping for a wonderful Easter feast after enduring six weeks of rigorous fasting, but he sinned by pridefully rejecting his master's words and instead seeking his own will. Fortunately, the disciple repented, for as St. John warned him, placing our own comfort ahead of God's glory can certainly start us down that wide and easy road which leads to destruction.[59] Self-indulgence is commonly seen as a mild and relatively unimportant moral weakness, but in fact, it can be a serious spiritual danger, for the teachings and example of the saints show that worldly things must be firmly put in their proper place if we are to give ourselves completely to God.

The life of St. Augustine gives us a striking illustration of how a love for God's creatures can lead to an unwillingness to acknowledge their Creator. It's well known that, before his conversion, Augustine was long enslaved to the passions and pleasures of illicit sex; for many years, he lived with the mother of his illegitimate son. However, the future saint also faced the temptation of gluttony; even after his conversion, he wrote: "The necessity [of eating and drinking] is sweet to me, and against this sweetness I must fight, so that I might not be made captive by it. . . . This much You have taught me: that I must look upon food as medicine."

[58] Cf. Ps. 78:19.
[59] Cf. Matt. 7:13.

Augustine deeply enjoyed life, including the legitimate plea-sures of friendship and learning. Nevertheless, his honesty forced him to admit that, in his heart of hearts, he experienced a profound emptiness and alienation. He wanted to find the truth, yet felt himself unable to let go completely of those things he cherished, for fear he might lose all, and so he hesitated and struggled with his conscience. In a famous and compelling passage from his *Confessions*, Augustine writes, "Late have I loved You, O Beauty ever ancient, ever new, late have I loved You! You were within me, but I was outside, and it was there that I searched for You. In my unloveliness, I plunged into the lovely things which You created. You were with me, but I was not with You. Created things kept me from You; yet if they had not been in You, they would not have been at all. You called, You shouted, and You broke through my deafness. You flashed, You shone, and You dispelled my blindness. You breathed Your fragrance on me; I drew in breath, and now I pant for You. I have tasted You; now I hunger and thirst for more."

St. Augustine not only came to realize that created things have no lasting value without their Creator; he also discovered that we, as creatures ourselves, must remain firmly rooted in God if our lives are to achieve their ultimate purpose. One might arrive at this truth intellectually, but God's grace is essential if we are to act upon it, for the pleasures of the flesh are capable of subverting even the best intentions. Augustine refers to this sad reality as *concupiscence*, which refers to a disordered desire for pleasure, even when it goes against our spiritual needs and our long-term benefit. Concupiscence is rooted in Original Sin; it's not part of human nature (as created by God), but it is part of our human condition, and as a result, all of us must wage an ongoing struggle against self-indulgence if we wish to place God's will first in our lives.

A similar, although less dramatic, conversion took place in the life of St. Francis of Assisi. He was a carefree, popular young man who drank deeply of worldly pleasures, but after his conversion, he freely chose to live in absolute poverty and simplicity, so that he might devote himself entirely to the demands of the gospel.

Another popular saint known for a life of simplicity and self-denial is Thérèse of Lisieux. The many penances she practiced during her nine short years in the convent are widely known. Most people, however, aren't aware that, aided by her family, she developed a sacrificial spirit while still a young child.

Returning home after a long walk one hot summer day, little Thérèse asked her older sister, "Give me a drink, Pauline, please." Pauline answered, "[This is] a good chance to make a sacrifice." Physical thirst and the attraction of self-sacrifice struggled with each other for a moment in Thérèse's young mind, and then she smiled and nodded in agreement — prompting Pauline to tell her to go and drink a glass of lemonade. "But what of my sacrifice?" asked the confused child, and her older sister explained, "You've already won the merit of that; now you will get the merit of obedience as well." (Needless to say, we shouldn't expect to be rewarded for our own acts of self-denial by being given the good thing we've just sacrificed; if it occurs, it's an unexpected blessing, but to plan on this happening takes away the merit of our act.) From an early age, Thérèse was trained in the way of self-giving; as her mother wrote in a letter when the child was only three, "Even Thérèse is anxious to make sacrifices. Marie has given her little sisters a string of beads on purpose to count their acts of self-denial. They have really spiritual but very amusing conversations together."

Forsaking the pleasures of this world in exchange for the joys of God's kingdom requires a change in perspective, and sometimes this can occur quite suddenly. An amusing story in this regard is told of Bl. James of Lodi, who lived in the fourteenth century. He was a self-indulgent young man who occupied himself with painting, singing, and dancing, while giving little thought to religion. One day he entered a church containing a replica of the Holy Sepulcher (the tomb of Christ). James jokingly said to a friend, "Let's see who is taller — Christ or I," and lay down next to the tomb. However, in that instant James underwent a dramatic conversion. From then on, he lived a penitential life, and his example inspired his equally indulgent wife, Catherine, to do the same. (Many of us surely wish that sanctity would always "rub off" that easily.)

One very common form of self-indulgence is the vice of laziness — a weakness some of the saints had to overcome. For instance, when Augustine's education was interrupted at age sixteen (due to his father's inability to pay for continued tutoring), the youth returned home with nothing to do, and it was then that he fell into the sin of unchastity (for, as the saying goes, "Idleness is the Devil's workshop").

St. William, Archbishop of York in the mid-twelfth century, had been somewhat indolent as a young man; it was only after he responded to his calling from God that he became more energetic. The same was true of St. Joseph of Cupertino, who had a justly deserved reputation for laziness and absentmindedness as a youth. Early attempts to find his place in the world — first as an apprentice to a shoemaker, then as a Capuchin lay brother — were failures. It was only after some behind-the-scenes string-pulling by his mother, and much prayer, penance, and hard work on Joseph's part, that the Franciscans finally let him study for the priesthood.

Many of the saints, of course, are known for their diligence and hard work, including St. Martha, who was anxious with all the details of hospitality when Jesus visited her home;[60] St. Isidore the Farmer, who got up early each morning so as to attend Mass, and then made the long hours of the day pass more quickly by praying as he worked; and St. Charles Borromeo, who became a cardinal while very young and — contrary to common practice — took his duties very seriously and worked faithfully and diligently in performing them.

[60] Luke 10:40.

More Saintly Solutions

St. Benedict is a notable example of one who took a balanced approach to work, for when he wrote the rule for his order, he emphasized *ora et labor*, ("prayer and work") while maintaining a spirit of moderation that allowed the monks under his supervision to thrive (even to the point of helping preserve Western culture and civilization during the so-called Dark Ages). Benedict believed that labor was not only dignified, but also very helpful in moral and spiritual growth, and so he required it of everyone who joined his communities, nobles as well as commoners.

It must be admitted that at least one case is recorded of diligent labor getting someone into deep trouble. The tenth-century monk St. Reinold was put in charge of a building project at his monastery and was so industrious that he shamed the stonemasons working alongside him. When he refused to slow the pace of his work, so as not to make the professionals look bad, the angry masons killed him (thereby giving the lie to the expression that "hard work never killed anyone"). St. Reinold is today honored as a martyr.

A more tactful, and thus more successful, approach was used by Bl. Giles of Assisi. He hated idleness, but was careful not to condemn it in others. The cardinal bishop of Tusculum enjoyed his company at dinner, but Giles always insisted on first earning his meal by working in the fields. On a very rainy day, the cardinal told Giles that for once he'd have to accept a free meal, as outdoor work was impossible. However, Giles politely excused himself and went into the kitchen. Finding it in a very dirty state, he happily gave it a good cleaning before returning to table.

Laziness is a snare to be avoided. So is over-indulgence in food and drink. Gluttony is bad not only for our bodies, but also for our souls; regular fasting is a powerful and valuable remedy, but it must be done in a spirit of moderation and humility. According to St. Melania, "Just as a bride decked out in full finery cannot wear black sandals, but adorns her feet in the same way as her body, so the soul needs fasting, accompanied by all the other virtues. If anyone is eager to practice fasting apart from the other virtues, she is like a bride whose body is naked, and who adorns only her feet."

The saints frequently practiced fasting themselves, and encouraged others to do so. Indeed, one Lent St. Maximus, Bishop of Turin, did so quite forcefully, warning his congregation, "You will get your reproof during the Liturgy if I smell food on your breath at the kiss of peace."

Fasting and other acts of penance, of course, must be undertaken with prudence, making due allowance for our individual needs and weaknesses. St. Francis and his brother monks used to practice severe fasting each Lent. One night the saint was awakened by a voice crying out, "I'm dying! I'm dying!" It turned out that one of the brothers was extremely ill and weak from hunger, so Francis immediately prepared some food for him, and gently rebuked him for overdoing his ascetical practices. Then, to spare the brother the humiliation of eating alone, Francis broke his own Lenten fast by eating with him — a wonderful example of properly arranged priorities. (Francis wasn't always successful in this regard, however; for many years he practiced extreme penances — so much so that on his deathbed, he confessed that he was guilty of greatly sinning against "Brother Body.")

Acknowledging our human weakness can be a sign of spiritual maturity. The thirteenth-century virgin St. Lutgardis had fasted at length in preparation for Holy Communion and afterward was absorbed in prayer and thanksgiving. However, the saint was also conscious of feeling very weak due to hunger, so in her honesty and humility she prayed, "Lord Jesus, now is not the right time for me to be occupied with Your delights. Go instead to Elizabeth [a fellow religious sister confined to the infirmary], who is so weak that she must be fed every hour. Take possession of her heart, and let me go to take some food to restore my strength." This prayer was answered; Lutgardis went off to her meal without feeling guilt, and the Lord healed Sr. Elizabeth, allowing her to return to her regular role as part of the community.

The discipline of fasting can be a powerful aid to our spiritual growth — so long as it's done in a spirit of moderation and humility. As archbishop of Canterbury, St. Thomas Becket lived very simply, but always provided a fine meal for his many guests — and in the interests of hospitality, would even put them at ease by drinking a little wine himself and tasting the main course. A visiting monk noticed this and smiled to himself. Guessing his thoughts, the holy archbishop said, "If I am not mistaken, Brother, there is more greediness in your eating beans than in my eating pheasant." The surprised monk could only nod in shamed agreement, for in fact his motto was "quantity, not quality," and he compensated for living on simple monastic food by always eating as much of it as he wanted.

The saints have a great deal to say about overeating and other forms of self-indulgence. According to John Climacus, "Gluttony is the hypocrisy of the stomach which complains of being empty when it is well fed, and bellows that it is hungry when it is full almost to bursting." Self-discipline is necessary when it comes to eating, for as St. Gregory the Great tells us, "It is impossible to engage in spiritual combat unless the appetite has first been subdued." Moreover, St. Thomas Aquinas warns us that "Irrational feeding darkens the soul and makes it unfit for spiritual experiences," and St. Ignatius of Antioch teaches that "If you become surfeited with food, or still more with drink, the peace of God will cease to act in you."

Our souls are affected to a degree by the condition of our bodies, and overindulgence in food can make it more difficult to fulfill our spiritual duties. That's why St. Bernard of Clairvaux advises, "Inordinate love of the flesh is cruelty, because under the appearance of pleasing the body, we kill the soul. Take even bread with moderation, lest an overloaded stomach make you weary of prayer."

There are two practical steps we can take to avoid gluttony. First, Padre Pio suggests, "Never rise from the table without having given due thanks to the Lord. If we act in this way, we need have no fear of the wretched sin of gluttony." Thanking God for His blessings reminds us of the need to use these blessings properly; and freely denying ourselves certain legitimate blessings makes it possible for God's grace to be active in our lives at a deeper level. This is why, as a second step, the fifth-century monk St. John the Dwarf stresses the importance of fasting, saying, "If a king wants to take a city whose citizens are hostile, he first captures their food and water, and when they are starving, he subdues them. So it is with gluttony. If a man is earnest in fasting and making himself hungry, the enemies that trouble his soul will grow weak."

Self-indulgence of any kind can be spiritually harmful. In regard to slothfulness, for instance, St. Gregory the Great warns that if we form the habit of neglecting our religious duties, it gradually becomes extremely difficult — if not impossible — to perform them later on. Quoting the book of Proverbs — "Slothfulness casts into a deep sleep"[61] — the saint notes that those who are slothful grow increasingly oblivious to their spiritually lukewarm condition.

Similar admonishments are given about the excessive use of alcohol. St. Basil the Great tells us, "Drunkenness is the ruin of reason. It is premature old age. It is temporary death." St. John Chrysostom asserts, "The drunken man is a living corpse," and an even stronger warning is given by St. Francis de Sales: "He who drinks wine out of necessity does no evil; but he who takes it to such an excess that he becomes intoxicated offends God mortally, loses his judgment, drowns his reason in the wine he drinks, and if he happens to die in this state, is damned."

[61] Prov. 19:15.

More Saintly Solutions

Messages such as these might seem overly alarming to us, but the saints were uncompromising in their belief that anything which could interfere with the workings of God's grace must be avoided and resisted. According to St. Catherine of Siena, "Self-love is a tree on which grows nothing but fruits of death, putrid flowers, stained leaves, branches bowed down, and struck by various winds." True spiritual growth requires us to discipline our bodily appetites, for in the words of St. Columban, "Humility makes you strong; self-denial makes you Christlike." This sentiment is echoed by St. Josemaría Escrivá, who asserts, "Where there is no self-denial, there is no virtue."

There are many benefits to a sacrificial way of life. St. Thérèse calls it "the food of real love," and St. Elizabeth Ann Seton states, "The reward of sacrifice is peace." Moreover, St. Louis de Montfort promises us, "The more you give yourself, the more God will give Himself to you."

There are many ways to fast: taking only bread and water one day a week, skipping a meal on occasion, eating only once a day, passing up dessert, or, in the case of children (and even adults), eating everything on our plate without complaint. Other forms of self-denial include getting up early on occasion so as to attend Mass or to spend extra time in prayer, turning off the television and using the quiet time for spiritual reading, being very careful and moderate in our use of alcohol, setting aside our convenience or desires for the sake of another person in need, and contributing as much money to charity as we spend on our own pleasures. As we begin practicing this sort of self-giving, we'll discover that we receive far more in return, for as we clear away the clutter of self-will and self-love from our hearts, we develop a greater capacity to be filled with God's peace.

Self-discipline is very important, but it mustn't become an end in itself. St. Francis of Assisi shares with us this hard-won piece of wisdom: "Just as we must beware of overindulging in eating, which harms body and soul, so we must beware of excessive abstinence even more, because the Lord desires mercy and not sacrifice." Francis's friend St. Clare echoes this advice, telling us, "Our body is not made of iron. Our strength is not that of stone. Live and hope in the Lord, and let your service be according to reason. Modify your holocaust with the salt of prudence." Similarly, St. Catherine of Siena reminds us, "Perfection does not consist in lacerating or killing the body, but in killing our perverse self-will."

Our Lord has told us that there is a proper time for acts of penance and fasting[62] and a proper way of performing them.[63] If we humbly surrender ourselves to Jesus, and allow His Spirit to guide us in all things, including our practices of penance and self-denial, we can be sure that we are pleasing in His sight.

For Further Reflection

"The pleasure that a person seeks by gratifying his own inclinations quickly changes into bitterness and leaves nothing behind but the regret of having been ignorant of the secret of true beatitude and of the way of the saints." — *St. Isidore of Seville*

"To enjoy, we must love, and to love, we must sacrifice." — *St. Elizabeth Ann Seton*

"Preoccupation with sensual comforts is another block to devotion, because a person who indulges too much in worldly delights does not deserve those of the Holy Spirit." — *St. Peter of Alcantara*

Something You Might Try

◆ According to St. Vincent Pallotti, we must "remember that the Christian life is one of action, not of speech and daydreams.

---

[62] Mark 2:19-20.
[63] Matt. 6:16-18.

Let there be few words and many deeds, and let them be done well." Thus, a regular practice of self-denial isn't something to talk about, but to implement. It's often helpful to begin with something small: calling an elderly neighbor to see if she needs anything every single time you go to the store, skipping one meal a week and giving the money saved to charity, or unplugging the television one evening every week and using the time for family activities or reading Scripture, or both. Once something like this has become a habit, self-discipline will more easily become a regular part of your life, leading to a greater overall awareness and experience of God's blessings.

♦ As most of us know from experience, our eyes are often "bigger than our stomachs." In this regard, St. Ignatius of Loyola offers this advice: "To remove all disorder, it is a very great help that after eating, when he does not feel hungry, the person should determine the amount he should eat at the next meal. Once the amount is fixed, no hunger and no temptation should make him go beyond it; on the contrary, in order the better to overcome every inordinate attachment and temptation from the Enemy, if he feels tempted to eat more, let him eat less." This course of action can be very helpful to those who are serious about practicing self-denial (or sticking to a diet), and it will soon demonstrate that most of us can happily live much more simply than we're accustomed to — thereby making more room in our lives for God, and giving us more resources to share with those in need.

Further Reading

Scripture: Proverbs 6:9-11; Proverbs 20:13; Proverbs 23:20-21, 29-35; Matthew 11:28-29; Luke 21:34; Galatians 5:19-21; 1 Thessalonians 3:7-10; 1 Peter 2:11-12.

Classics: St. Augustine, *Confessions*; St. Thérèse of Lisieux, *The Story of a Soul*; St. Alphonsus Liguori, *Thoughts on* *the Holy Spirit;* St. Francis de Sales, *An Introduction to the Devout Life.*

Contemporary Works: Rudolf Allers, *Self-Improvement;* Ted Lawson, *Understanding Alcoholism.*

Dearest Lord, teach me to be generous;
teach me to serve You as You deserve;
to give and not to count the cost,
to fight and not to heed the wounds,
to toil and not to seek for rest,
to labor and not to seek reward,
save that of knowing that I do Your will.

St. Ignatius of Loyola

Shyness

Fear not, for you will not be ashamed;
be not confounded, for you will not be put to shame.
Isaiah 54:4

According to an ancient legend, after Jesus died, He "descended to the dead" and went down to limbo to free the souls of all the just people who had been waiting there for many years or even centuries. These just persons had some awareness of everything that was happening on earth, and they became very excited as the plan of salvation drew to a climax. Soon the gates of Heaven — which had been closed to all humanity because of Original Sin — would be thrown open, and their deepest yearnings would be fulfilled. When Jesus suddenly stood among them, all the just rushed forward to offer their greetings and expressions of thanks: Adam, Eve, Abel, Noah, Abraham, Isaac, Jacob, Joseph and his brothers, David, Ruth, Judith, John the Baptist, and innumerable others. Jesus smiled at them with great love, but He kept looking for someone else. Finally He saw him, modestly standing in the background. The Lord hurried over to him and embraced him, rejoicing in His loving reunion with His foster father, St. Joseph.

Joseph may or may not have been shy by nature; it was certainly characteristic of him to remain behind the scenes and avoid drawing attention to himself. This has been true of a number of saints; shyness is no impediment to holiness. Certainly there have been very outgoing and social saints, such as Teresa of Avila, among others — persons who were completely at ease in the presence of large crowds or intimate groups, who said what they thought and who attracted others by the force of their personalities. Jesus Himself was such a person. However, not everyone is called to such a lifestyle (nor is everyone capable of it). Biblical stories naturally draw our attention to the people who made a name for themselves, who — whether sinners or saints — tended to be present in a way that couldn't be overlooked. Sometimes we have to read between the lines, or look to the periphery of the scene, to spot some of the others who were there.

As an example, consider the brothers Peter and Andrew. Both were apostles, but their temperaments were quite different. Peter was outgoing, impetuous, and anything but shy — making him, in spite of his weaknesses and sins, a logical choice as the leader of the Apostles. In all likelihood, Andrew was quite different. The Gospels don't directly tell us so, but he seems to have been much quieter and more reserved. (With someone like Peter as a brother, this is hardly surprising; indeed, it would have been surprising had it been otherwise.) Nonetheless, Jesus chose him, and He knew what He was doing. Along with St. Paul, Andrew and all the other apostles — unique men with a wide range of talents and temperaments — became, through their empowerment by the Holy Spirit, the greatest and most important missionaries in history.

Several of the saints were known to be shy by nature. This was true, for instance, of St. Gregory of Nazianzus, a close friend of the fourth-century bishop St. Basil the Great. Basil had a strong, outgoing personality, but Gregory was quiet and sensitive. Both were great scholars, but Basil was more suited to an active life and to involvement in the religious issues and controversies of the day. Gregory was happier in a monastery. Even so, Basil, as Bishop of

Caesarea, appointed his friend as bishop of the small city of Sasima; instead of taking up his new duties, however, Gregory remained in Nazianzus — which led to a temporary rift between the two friends. (Basil hadn't realized that this sort of responsibility wouldn't come easily or naturally to his friend; Gregory, for his part, didn't understand that his friend recognized within him a potential for leadership.)

A few years after the temporary falling-out between Basil and Gregory, St. Gaudentius, a shy young priest from the Italian city of Brescia, went on a pilgrimage to Jerusalem, not only for religious reasons, but also to deflect attention from himself, for people were beginning to notice his many admirable qualities. Gaudentius's attempted flight into obscurity failed, for while he was away, the bishop who had educated him, St. Philastrius, died, and the people immediately chose Gaudentius as his successor. Indeed, they were so determined that they solemnly swore not to accept anyone as their bishop but him. The shy and overwhelmed Gaudentius tried to escape the responsibility, but the other bishops of Italy insisted that his election was a call from God and threatened to excommunicate him if he refused to accept it. Gaudentius reluctantly acceded and was consecrated as bishop by St. Ambrose around the year 390.

Quite a few of the saints, of course, have felt drawn to lives of solitude and prayer, but this is not always an option for shy people, nor is it necessary. Introverted persons can become more comfortable interacting with others and with living something of a public life. This was true of several of the saints, including the great theologian St. Thomas Aquinas. As a youth, he was so quiet and withdrawn that his fellow students mockingly called him "the Dumb Ox," yet, as his personality developed along with his amazing intellect, he came to enjoy the company of others.

St. Hugh, the future Bishop of Grenoble in the twelfth century, was an extremely bashful young man. Out of modesty, he concealed his great talents and learning, but his courtesy and self-effacing manner favorably influenced everyone who knew him. (In a sense, he made a virtue out of necessity, for his shyness and reluctance to talk about himself was usually interpreted as great humility.)

St. Elizabeth Bichier des Ages was also very shy as a child, but with the help of divine grace, she managed to establish a new religious order early in the nineteenth century — a highly impressive achievement for someone often uncomfortable with social interactions.

Another naturally shy saint is a seemingly unlikely one: St. Peter Claver, who spent his life working among the slaves of South America. He became a Jesuit priest in 1616 and, in spite of his lack of self-confidence, was soon involved in ministering to the black captives brought over from Africa. He enlisted assistants, boldly confronted landowners who mistreated their slaves, and did everything possible to meet the physical and spiritual needs of the Africans. Peter's life is a wonderful illustration of God's power to give His servants the spiritual and personal resources needed to accomplish their mission in life.

Being shy and withdrawn can make it harder to do one's part in spreading the gospel, but it's by no means impossible; as the prophet Jeremiah discovered, the closer we come to the Lord, the more we feel compelled to share His word.[64] Those who are usually quiet can often hear the Lord in ways that escape people who are always talking, and if they truly desire it, God will help them bring forth the gifts they hold deep within themselves.

For Further Reflection

"For in truth, no man is really weak and timid who knowingly leans upon the assistance of God." — *St. Francis de Sales*

[64] Jer. 20:9.

"Quiet is the first step to sanctification." — *St. Basil the Great*

"Do not be too timid and squeamish about your actions. All life is an experiment." — *Ralph Waldo Emerson*

Something You Might Try

♦ A good means of meeting people in a nonthreatening setting is simply to volunteer in your church or local community. If you're shy, you might find it hard to attend social gatherings (even when hosted by your parish), because you might not know anyone and may end up standing alone or feeling left out. If you're present for an activity or project, however (such as a fish fry, a rummage sale, a festival, or a car wash), you can ask the person in charge how to help. Keeping busy with the work can help you avoid awkwardly standing around with nothing to do, and allow you gradually to enter into conversation and fellowship with the other volunteers. Once you've begun to meet people that way, it will become easier to be involved in other activities and to continue widening your circle of acquaintances. (Besides, your parish and local community groups are always in need of more volunteers!)

♦ Sometimes an effective way to mingle at a party or event where you don't know anyone is to look for someone else who also appears shy or left out. Summon your courage, ask your guardian angel to help you find the right words, and go over and talk to him or her. If nothing comes of it, you haven't lost anything, but you may just meet someone who would welcome the chance to enter into a conversation.

Further Reading

Scripture: Psalm 34:6; Sirach 41:14.

Contemporary Works: Rudolph Allers, *Self-Improvement;* Russell Abata, *A Christian's Guide to Self-Esteem.*

O Lord, You are the Eternal Word,
so I ask You to help me in my words.
Many times I don't know what to say to others;
I'm afraid of embarrassing myself
or of saying something that others
will find foolish or offensive.
I really don't always want to be alone,
but sometimes it's easier that way.
I know I should be more outgoing,
and I know You've given me gifts
that You want me to share with others.
It's hard, Lord;
I know it's important, but it's hard.
Please help me;
please send me friends
who will accept me as I am,
who will be comfortable with me
and who will allow me
to join in and contribute
when I feel ready to do so.
I thank You, Lord,
for the gifts You have given me —
gifts that most people don't know about —
and I ask Your assistance
as I attempt to use them for the benefit of others.
Strengthen me, O Lord, and give
me the courage and confidence
to become the person You desire me to be.

Speech Impediments

The mind of the rash
will have good judgment,
and the tongue of the stammerers
will speak readily and distinctly.

Isaiah 32:4

Once there was a young man named Mark who was classified as having a severe learning disability. He didn't know how to read or write, and he had difficulty speaking. Nevertheless, he was a great evangelist and managed to bring many people to Christ. His method was simple: arming himself with religious tracts or pamphlets, he'd approach strangers and, in his slurred, halting speech, say to them, "Hello, my name is Mark. I can't read. Will you please read this to me?" Most people would grant his request — and quite a few of them, being deeply moved by the religious message they read aloud, gave their lives to Christ.

This true story reminds us that God can use anyone to share the Good News of salvation — including persons suffering from a speech impediment. Some scholars speculate that Jeremiah, one of the greatest Old Testament prophets, suffered from stuttering, for when he was called by the Lord, he answered, "I do not know how to speak." God, however, reached out and touched the prophet's lips, saying, "I have put my words in your mouth."[65] Jeremiah was thus able to proclaim the message the Lord had given him.

The same thing was true for a number of the saints. Speaking didn't come easily to them, but divine grace made it possible for them to fulfill their mission.

Some of the saints were naturally eloquent, capable of inspiring people by their preaching. St. Anthony Claret, for instance, was a speaker of exceptional magnetism. As a young missionary priest in nineteenth-century Spain (and later as archbishop of Santiago in Cuba), he attracted large crowds. Anthony's preaching brought about many conversions, and people were willing to wait in line for hours or even days to have him hear their confessions.

St. Francis de Sales, St. Peter Canisius, and St. John Chrysostom were also known for their powerful and eloquent preaching; indeed, *Chrysostom* is a nickname meaning "golden-mouthed." Another great religious orator was the fifth-century bishop St. Peter Chrysologus ("golden speech"), whose sermons were very short, as he didn't want to wear out his listeners. It's interesting to note, however, that sometimes Peter preached with so much passion and conviction that he rendered himself speechless.

Other saints were speechless for different reasons. St. Bridget of Sweden was unable to speak until she was three years old, and St. Charles Borromeo stuttered as a youth. He was accordingly considered somewhat slow, but he did well in his studies and was ordained a priest. Hard work helped him eventually conquer his speech impediment, although he never overcame it completely. This made it hard for him to preach, but he persevered and, as Cardinal of Milan, played a vital role in helping the Church implement the reforms of the Council of Trent.

Several of the saints were miraculously cured of speech impediments. At the end of the seventh century, for instance, young St.

[65] Jer. 1:6, 9.

Bede suffered from this handicap. Someone suggested that he venerate a relic of St. Cuthbert, and the desired miracle occurred: his speech was completely restored. (In gratitude, Bede later wrote Cuthbert's biography.)

Some seven hundred years later, Bl. John Dominici's desire to enter the Dominican Order was almost frustrated because of his speech impediment; and even after he was ordained, he wasn't allowed to speak in public. It was only after he prayed to the recently deceased St. Catherine of Siena that this handicap disappeared.

Not all verbally challenged saints were so fortunate, of course. In the tenth century, Bl. Notker Balbulus had a stuttering problem (and in fact, *Balbulus* is a nickname meaning "the stutterer"), and in the seventeenth century, St. Anthony Grassi had to give up preaching at age eighty, for when he lost his teeth, he could no longer make himself understood.

Saints like these put us in mind of Zechariah, the father of John the Baptist, who was temporarily struck mute for failing to believe the words of the angel Gabriel.[66] Zechariah's difficulty in speaking, however, was entirely of his own doing; those who suffer any physical or emotional difficulty in speaking are instead coping with one of the crosses the Lord has given them.

It isn't necessary for all of us to proclaim the gospel with eloquent words; at least as important is the example we give. This truth is expressed by the saying, "I can't hear what you're saying because your words are being drowned out by your deeds"; that is, if we're not living as Christians, no amount of eloquence on our part will attract others to Christ. Not every Christian is called to speak the gospel, but all of us are called to *live* it. The young man named Mark somehow understood this; his difficulty in speaking was no impediment to sharing his Faith. May all of us prove to be as wise as he.

[66] Luke 1:20.

For Further Reflection

"Preach the gospel at all times. If necessary, use words." — *St. Francis of Assisi (In other words, there's a way of proclaiming the gospel without words — through our example. Even if it's physically difficult for you to speak, you can influence others through your kindness and love.)*

"Though our lips can only stammer, we yet chant the high things of God." — *St. Gregory the Great*

"He who is educated and eloquent must not measure his saintliness merely by his fluency. Of two imperfect things, holy rusticity is better than sinful eloquence." — *St. Jerome*

Something You Might Try

♦ St. Peter of Verona once encountered a boy who had been unable to speak since birth. He had the lad open his mouth, and blessed his tongue "In the Name of the Father, and of the Son, and of the Holy Spirit." The boy immediately responded, "Amen" and, from then on, had perfect use of his speech. Praying aloud doesn't always work miracles (as the stories above about saints with ongoing speech impediments show), but it's a way of glorifying God — even if our voices falter — and of strengthening ourselves to bear the particular crosses He has chosen for us.

Further Reading

Scripture: Exodus 4:10-12; Luke 21:15.

Contemporary Works: Rudolf Allers, *Self-Improvement.*

꩜

Lord, I understand the hesitations
of Moses and Jeremiah when You called them;

I appreciate the difficulties experienced by
Zechariah, St. Bridget, St. Charles, and all
Your servants who have had difficulties speaking.
My speech impediment often fills me
with frustration and weariness.
I would so much like to be able to speak easily and clearly,
to express my ideas and thoughts and feelings with ease,
and to have others listen to and respect me.
Instead, I struggle. I know You've given me
this cross to bear, O Lord, so I realize that it has value,
and that by doing my best with it, I can come closer to You.
I submit myself to Your will even as I beg for Your help.
If You wish, O Lord, You can free me;
if this isn't Your will, You can sustain me.
In either case, I trust in You.
Help me to proclaim Your mercy and love
by the way I live; help me to share Your
Good News by my example.
Be with me in this and every other
burden and challenge. Amen.

Spiritual Dryness

My soul thirsts for God, for the living God.
When shall I come and behold the face of God?

Psalm 42:2

A little girl was in the habit of praying every night before she went to bed, but it seemed — at least in her mind — that her prayers weren't being answered. Therefore, she told her mother, "Mommy, I'm not going to say 'Amen' to my prayers anymore. Instead, I'm going to say 'RSVP.' "

Many of us are like that little girl: we wonder at times if our prayers are being heard, and we'd appreciate, if not an immediate answer, at least an acknowledgment that God has noted our request. It's a wonderful thing to experience God's consolations, feeling a strong sense of His presence and knowing in our hearts that we're deeply cherished by Him. Being able to rely confidently on the love of our heavenly Father helps make life a joyful experience, but that certainty and peace is sometimes unavailable to us. We'd like God to give us an RSVP to our prayers, telling us at the very least whether He's going to respond eventually. Far more often than not, however, we're denied this consolation.

Almost everyone seriously committed to growing closer to God sooner or later experiences a time of spiritual dryness, in which prayer is difficult and unsatisfying, distractions threaten to over-whelm our holy thoughts and intentions, and in which only sheer willpower can make us attend Mass or read Scripture or various other spiritual books. The fulfillment of our religious duties appears to be pointless and even oppressive, spiritual progress seems illusory, and the omnipresent God Himself seems far away — as if He had deliberately turned His face from us. It may console us to know that such experiences are not unusual, nor are they necessarily an indication of some great moral failing on our part. Aridity of this sort, however, can be so unpleasant and discouraging that to cope with it, we need whatever advice and assistance we can find. So it's good news that the saints have much to share with us on this subject.

Writing about the experience of terrible spiritual desolation and dryness, St. Alphonsus Liguori, in his classic *The Way of Salvation and of Perfection,* describes the suffering of one fifteenth-century mystic: "Behold what St. Catherine of Genoa used to say, when suffering aridity to such a degree that it seemed to her as if God had abandoned her, and that nothing remained to her as a ground for hope; it was then that she would say: 'How happy I am in this state, so deplorable even as it is! May my heart be broken down to ruins, provided that my Love be glorified! O my dearest Love, if from this unhappy state of mine is produced but a single atom of glory for You, I pray that You would leave me thus for all eternity!' And saying this, she would burst into a flood of tears in the midst of her desolation."

Other saints have experienced a similar degree of spiritual suffering — and made a similar, heroic act of faith. St. Pio, for instance, in a letter to his spiritual director, once wrote, "Dear Father, when will the sun shine in the heavens of my soul? Alas, I see myself astray in the deep dark night through which I am passing. But praise be to God, who never abandons anyone who hopes and places his trust in Him!" The Lord does indeed fulfill our hopes in Him, but He sometimes seems to withdraw from us so that we might grow in our yearning for Him, and also that we might be more aware of our absolute need for His help. When St. Margaret of Cortona was going through a difficult experience of aridity, our Lord is said to have explained to her, "I am concealing myself from you so that you can discover by yourself what you are without me."

A number of saints had to endure prolonged experiences of spiritual dryness, including St. Elizabeth Ann Seton, St. John of the Cross, St. Rose of Lima, St. Margaret Mary Alacoque, St. Anthony Claret, and St. Jane Frances de Chantal. The fourth-century founder of monasticism in Palestine, St. Hilarion, practiced great self-denial, eating very little and sleeping in a crude hut. This virtuous lifestyle, however, did not preserve him from intense temptations and prolonged aridity. The saint responded in the only proper way: by continuing to trust in God and by persevering in spite of all difficulties.

Genuine spiritual growth is a demanding and lifelong process. According to the great Franciscan scholar St. Bonaventure, those who truly seek God must pass through three stages: purification from sin, which results in what he calls "the calm of peace"; illumination or enlightenment, leading to "the splendor of truth"; and finally, union with God, which brings us to the "sweetness of love."

However, there exists within each of these stages, and particularly in between the stages, the possibility of great spiritual anguish. Just as an unborn child doesn't want to leave the comfort and security of the womb, so the soul finds it difficult to leave behind the consolations and certainty of one stage of spiritual development to move to a higher one. God is well aware that in our human weakness, we need to be challenged — sometimes in intense and uncomfortable ways — if we are truly to grow. This means, therefore, that spiritual aridity can be a sign of divine favor toward a person who truly wishes to serve Him.

Some of the saints use helpful images in describing the process of spiritual growth. St. Peter Damian, for instance, compares our imperfect awareness of God's presence to a flying fish, which springs into the air but immediately falls back into the sea. In the same way, he says, our souls — in moments of grace, prepared for by our faithful prayer and good deeds — briefly arise to the contemplation of the divine presence, but quickly fall back into the sea of everyday concerns.

A different, more modern image, is used by St. Thérèse of Lisieux. In her humility, she considered herself incapable of the great spiritual feats accomplished by earlier mystics and saints, so she said that instead of climbing the arduous steps to the top of Mt. Carmel (symbolizing the spiritual journey to Heaven), she needed to take the elevator — that is, to be lifted up to God's presence solely by His grace. This utter reliance on divine providence means, of course, that a person must surrender completely to God, patiently enduring whatever trials and challenges He may choose to send or allow.

St. John of the Cross wrote of the Dark Night of the Soul — a time of prolonged and intense spiritual anguish and restlessness. Most people don't fully undergo this experience, but even so, the saint's words on the subject have some relevance here. St. John tells us, "Since God puts a soul in this dark night in order to dry up and purge its sensory appetite, He does not allow it to find sweetness in anything." Part of the reason for this, as the great mystic notes, is that when our prayer is joyful and satisfying, we might easily come to love the consolations of God more than God Himself; by completely withdrawing these things from us, the Lord is helping us learn to love Him for His sake alone.

A similar idea is expressed by the great doctor of souls, St. Francis de Sales: "If God has stripped you of the sense of His presence, it is in order that even His *presence* may no longer occupy your heart, but Himself."

Offering an even more practical diagnosis, St. Francis continues, "If I am not mistaken, when we say that we can't find God and that He seems so far away, we only mean that we can't feel His presence. . . . Many people do not distinguish between God and the feeling of God, between faith and the feeling of faith — which is a very great problem. It seems to them that when they do not feel God, they are not in His presence. This is a mistake. A person . . . about to suffer martyrdom for God . . . does not actually think of Him but rather of his pain. . . . Although the feeling of faith may be wanting, he makes an act of great love. There is a difference between . . . being in God's presence and having the feeling of His presence. God alone can give the latter."

An important but often overlooked spiritual truth is simply this: God's grace does not depend on human feelings. If we desire to please Him, we receive God's blessing, even when we don't realize it or feel any different. Therefore, spiritual desolation doesn't indicate any failure on our part. Indeed, St. Teresa of Avila writes, "As to the aridity you are suffering from, it seems to me our Lord is treating you like someone He considers strong: He wants to test you and see if you love Him as much at times of aridity as when He sends you consolations. I think this is a very great favor for God to show you." Teresa also advises us, "Don't let aridity distress you; perfection has nothing to do with such things — only with virtues. Your devotion will come back when you're least expecting it."

In order that true spiritual growth may occur, a certain amount of change is necessary within our souls. Padre Pio uses a simple analogy to express this idea: "Sometimes you feel the winter of so much sterility, distraction, listlessness, and boredom. . . . You would like it to be eternally spring and summer. But no, these rotations are necessary, both internally and externally. Only in Heaven will everything be spring as regards beauty, autumn as regards enjoyment, and summer as regards love. There will be no winter, but here winter is necessary in order to practice abnegation and those beautiful virtues. . . . Do not fear the storm that roars around your heart, because to the degree the winter is rigid and stormy, on an equal basis will the spring be beautiful and rich with flowers, and the harvest more abundant."

The saintly Capuchin offers us this further advice: "Don't be bewildered if the night becomes deeper and darker for you. Don't be frightened if you are unable to see, with the eyes of the body, the serene sky that surrounds your soul. But look above, elevating yourself about yourself, and you will see a shining light, that participates in the light of the eternal Sun." To achieve this consolation, Padre Pio tells us, we must persevere in our prayers and spiritual devotions even when they're dry and unsatisfying to us, for this will demonstrate and, indeed, increase our love for God.

Moreover, he assures us, "Don't worry about your spirit, for it is by no means true that you have lost the path. The one on which you are walking is the true and safe way, and will lead you to the port of salvation." Padre Pio also advises us, "Don't be upset by aridity. . . . [Remember] what the Divine Master said: 'Blessed are the poor in spirit, for theirs is the kingdom of Heaven.' "[67]

How are we to pray when prayer is difficult? According to St. Jane Frances de Chantal, "You adore Him better by your silence than by your speeches. If you are incapable of anything whatever, then suffer. If you cannot pray by effort, then you will pray by endurance. In such an extremity, turn your face toward the Blessed Virgin, or toward any of the saints. Beg them to make your prayer for you, or to grant you some share in that prayer which they utter forever in Heaven." The saint also instructs us, "There are people who want to have experiences of God's closeness in prayer as a means of growing holy . . . but nevertheless He permits them to be dry and parched, powerless and blind to the extent that they don't

[67] Matt. 5:3.

even know what they're doing. Well, then, let's look for our perfection in this darkness and obscurity, by humility, patience, and resignation. . . ."

For Catholics, the most powerful and reliable source of divine grace — especially in times of spiritual turmoil and restlessness — is the Eucharist. Attending Mass, and receiving the Body and Blood of Christ, nourishes our souls and enables us to persevere on our spiritual journey and to overcome the trials and difficulties of daily life.

During a time of suffering and aridity, St. Faustina Kowalska wrote, "One thing alone sustains me, and that is Holy Communion. From it I draw my strength; in it is all my comfort. . . . Jesus concealed in the Host is everything to me. From the tabernacle I draw strength, power, courage, and light. . . . I would not know how to give glory to God if I did not have the Eucharist in my heart."

As the above examples and words of advice make clear, times of spiritual dryness are not a punishment or an indication of divine displeasure, but rather an invitation from God to enter into a new and deeper stage of our relationship with Him. Answering this call is challenging, but ultimately very rewarding. In the words of Ven. Solanus Casey, "As manifested in the lives of the saints, if we strive and use the means God has given us, we, too, can ascend to great sanctity and astonishing familiarity with God, even here as pilgrims to the Beatific Vision." One day we will see God face-to-face, and on that day we will truly give thanks for all the spiritual trials and struggles we encountered in this life.

For Further Reflection

"If any one of you be for a time cast down with weariness of spirit or afflicted with aridity of heart so that the torrent of devoted love seem to be dried up . . . realize the Lord's way. For a time, He will draw away from you that you may seek

Him with greater ardor and, having sought, may find Him with greater joy and, having found, may hold Him with greater love and, having held, may never let Him go." — *Bl. Jordan of Saxony*

"Man's greatness lies in being faithful to the present moment. We must be faithful to the present moment, or we will frustrate the plan of God for our lives." — *Ven. Solanus Casey (Thus, the spiritual difficulties we're experiencing may in fact be part of God's design — perhaps a preparation for a new challenge or mission in life, or the surest way of overcoming a particular fault or bad habit that's hindering our continued growth, or a way of making us more appreciative of a blessing or consolation we're about to receive. Being faithful to the present moment — by persevering in prayer even when it's not easy — allows God's wonderful plan to continue to unfold in our lives.)*

"One single act done with aridity of spirit is worth more than many done with feelings of devotion." — *St. Francis de Sales*

Something You Might Try

♦ In her *Diary*, St. Faustina Kowalska recorded this insight: "O my Jesus, how very easy it is to become holy; all that is needed is a bit of goodwill. . . . Faithfulness to the inspirations of the Holy Spirit — that is the shortest route." We might have our doubts that it's actually very easy to become holy, as the saint claims, but she's certainly correct in stating that the shortest path to perfection is to follow every inspiration of God's Spirit. This is simply a matter of uttering a silent prayer — "Holy Spirit, give me the words to say," or "Tell me what to do" — and then acting on the sense or guidance that we receive. As we form this habit, we'll become more aware of the many promptings or inspirations of the Holy Spirit that occur each day, while also strengthening our souls for the possible times of aridity and desolation that may come.

◆ St. Pio offers these practical words of advice: "Trust in Jesus and do not be afraid, for you have no reason whatever to fear. Our most tender Savior has not forsaken you, but is showing His love for you. . . . The evil one wants to persuade you that you are the victim of his attacks and are abandoned by God. Don't believe him. Despise him in the Name of Jesus and His most holy Mother." Thus, it can be helpful to see desolation within the larger context of the ongoing spiritual war that Satan wages against us, and in this regard, Jesus promises that "he who endures to the end will be saved."[68]

Further Reading

Scripture: Psalm 13:2-4; Psalm 42:1-3; Isaiah 58:9; Mark 13:13; Romans 8:38.

Classics: St. Alphonsus Liguori, *The Way of Salvation and of Perfection*; St. Alphonsus Liguori, *Conformity to the Will of God*; St. Alphonsus Liguori, *The Practice of the Love of Jesus Christ*; St. Francis de Sales, *An Introduction to the Devout Life*.

⌒

O my crucified Jesus!
You already know that,
out of love for You,
I have left all;
but after You have caused
me to leave my all,
I find that You Yourself
have left me, too.
But what am I saying,
O my Love?

[68] Matt. 24:13.

Have pity upon me;
it is not I who speak;
it is my weakness that
makes me speak thus. . . .
I wish to love You
with all my strength;
but what can I do myself?
Your Blood is my hope.
O Mary, Mother of God, my refuge!
Neglect not to pray for me
in all my tribulations.
First of all, in the Blood of Jesus Christ,
and then in your prayers,
do I trust for my eternal salvation.
"In You, O Lady, have I hoped,"
I will say to you with St. Bonaventure;
"I shall not be confounded forever."
Obtain for me the grace
ever to love my God in
this life and in eternity,
and I ask for nothing more.

St. Alphonsus Liguori

Spiritual Warfare

*I saw Satan fall like lightning from Heaven. Behold, I have
given you authority to tread upon serpents and scorpions, and
over all the power of the enemy; and nothing shall hurt you.*

Luke 10:18-19

St. John's Gospel tells us, "The light shines in the darkness, and
the darkness has not overcome it."[69] Jesus is the true light of life,
and He calls His followers to be children of the light and to share
the light of faith and love with the world.[70] Satan, as the Prince of
Darkness, isn't able to overcome the light, but that doesn't keep
him from attacking and tormenting God's children whenever
possible. All of us, of course, are constantly being tempted by
the Devil and his evil spirits, but occasionally some people may
undergo an even more direct diabolical assault. This was the case
for many of the saints, and their example of courageous perseverance and fidelity can be an inspiration to us in our own struggle
against evil.

The story of the great desert father St. Anthony of Egypt (as
recorded by St. Athanasius in his *Life of St. Anthony*) shows that

[69] John 1:5.
[70] See Matt. 5:14.

the Devil can be a wily and dangerous adversary and, more important, that those who place their trust in God will ultimately prevail. As a young man, Anthony gave his possessions to the poor and went into the desert to live as a hermit. His rapid growth in holiness attracted Satan's attention, and the enemy of all that is holy began tempting him in various ways: first by suggesting the many good works Anthony might have accomplished with his wealth had he remained in the world, then by attempting to make him dissatisfied with his calling from God. Failing in these first assaults, Satan tormented him day and night with obscene temptations; Anthony responded with increased prayer and fasting, and by keeping close watch over his senses. Next the Devil appeared to him in a visible form, first as a beautiful woman seeking to seduce him, then as a powerful brute threatening to destroy him. Anthony vanquished him by standing firm, and the Devil withdrew — but only for a time.

St. Anthony, seeking a more remote location for his solitary lifestyle of prayer and penance, withdrew to an old cemetery, where a friend occasionally brought him bread. Satan was again allowed the opportunity to attack Anthony, which he did by creating frightening noises, appearing in repulsive forms, and even beating the saint physically. In fact, Anthony was once assaulted so severely that his friend, arriving moments afterward, feared he was dead. Coming to himself, Anthony cried out, "Where were You, my Lord and Master? Why were You not here from the beginning of this conflict to render me assistance?" The saint heard the Lord answer, "Anthony, I was here the whole time; I stood by you and beheld your combat; and because you have manfully withstood your enemies, I will always protect you and will render your name famous throughout the earth" — a promise, of course, that was kept in a glorious way.

Other saints also experienced a higher-than-normal degree of attention from the Devil, including St. Rose of Lima, who often suffered terrifying visions and physical beatings. On the advice of her confessor, she fought back in an unusual way: by laughing in the Devil's face. An infuriated Satan, finding that he was unable to destroy Rose as he then wished to do, suddenly departed in impotent rage. St. Genevieve, although never beaten physically, was also subject to devilish harassment, as was St. Catherine of Palma, whose forceful protests to the Devil's lewd suggestions often disturbed the sleep and meditation of the other nuns in her convent.

St. Nicholas of Tolentino was visited by Satan, who beat him with a stick, and for some centuries afterward, the stick was on display in his church. An even more amazing trophy of saintly triumph over the Devil can be seen at the Mayfield Convent in East Sussex, England: the blacksmith's tongs with which St. Dunstan is said to have caught the Devil by the nose when he tried to tempt the saint under the form of an attractive woman.

St. Martin de Porres was visited by the Devil on three occasions. The first time the evil spirit appeared as a man who attacked Martin at the bottom of a flight of stairs, but the saint wasn't intimidated into lessening his prayers or his acts of charity. On another occasion, while a friend was staying with Martin in his cell, the door suddenly opened, and Satan and other demons rushed in. To the horror of the guest, they attacked Martin and set the cell on fire, but did no lasting harm, and afterward the room reverted to its normal appearance. For the third and final assault, which occurred shortly before the saint's death, the Devil changed his tactics; he began praising Martin and telling him how holy he was, hoping to ensnare him in the sin of pride. Martin resisted this final temptation through prayer, resulting in an appearance by the Virgin Mary and Sts. Dominic and Vincent Ferrer, whose presence forced Satan to flee.

One of the greatest saints of the nineteenth century — St. John Vianney, the holy French priest known as the Curé d'Ars — was also the victim of one of the longest and most determined diabolical assaults on record. For more than thirty years, day and night, the Devil attempted to deflect St. John from his efforts to rekindle the spiritual fervor of his small parish; the long hours the saint spent in the confessional, reconciling sinners to God — sometimes through his divinely given gift of reading souls — was rightly perceived by the Devil as a direct attack upon his evil kingdom, and as something to be resisted with all possible vigor. (Indeed, the Devil supposedly admitted that if there were another three such saints in the world, his kingdom would be undone.)

During his many attacks upon the humble parish priest, Satan interrupted St. John's sleep by making hideous noises, yelling insults at him, and beating him physically; and several of these attacks were witnessed by others who were present. Once the Devil even set the saint's bed afire, and when the evil spirit was particularly violent, St. John took that as an indication that a particularly notorious sinner would appear in his confessional the next day. (This can be an important lesson for us: strong opposition from the Devil might be a sign that our spiritual activities or acts of service in God's name are causing him serious trouble.) Over time St. John learned to take everything in stride; when a neighboring pastor said, "You must get very frightened," the saint responded, "One gets used to everything, my friend. The grappin [St. John's term for the Devil] and I are almost mates."

The only recorded experience to rival or exceed that of St. John Vianney belongs, of course, to St. Pio of Pietrelcina, one of the holiest men of the twentieth century. Satan reserves his worst attacks for those who can do him the greatest harm; and prolonged demonic harassment was part of the price the holy Capuchin friar paid for his profound spiritual influence on countless thousands of people throughout the world. Padre Pio was frequently attacked and physically beaten at night. On one occasion, he saw his bed surrounded by fearsome creatures who mockingly shouted, "See, the saint is retiring!" Padre Pio bravely answered, "Yes, in spite of you!" — and for his holy defiance, was thereupon seized and thrown to the floor.

In a series of letters to his spiritual director, written in 1912 and 1913, Padre Pio noted, "Bluebeard [his term for Satan] will not give up. He has appeared in almost every form. . . . Who knows how many times I have been thrown from my bed and dragged around the room. . . . That 'good for nothing' did nothing but beat me from about ten o'clock, when I went to bed, until five in the morning. Many were the diabolical suggestions that he placed before my mind, thoughts of despair, of a lack of faith in God; but long live Jesus, because I defended myself by repeating to Jesus: *Your wounds are my merits.* . . . I cannot tell you in what fashion those miserable creatures continue to persecute me. Sometimes I feel as if I am close to dying. . . . I had recourse to my angel, and after making me wait awhile, there he was beside me to relieve me, and with his angelic voice, sang hymns to His Divine Majesty. . . . For twenty-two consecutive days, Jesus has allowed them to vent their anger on me. My body, dear Father, is completely bruised by the many blows it has received at the hands of our enemies. More than once they went so far as to pull off my nightshirt and persecute me in that state. Now tell me, wasn't it Jesus who helped me in those sad moments in which, utterly destitute, the devils tried to destroy me, body and soul?"

Satan's almost incredible attacks upon the saintly Capuchin weren't limited to physical assaults; the Devil employed deception occasionally. Once, while ill in bed, Padre Pio apparently saw his former confessor enter the room. The apparition ordered him to give up his many penances because God allegedly disapproved of them. Suspicious of this message, Padre Pio ordered his visitor to call out, *"Viva Gesù!"* ("Long live Jesus!"), causing the creature to vanish instantly. The same thing happened when Satan tried to disguise himself as Padre Pio's guardian angel.

More Saintly Solutions

Quite often, the Devil interfered with letters sent to the saint from his spiritual director. One letter was unreadable because of a large ink blot, but when Padre Pio (at the suggestion of his angel) sprinkled it with holy water, the blot immediately disappeared. On another occasion, as he was about to open a letter, a group of demons ordered the Capuchin to throw it into the fire. When the saint made no response, they tried to bargain with him: "We want this merely as a condition for our withdrawal. In doing so, you will not be showing contempt for anyone." Padre Pio's continued refusal thereupon prompted another physical attack by the evil spirits.

On occasion, St. Pio complained about his sufferings, but according to him, his guardian angel answered, "Thank Jesus, who is treating you as one chosen to follow Him closely up the steep ascent of Calvary. [O] soul confided by Jesus to my care, I behold with joy and deep emotion this behavior of Jesus toward you. Do you perhaps think I would be so happy if I did not see you ill-treated like this? I, who in holy charity greatly desire your good, rejoice more and more to see you in this state. Defend yourself, always reject and despise the Devil's evil insinuations, and when your own strength is not sufficient, do not be distressed, beloved of my heart, for I am close to you."

Few people are given or desire the honor of imitating Jesus by receiving such prolonged and malevolent attention from the Devil, and we can certainly be forgiven for not willingly seeking out this potential means of growing in grace, but all of us experience ongoing temptations by evil spirits, and the advice of the saints can be very helpful in resisting and overcoming these assaults. St. Ignatius of Loyola, a former soldier, compared the Devil to a shrewd military commander preparing to assault a fortress; rather than directly attacking the strongest point of the defenses, such an enemy would look for a weak point and, then, without alerting the defenders beforehand, launch his assault there.

We might say that we're defending the fortress of our souls, and the four "walls" of this fortress consist of our relationships with God, as expressed in prayer; with the Church, as expressed in our reception of the sacraments and our participation in the life of the faith community; with our neighbor, as expressed in our acts of Christian charity; and with society, as expressed in our commitment to be good citizens and work for a better world.

St. Ignatius stresses that all four walls must be strong, because Satan's attack — in the form of spiritually dangerous temptations — could come from any direction, particularly, of course, in the area where we're weakest. Moreover, the saint emphasizes, the Devil is quite happy to see us focus our attention on making a strong wall even stronger, so long as we continue to neglect a weaker one. Indeed, the Devil will even tempt us to make greater efforts in our areas of strength, thus distracting or discouraging us from using God's grace to address our areas of weakness.

Preventing this, St. Ignatius says, requires that we humbly rely upon God's grace to show us what we must do, and that — after an honest self-appraisal — we direct our efforts to those areas in which we need to improve, rather than returning to our safe and comfortable areas of earlier success. Thus, for example, a woman heavily involved in her parish to the neglect of her family must resist the Devil's apparently pious temptation that she take on even more duties at church, and instead use God's grace to reorder her priorities. A man so busy working for social justice that he has no time to pray must not let himself be fooled by the Devil's suggestion that, at the expense of his spiritual duties, he take part in yet another protest march. A teenager who has been behaving in a beastly manner toward a classmate mustn't excuse herself on the basis that she spends more time in church than anyone else in her school. As St. Ignatius warns, Satan tries to use our strengths against us, making it essential that we try to do all things with humility.

St. Teresa of Avila, in her great spiritual work *The Interior Castle,* writes, "If the soul invariably followed the will of God, it is clear that it would not be lost. But the Devil comes with his artful wiles and, under color of doing good, sets about undermining it in trivial ways, and involving it in practices which, so he gives it to understand, are not wrong; little by little he darkens its understanding, and weakens its will, and causes its self-love to increase, until in one way or another he begins to withdraw it from the love of God and to persuade it to indulge its own wishes. . . ." Satan knows that good people can't be tempted to do clearly evil things, so he's much more subtle in his attacks. To overcome his wiles, St. Teresa, like St. Ignatius, recommends that we practice humility, for this virtue, totally foreign to the Devil's proud spirit, unmasks his wiles and short-circuits his assaults. Teresa also advises that when we pray for God's help, we do so in a spirit of confidence, for God wants us to conquer the adversary, as our success gives Him greater glory.

Contrary to the belief of many worldly people today, evil as a personified force does exist and is capable of causing great harm, but God's power is infinite; He's always willing to help and protect us and will never let us be attacked beyond our strength to resist. In the unlikely event that we experience demonic harassment above and beyond the normal course of temptations, we can be victorious through our use of the spiritual resources of the Church, the intercession of the saints — especially the Virgin Mary — and reliance upon our guardian angels. As Jesus promises, those who persevere to the end will be saved,[71] and those who place their trust in Him have nothing to fear.

For Further Reflection

"The power of Satan is . . . not infinite. He is only a creature, powerful from the fact that he is pure spirit, but still a creature. He

---

[71] Mark 13:13.

cannot prevent the building up of God's reign. Although Satan may act in the world out of hatred for God and His kingdom in Christ Jesus, and although his action may cause grave injuries — of a spiritual nature and, indirectly, even of a physical nature — to each man and to society, the action is permitted by divine providence which with strength and gentleness guides human and cosmic history." — *Catechism of the Catholic Church, par. 395*

"So often have the accursed creatures tormented me and so little am I afraid of them, now that I see they cannot stir unless the Lord allows them to. . . . Every time we pay little heed to them, they lose much of their power and the soul gains much more control over them." — *St. Teresa of Avila (Thus, as we engage in spiritual warfare, it's important that we focus on God's loving power to protect us, rather than on the Devil's limited power to harm us.)*

"Never forget your guardian angel who is always close to you, who never leaves you, no matter how badly you treat him. O unspeakable excellence of this good angel of ours! . . . How consoling to know one is always under the protection of a heavenly spirit who never abandons us, not even when we are actually offending God. How delightful is this great truth to the one who believes. Who is to be feared, then, by the devout soul who is trying to love Jesus, when accompanied by such an illustrious warrior?" — *St. Pio of Pietrelcina*

Something You Might Try

◆ Many of the saints had loving and intimate relationships with their guardian angels, including St. Joseph of Cupertino, St. Mary Magdalene de Pazzi, St. Faustina Kowalska, and, of course, St. Pio. The holy Capuchin friar of Pietrelcina advises us, "When it seems to you that you are alone and abandoned, don't complain that you are without a friend to whom you can open your heart and confide your woes. For goodness' sake, don't forget this invisible companion who is always there to listen to you, always ready to console you." Thus, whenever we face a spiritually dangerous situation, or undergo any other difficulty, we should make a point of invoking the assistance of the angel assigned to us by God.

♦ Demonic harassment (as opposed to standard temptations by the Devil) isn't a problem experienced by most Christians, but it's certainly a possibility. Cases of full-fledged possession, which are relatively rare, can be resolved (through exorcism) only by a duly authorized priest, but Jesus gave all His followers authority over evil spirits.[72] The easiest way to exercise such authority is through a simple binding prayer — that is, whispering or saying silently, "Evil spirit, I bind you in the Name of the Lord Jesus Christ." Such a prayer is appropriate whenever you feel spiritually uncomfortable or have a sense that something affecting you or another person "isn't quite right." In more serious cases, when sinister and unexplainable events occur, or when someone seems to be attracting misfortune, it often turns out that the person is guilty of an unconfessed mortal sin. (Serious sins can provide an opening for greater evil or negative influences to take root in our lives.) Many times, all that's needed for the person to break these chains is to make a good confession in the sacrament of Reconciliation. It's also helpful to sprinkle rooms and objects with holy water, to carry or wear blessed sacramentals (rosaries, scapulars, and religious medals), and to pray for the intercession of the angels and saints, particularly St. Michael the Archangel and the Blessed Virgin Mary.

Further Reading

Scripture: Matthew 13:39; Luke 8:12; John 8:44; Ephesians 4:25-27; Ephesians 6:11-17; 1 Peter 5:8-9; Revelation 12:1-9.

---

[72] Mark 16:17.

Classics: St. Athanasius, *Life of St. Anthony*; St. Ignatius of Loyola, *Spiritual Exercises*; Lorenzo Scupoli, *Spiritual Combat*.

Contemporary Works: Mother Nadine Brown, *God's Armor*; Paul Mihalak, *The Nature of Angels*; Terry Ann Modica, *Overcoming the Power of the Occult*; Joan Carroll Cruz, *Angels and Devils*; Gerald Vann, *The Devil and How to Resist Him*; Gabriele Amorth, *An Exorcist Tells His Story*; Gabriele Amorth, *An Exorcist: More Stories*.

⌒

St. Michael the Archangel,
defend us in battle,
be our safeguard against the
wickedness and snares of the Devil.
May God rebuke him, we humbly pray,
and do thou, O Prince of the Heavenly Host,
by the power of God, cast into Hell
Satan and the other evil spirits
who prowl about the world
seeking the ruin of souls.

Pope Leo XIII

Stubbornness

A stubborn mind will be afflicted at the end, and whoever
loves danger will perish by it. A stubborn mind will be
burdened by troubles, and the sinner will heap sin upon sin.

Sirach 3:26-27

About the year 580, there was a seven-year-old boy named Zosimus whose parents were prosperous farmers on the island of Sicily. His family had taken him to live at the nearby monastery of St. Lucy, near the city of Syracuse. Young Zosimus's duties were primarily those of tending to and guarding the relics of St. Lucy, a virgin who had been martyred in Syracuse in 304. Having been accustomed to roaming freely through his family's farm and the surrounding countryside, Zosimus didn't welcome this assignment. Moreover, the boy had a stubborn streak, which was manifested one day when the abbot assigned him a particularly disagreeable task. Rebelling, Zosimus ran away and went home. His angry parents, however, took him back to the monastery, where they and the monks made him quite aware of how much trouble he had caused. Even they couldn't have guessed, however, what further penalty the boy was to experience as a result of his stubbornness.

That night Zosimus dreamed that St. Lucy rose from her shrine and turned toward him with a severe, threatening expression. As the boy looked on in terror, St. Lucy, in that ominous manner characteristic of nightmares, approached with vengeful intent, but then our Lady appeared and saved him by promising in his name that he would never again commit such an offense. The thoroughly frightened boy took this dream as a message and a warning. St. Zosimus accepted his vocation and lived faithfully as a monk for the next thirty years, and was then chosen as Bishop of Syracuse.

It might seem that a punishment for stubbornness and neglect of duty such as Zosimus experienced in his dream is both unlikely (would St. Lucy really have threatened a child?) and extreme (after all, the boy was only seven years old); however, aside from the fact that what Zosimus experienced was only a dream, it should be remembered that stubbornness isn't always a minor fault or (among children in particular) an endearing characteristic or personality quirk.

An ongoing refusal to submit to legitimate authority can create severe obstacles to our spiritual growth. Stubbornness — which is a way of saying that what we want is most important, or that we alone know what's best — often interferes with God's plan for us. Being stubborn combines elements of pride, willfulness, and self-indulgence, and these are all moral failings we must resolve to overcome. As St. Bernard asks, "Where is all disturbance of mind, if not from following one's own desire?" Holiness and happiness require that we learn how to surrender ourselves to God's will, but many of us find this a hard lesson to master.

Some of the saints tended to be stubborn by nature. As a young girl, the nineteenth-century Carmelite nun Bl. Elizabeth of the Trinity was very strong-willed — so much so that her relatives called her "a little devil." When she was three, she brought a doll to church, and before Mass, the priest obtained permission from Elizabeth's mother to use the doll in the Christmas manger scene. Little Elizabeth, unaware of these arrangements, was shocked to see the priest carrying the doll away, and — to her mother's intense embarrassment — shouted, "Bad priest! Bad priest! That's my doll!"

The death of her father when she was seven helped Elizabeth become spiritually aware, however, and this process was intensified when she received her First Communion and Confirmation at age ten. At age fourteen, Elizabeth, choosing Christ as her Spouse, made a private vow of virginity, and sought to enter the Carmelite Order. Her mother did everything she could to oppose this course, but in the end her daughter's holy stubbornness won out.

Several centuries earlier St. Rose of Lima drove her parents to distraction by her determination to follow a life of prayer and solitude, and consistently rejected their efforts to arrange a marriage for her. For ten years, they insisted that she marry, but Rose refused; for ten years, she sought permission to enter a convent, which they wouldn't allow. Finally they came to a grudging agreement: Rose would live at home as a member of the Third Order of St. Dominic (intended specifically for laypersons), while practicing as much as possible a life of penance and solitude.

Rose's determination paid off, but it's possible to take a good thing too far. As one of her penances, she customarily wore a crown of thorns. When her confessor urged her to shorten the thorns somewhat (so as to inflict less suffering on herself), she defiantly drove the thorns in even deeper. Rose's desire to suffer in Christ's Name may be commendable, but on this occasion she forgot one important point: obedience — especially when it goes against our inclinations — is the sacrifice most pleasing to God.

This truth is shown rather dramatically and forcefully in a story about St. Columba, the great sixth-century Irish missionary and abbot. Upon the death of King Conall in Scotland, Columba was asked by the people to choose and crown the king's successor. The saint decided upon Conall's eldest son, Iogenan, but for three nights in a row an angel appeared in a dream bearing a glass tablet, on which was written a command that Aedhan, the youngest son, should instead be made king. Most people — let alone most saints — would recognize this as a message from God, and respond accordingly, but that reckons without traditional Irish stubbornness. The saint refused. God always has the last word, however. On the third night, the angel is said to have responded to Columba's stubbornness by scourging him. Finally getting the message, Columba relented and agreed to Aedhan's coronation.

Another story involving the stubbornness of St. Columba describes a visit he paid to his former teacher St. Finnian of Moville. Finnian showed his guest a newly obtained manuscript of the four Gospels. Columba, desiring a copy for his own monasteries, secretly went into the library every evening and, by the light of a candle, carefully traced the beautiful letters onto his own parchment. When Finnian discovered this, he was furious, and he demanded that his former student give him the copied manuscript. Columba refused, so the matter was taken to Dermott, the local king. Dermott stated, "To each cow her calf, and to each book its copy." Columba had to give in, but he was very angry.

Later one of his relatives, who had accidentally caused someone's death, took refuge with Columba, but Dermott's men violated the sanctuary of the monastery and took him away. Columba's fury could no longer be contained; he urged his kinsmen to revolt against Dermott. After a bloody battle in which three thousand warriors lost their lives, a Church synod was convoked, and Columba was excommunicated — but St. Brendan of Birr stepped up to Columba and kissed him. This gesture of forgiveness inspired the synod to revoke its punishment.

Columba, however, was filled with guilt, and when he confessed his sin to St. Molaise, a severe penance was imposed: Columba was never again to set eyes on his homeland; instead, as a missionary, he was to win as many souls for Christ as were slain in battle. Columba, realizing what his stubbornness had caused, sadly agreed. (On one occasion, he did return to Ireland, however, so as to intercede to prevent an injustice from being done, but he was careful to wear a blindfold, so that he didn't actually see his homeland.)

Other recorded instances of saintly stubbornness manifest a more positive outlook, for it is a good thing to be single-minded in doing the will of God, in spite of all opposition. It's necessary, though, for this determination to be linked to a genuine spirit of humility and Christian charity.

We see this impressive combination in the life of St. Catherine of Siena. As she was the youngest of twenty-five children, it was only natural that her parents wanted her to marry into wealth, but Catherine, at a young age, decided to dedicate her life to God. Her mother nagged her about making herself pretty and charming, so as to attract a suitor. Catherine, however, responded by cutting off her beautiful hair to prevent this. In punishment, she was forced to wait on everyone else in the family and was given the hardest household tasks. The teenage Catherine accepted this situation with cheerful obedience, and this finally led to her father's decreeing that she be given what she desired: the opportunity to live as a recluse in her own room, spending all her time in prayer and solitude. (In this she verified the words of St. John of Avila: "Humility and self-contempt will obtain our wish far sooner than will stubborn pride.")

Other saints known for their unyielding character include St. Thomas Becket, whose obstinacy enabled him to withstand King Henry II's efforts to undermine Church authority in twelfth-century England, and St. Peter Claver, who spent his life ministering to black Africans brought over to the Spanish empire in South America as slaves. A friend of Peter described him as "pig-headed and difficult," and these traits served him well in his efforts to alleviate some of the slaves' sufferings and to defend their rights as human beings against harsh and uncaring owners.

Another somewhat willful saint was St. Hedwig, whose many penances included going barefoot in winter. An abbot once gave her a pair of shoes and ordered her, under pain of holy obedience, never to appear in public without them. Hedwig fulfilled this command, while continuing her preferred form of penance, by constantly carrying the shoes under her cloak, rather than wearing them as the abbot had intended.

Sometimes the saints had to be stubborn to answer God's call, for parents' ambitions for their children don't always correspond to their actual vocation. In the sixteenth century, St. Aloysius Gonzaga seemingly had a bright future in front of him. He came from a noble family, and for a time served as a royal page in the court of King Philip II of Spain. His father envisioned his son as a great military leader, but young Aloysius — inspired by a book detailing the success of the Jesuit missionaries in India — conceived a fervent desire to enter the relatively new Society of Jesus. His father was so appalled that he not only forbade this, but also enlisted the help of some important Church leaders to dissuade the youth from throwing his life away in such a manner. Aloysius stood firm, and for four years, father and son were locked in a battle of wills. Finally the young man was given reluctant permission to enter the Jesuit novitiate in Rome. Once there, however, Aloysius was required to do some things he wouldn't have chosen for himself, such as eating and resting more, and praying less, than he was accustomed to, but he obeyed in a spirit of humility.

The fifteenth-century virgin Bl. Christina of Spoleto, as a child, strongly desired the religious life, but when she was ten, her parents announced their intention to arrange for her eventual marriage. Christina flatly refused, and for two years, there was an impasse between parents and daughter. As Christina was about to be forced into marriage at age twelve, she ran away from home with the help of a servant girl and eventually achieved her goal of becoming a nun.

Two centuries earlier Bl. Philippa Mareri withstood pressure to marry from her parents and brother by cutting off her hair, wearing unattractive clothes, and living as a recluse in her room. When her brother tried to force her to change her mind, she ran away with a few companions. (Philippa's brother later begged her forgiveness and helped her establish an abbey.)

On occasion, parents support the efforts of their children to do God's will, even when they know this will cause suffering and grief. In the third century, a young man named Maximilian refused to be drafted into the Roman army. In spite of threats of severe punishment, he stood firm, saying, "My army is the army of God, and I cannot fight for this world." His father, a retired soldier himself, was sent for and told to correct his son, but he answered, "He knows what he believes, and he won't change his mind." St. Maximilian was beheaded, and his father, although grieving, also expressed joy that he had been allowed to send such a gift to Heaven.

This story is a good example of what holy stubbornness should be: both Maximilian, in his refusal to violate his conscience, and his father, in his unwillingness to pressure or lead him astray, demonstrate an awareness that God's will must always come first. A strong and courageous character is of inestimable value in a world that actively threatens and opposes all true servants of God. Let us follow the example of the saints by being stubborn not for ourselves, but for God — for this can turn a vice into a virtue.

For Further Reflection

"Our greatest fault is that we wish to serve God in our way, not in His way — according to our will, not according to His will. . . . This is certainly the greatest obstacle we can raise to our own perfection, for it is beyond doubt that if we wish to be saints according to our own will, we shall never be so at all. To be truly a saint, it is necessary to be one according to the will of God." — *St. Francis de Sales*

"The merit of renouncing one's own will is invariably greater and more precious than getting one's own way." — *Bl. John Ruysbroeck*

"In the royal galley of Divine Love, there is no galley slave: all the rowers are volunteers." — *St. Francis de Sales*

Something You Might Try

◆ As novice-mistress, St. Thérèse of Lisieux realized she had to be very gentle with some novices, and quite firm with others. Regarding the latter, she wrote, "God has given me one grace — I'm not afraid of a fight; I have to do my duty, come what may. More than once these people have protested, 'If you want to get anything out of me, you'll have to go gently; blustering won't get you anywhere.' Unfortunately, I needn't be told that nobody is a good judge in his own cause! When some doctor decides that a child has got to have a painful operation, there will be plenty of screaming, and he will be told that it's hurting worse than the pain did; but how glad the child is, a day or two later, to be well again, able to play and run about! And so it is with souls; they soon come to realize that a dose of medicine does more good than sugar, sugar all the time; and they aren't afraid to admit it." We, too, must become like those souls who realize that God always knows what's best for us, and that quite often He uses other people to express this truth. If you're naturally stubborn, conduct this experiment: decide to give in every other time when you're told or asked to do something you don't want to do, and then keep track of which way works better — yours, or God's.

◆ If you tend to react negatively when people tell you to do something, consider this approach. When someone who has the right to do so (a person in legitimate authority, or a loved one) gives an order or suggestion, try to see it as a request from the Lord. If you can decide that you're doing this action for His sake, even if not for the person requiring it, you may find it much easier to respond.

Further Reading

Scripture: Mark 16:14; Hebrews 3:7-9.

Classics: St. Thérèse of Lisieux, *The Story of a Soul*.

Contemporary Works: Rudolf Allers, *Self-Improvement*.

Lord, sometimes my stubbornness
can be good, as when I stick up for
my beliefs and refuse to let anyone
or anything dissuade me.
Many times, however, my stubbornness
isn't so noble; in fact, it can get me into
trouble for no good reason and even
make me difficult to live with,
causing unnecessary suffering
and difficulty for others.
Please help me overcome this fault —
but in a way that allows me
to keep that which is good
while uprooting that which is harmful.
I want to hold on to my strong character
and sense of determination,
but I also want to become
sensitive and compassionate,
learning to think of other
people's needs and feelings,
instead of focusing only on my own.
Touch my hardened heart, O Lord,

and make me gentle and caring,
flexible and responsive,
and ever willing to consider
the possibility that sometimes other
people have a better understanding
of what's best than I do.
Give me opportunities to be
humble and submissive,
and instruct my guardian angel
to give me a friendly poke whenever
I revert to my old ways.
Lord, You are the Source of
all love and peace:
help me to live in peace
with the world around me. Amen.

Uncertainty

Thou dost guide me with Thy counsel,
and afterward Thou wilt receive me to glory.

Psalm 73:24

Many inspiring inscriptions are to be found in the catacombs of Rome. These underground cemeteries memorialize early Christian saints, martyrs, and unknown spiritual heroes who were willing to risk persecution, imprisonment, and even death to answer God's call. The powerful Roman Empire has long since faded away, but the glory of those who refused to render unto Caesar what belongs solely to God will last for all eternity. In most cases, we know nothing of these brave souls other than their names, inscribed on their tombs, but these few words, and the Christian symbols chiseled along with them, bear witness to a spiritual power that no earthly force could hope to conquer.

Not all the inscriptions tell the tale of a victorious faith, however. There's one unfortunate memorial containing the words *audienti protractae*, meaning "to the listener who overdid her time." Scholars tell us that the listener referred to was probably a catechumen, a girl who was listening to the teachings of the Church in preparation for Baptism. However, for some unknown reason, she delayed being baptized, and sudden death (of a cause unknown to us) caught her spiritually unready. She wasn't a martyr, receiving the baptism of blood (for this would surely have been noted), and the customary inscription *in pace* ("in peace") was omitted from the inscription on her tomb; but at the same time, she was not a lapsed Christian who left the Church (for in that case, she wouldn't have been buried among believers). It seems that this unfortunate and indecisive young woman heard the gospel, was attracted by it, and considered its demands quite seriously, but could never make up her mind to respond. She listened too long and didn't commit herself to act.

Jesus warns us, "Not every one who says to me, 'Lord, Lord,' shall enter the kingdom of Heaven, but he who does the will of my Father who is in Heaven."[73] Our faith must be a living faith if it is to save us. St. James instructs us, "Be doers of the word and not hearers only, deceiving yourselves."[74] We must actively respond to God's call, instead of merely listening to it; but this confronts us with an important, and often difficult, question: how do we know for sure what the Lord is asking of us?

It's quite common for followers of Jesus to have a sincere desire to know and do His will, and yet be unsure of exactly what this means in particular circumstances. When we have to choose — particularly in regard to important issues — how do we discover what God wants us to do? Does the Lord make known His will to us? Can we be sure our decisions truly are based on His desires, rather than our own piously disguised personal inclinations?

These and related questions revolve around the issue of discernment, which means discovering God's plan for us, or choosing from among two or more morally acceptable alternatives whenever an important decision has to be made. Some degree of uncertainty, or a need for divine guidance in specific instances, has

---

[73] Matt. 7:21.
[74] James 1:22.

always been present in humanity's relationship with God. The book of Exodus, for instance, speaks of the *ephod, urim,* and *thummin.*[75] The *urim* and *thummin* were apparently some sort of lots, cast by the high priest to discover the Lord's will in doubtful matters, and the *ephod* was the breastplate in which they were carried. This interpretation is supported by Proverbs 16:33, which states, "The lot is cast into the lap, but the decision is wholly from the Lord." Moreover, the Apostles were familiar with this tradition, for when it was necessary to replace Judas Iscariot to maintain the number of twelve, St. Matthias was chosen by lot.[76] The casting of lots is no longer a common religious practice, but there are still many instances in which we must discern God's will, and we can profitably look to the saints for help in this regard.

Sometimes one's entire life-direction becomes clear in an instant. For example, upon hearing a sermon on foreign missions when he was fifteen, St. John Gabriel Perboyre announced, "I mean to be a missionary!" The youth pursued his desire with unwavering determination, was ordained a priest, and went to China, where he died as a martyr at the age of thirty-eight.

At the age of twenty-one, Bl. Anne-Marie Jahouvey had a vision in which St. Teresa of Avila presented a number of foreign children to her, saying, "God wants you to found a congregation to care for these children." Anne-Marie acted upon this revelation with complete assurance, and this confidence remained with her throughout her life (for in her correspondence, she frequently stated, in regard to one project or another, "I know this is what God wants me to do").

It certainly isn't unknown for God to reveal His will in an unmistakable fashion — although sometimes the message is given in a symbolic or unexpected way. The Pope and martyr St. Fabian,

[75] Exod. 28:15-30.
[76] Acts 1:23-26.

for instance, was "elected" in an unusual manner. When Pope St. Anterus died in 236 (after reigning for barely a month), the clergy and people of Rome gathered to decide upon his successor. Fabian, a Christian layman, happened to be returning from his farm outside the city when a blue dove flew down and settled on Fabian's head. The conclusion was obvious and unanimous: Fabian was Heaven's choice as Pope. (An inspired choice it proved to be: he ruled with wisdom and firmness for the next fourteen years.)

In the ninth century, St. Donatus found himself acclaimed as bishop of Fiesole under similar circumstances. He was returning from a pilgrimage just as the people and their clergy were praying for divine guidance in choosing their new chief shepherd. At that moment, as Donatus entered the church, all the bells suddenly began ringing, and all the lamps and candles were kindled without any human hands involved. Naturally, this supernatural intervention was seen as a sign from Heaven, and Donatus was immediately chosen as bishop.

Scripture gives us several instances of God's will being made known in a dream, as happened to St. Joseph on two occasions,[77] and other saints had similar experiences. St. Cuthbert, for example, had a vision as a teenager which he interpreted as a message that he should enter a monastery — which he promptly did.

A famous story about St. Patrick tells of his vision in which a man from Ireland named Victoricus gave him a letter to read, and as he did so, he heard many Irish voices calling out as one: "We beg you, holy youth, to come and walk once more among us." This convinced the saint that God wanted him to return to Ireland (where he had spent six years as a slave before escaping) and there preach the gospel.

Another youthful recipient of a heavenly message was St. Nicholas of Tolentino. While praying, he saw a vision of angels

[77] Matt. 1:20; 2:13.

who began chanting, "To Tolentino, to Tolentino." The eighteen-year-old immediately set out, became a friar there, and remained in the town for the rest of his life.

The election of the great bishop St. Ambrose occurred in an unusual manner — one apparently inspired by Heaven. When the Bishop of Milan died in 374, the people of the city gathered to elect his successor. Ambrose, as governor of northern Italy, was present at the assembly in his official capacity; when he began to speak, a small boy — who was actually, according to legend, an angel in disguise — shouted, "Ambrose, bishop!" Caught up in this inspiring thought, the entire crowd shouted in response, "Ambrose, bishop!" and — over his protests (for he was only a catechumen, and not yet baptized) — Ambrose was elected by acclamation.

Another saint who received God's call in an unusual way was St. Austreberta. As a girl, she looked at her reflection in a pool of water. When she saw a veil covering her head (something she wasn't physically wearing at the time), she was convinced that God was calling her to a religious life.

Other saints who received direct signs include St. Francis de Sales and St. Jane Frances de Chantal, who, upon seeing each other for the first time, immediately recognized one another from a vision each had received regarding their future shared ministry; St. Thérèse of Lisieux, who asked God that a nun opposing her entry into the convent change her mind as a sign that her recently deceased father had gone straight to Heaven, and whose request was answered; the Franciscan friar St. Bernadine of Siena, who discovered his vocation as a powerful preacher after a novice proph-esied three times that he was to "go to Lombardy, where all await you"; St. Catherine Labouré, whose decision to enter the Sisters of Charity of St. Vincent de Paul was confirmed when she realized the holy priest she had seen in her dreams several times was in fact the (long-deceased) founder himself; and St. Alphonsus Liguori, who fervently prayed for the assistance of the Virgin Mary before every important decision, and who agreed to be consecrated a bishop only after our Lady appeared to him and told him this was God's will.

The Lord is quite capable of revealing His will through coincidences, mistakes, and even jokes. In the sixteenth century, for instance, St. Thomas of Villanova became Archbishop of Valencia because of a clerical error; his name was mistakenly put on a list of nominees for the position, instead of the name of another religious. Two centuries earlier, Bl. Roger LeFort was upset with the poor quality of candidates seeking to fill the vacant bishopric of Orleans, so he jokingly offered himself for the position. To Roger's shock, his jest was taken seriously and was popularly received, and he found himself elected bishop, in spite of his own protests. (Thus, it's not always safe to tell jokes in church, for the Lord's sense of humor trumps our own.)

A number of the saints have accepted ecclesiastical appointments very reluctantly, doing so only because their selection seemed to be God's will. When St. Augustine returned to Africa after his conversion, he lived a quiet, monastic-like life, and, knowing how his mentor, St. Ambrose, had been elected bishop, he was careful to avoid traveling to towns with vacant bishoprics or pastorates. One day he entered the church in Hippo, feeling perfectly safe in doing so, as Valerius, the city's bishop, was in perfect health. However, Valerius — casting telling glances in Augustine's direction — began speaking about how, due to his Greek background, he needed a priest who could preach in better Latin than his own. Knowing full well what was happening, the congregation began urging the unsuspecting Augustine to accept Ordination. His tears and arguments were useless. When he couldn't change the minds of the bishop and his people, Augustine reluctantly accepted this unexpected event as a manifestation of God's will.

St. Anselm showed a similar reluctance in the eleventh century, first when he was elected abbot, and later when he was appointed Archbishop of Canterbury. In each case, he practically had to be forced to accept what he later recognized as divine providence.

At least one instance is recorded of a saint acting on what he thought was divine inspiration, when in fact it was only an act of human deception. In the papal conclave of 1294, the hopelessly deadlocked cardinals finally agreed, almost in desperation, on a compromise candidate: a very holy — but as it turned out, totally unqualified — hermit named Peter of Morrone. The frail, eighty-year-old man refused to accept his election at first, and finally did so only when the cardinals insisted that God required it of him for the good of the Church. The reluctant Pope, known to history as St. Celestine V, ate nothing but bread and water, had a crude wooden cell built in a corner of the magnificent papal apartments, and began giving away the Church's treasure to the poor. He was overwhelmed by the many responsibilities of his office, however, and some of the cardinals soon began to regret their choice. One of them, Cardinal Benedetto Caetani, felt it was his duty to save the Church from a potentially disastrous papacy, so he inserted a speaking tube through a hole in the saint's cell, and for several consecutive nights identified himself as the Holy Spirit and directed the Pope to abdicate. A deceived but sincere Celestine was only too happy to agree (although after his resignation, the new Pope, Boniface VIII — the former Cardinal Caetani — had him arrested and imprisoned, lest Celestine become a rallying point for Boniface's many enemies).

Deception — whether human or diabolical — can make it more difficult to know God's will; however, the Lord does reveal His truth to those who persevere in seeking it. As a young man, St. Albert the Great heard a sermon by Bl. Jordan of Saxony, and as a result was attracted to the Dominican Order. Albert hesitated to enter, however; he remembered our Lord's words of condemnation regarding those who begin plowing but keep looking back[78] and was afraid that if he entered the order, his unworthiness and weakness might cause him to leave. The assurance Albert needed came in another sermon by Bl. Jordan; the Dominican explained that sometimes the Devil seeks to prevent us from answering God's call by wrongly convincing us that we won't be able to persevere. Enlightened by this insight, Albert acted decisively and entered the order, and from then on, in all his doubts and difficulties, he prayed for and received the guidance and assistance of the Blessed Virgin Mary.

The saints had various ways of making important decisions. For instance, the Jesuit missionary St. Francis Xavier wrote, while in India, "In this holy house of St. Thomas I made it my business to pray to God that He would let me feel in my soul His most holy will, being determined myself to carry it out, as He who gives the inclination will also give the strength to follow it. God, in His wonted mercy, did remember me, and it was with great interior consolation that I felt and knew His will to be that I should go to Macassar. I am sure that God our Lord is going to show me much mercy in this journey, as He has made me feel with such great satisfaction of my soul and spiritual consolation that this is His most holy will."

St. Ignatius of Loyola, who has much to say on methods of discernment, stresses the importance of seeking God's confirmation once a decision has been made. In a journal entry from 1544, the saint wrote, "Later, while preparing the altar and vesting [for Mass], I had a strong impulse to say, 'Eternal Father, confirm me; eternal Son, confirm me; eternal Spirit, confirm me; Holy Trinity, confirm me; my only God, confirm me!' I said this with great earnestness and with much devotion and tears, very often repeated

---

[78] Luke 9:62.

and very interiorly felt. . . . I finished the Mass and spent a short time in vocal prayer: 'Eternal Father, confirm me . . .' with a flood of tears spreading over my face. Today, even as I walked through the city, with much joy of soul, I represented the Most Holy Trinity to myself. I felt confirmed about the past." As Ignatius knew, a sense of peace and joy after we've made a decision will many times indicate that we're in conformity with God's plan.

A confirmation of the Lord's will doesn't always come quickly or easily, but those who persevere in their efforts to discover it will not be disappointed. After all, Jesus promises us, "Ask, and it will be given you; seek, and you will find; knock, and it will be opened to you."[79]

An assurance that we truly are doing God's will, however, does not mean that everyone else will accept our mission as divinely inspired. Quite often the contrary is the case, as many of the saints learned.

St. Colette, for instance, received a vision of St. Francis of Assisi, who entrusted her with the God-given assignment of reforming the Poor Clares. Colette prudently sought the advice of her spiritual director, who accepted the vision's authenticity and urged her to act upon the message. The sisters themselves, however, were greatly offended by Colette's efforts at reform and undermined her work with unrelenting opposition and hostility.

Our task is to do our best to discover God's will and to carry it out — not to worry about the possibility of failure. As Bl. Teresa of Calcutta frequently stated, "The Lord does not ask us to be successful, but faithful." Such an approach can give us great peace of mind, as illustrated in a story about Mother Teresa's namesake St. Teresa of Avila. The Lord had revealed that He wanted her to begin her mission of founding reformed convents within the Carmelite Order. She made all the necessary arrangements to start

[79] Matt. 7:7.

this project, but at the last minute, one of her superiors ordered her not to proceed.

Most people would have been confused and upset at this juncture, but as St. Teresa explained, "God was so gracious to me that none of this worried me in the slightest. I gave up the project as easily and happily as though it had cost me nothing. This nobody could believe, not even the very persons, given to prayer as they were, with whom I had to do: they supposed I must be very much distressed and ashamed; even my confessor could not really believe that I was not. It seemed to me that I had done all I possibly could to fulfill the Lord's command and that therefore I had no further obligation. So I remained in my own house, quite content and happy. I could not, however, give up my belief that the task would be duly accomplished, and although I was unable to forecast the means and knew neither how nor when the work would be done, I was quite sure that it would be done in time." Teresa's confidence was well founded, for the project was indeed soon undertaken successfully through the unexpected influence of others.

God doesn't require us to know everything in advance; He simply asks that we do our best, here and now, to discover and carry out His will. Discernment is necessary, according to St. Columban, to find our way through the darkness of doubt and confusion that surrounds us. It's also important as a way of avoiding unnecessary effort and sacrifice. St. Mark the Ascetic tells us, "Many have gone through great feats of self-mortification and endured much labor and sweat for the sake of God; but their self-will, lack of judgment, and the fact that they do not deem it necessary to seek salutary advice from their brethren, make these labors useless and vain."

Furthermore, St. Ambrose warns us not to trust outward appearances, which are often deceiving, but to seek the light of God's truth as we make our decisions.

What must we do to follow the promptings of the Holy Spirit? What is required of us if we truly wish to discern God's will?

According to St. John Climacus, "Discernment is — and is recognized to be — a solid understanding of the will of God in all times, in all places, in all things; and it is found only among those who are pure of heart, in body and in speech." If we're in a state of serious sin, it's impossible to claim we're answering God's call. The Lord's will for us in such a case is that we first repent and receive His forgiveness (particularly through the sacrament of Reconciliation); only then will we be ready to begin the process of discernment.

In addition to being in a state of grace, it's also necessary to be firmly rooted in humility. St. John Cassian observes, "True discernment is attained when one is really humble."

According to St. Anthony of Egypt, "God guides all by the action of His grace. Therefore, do not be lazy or lose heart, but call to God day and night to entreat [Him] to send you help from above to teach you what to do." This further advice is offered by St. Anselm: "When you resolve upon or prepare to do anything of importance, you must ask yourselves: Does God approve my determination to do this, or does He not? If your conscience answers you: I am certain that God approves this desire of mine, that He is pleased with my intention, then whether you can or whether you should carry out this plan, you should hold fast to your intention. But if your conscience warns you that God does not wish you to persevere in your project, then you must abandon it with all your might; and if you really and truly want to be rid of it, you must as far as possible shut out from your heart all thought and remembrance of it."

Because the Devil tries to confuse us, it's very important that we not only seek the Lord's guidance, but also be aware of whether we feel His peace. St. Barsanuphius warns, "When you intend to do something and see that your thought is perturbed, and if, after invoking God's Name, it remains perturbed even by a hair's breadth, know from this that the action you mean to commit is from the evil one, and refrain from committing it."

Troubled feelings and distractions can interfere with making good decisions, but St. Thomas More offers a solution: "If I am distracted, Holy Communion helps me to become recollected. If opportunities are offered by each day to offend my God, I arm myself anew each day for combat by the reception of the Eucharist. If I am in special need of light and prudence in order to discharge my burdensome duties, I draw nigh to my Savior and seek counsel and light from Him."

Common sense suggests that when we want to make a choice pleasing to God, we ask for His guidance and assistance. St. Josemaría Escrivá tells us, "Never make a decision without stopping to consider the matter in the presence of God." Everything we do must be rooted in Christ, and all our daily actions and decisions should be undertaken for His glory. St. Anthony Claret offers a unique way of reminding ourselves of this truth: "I will imagine that my soul and body are like the two hands of a compass, and that my soul, like the stationary hand, is fixed in Jesus, who is my center, and that my body, like the moving hand, is describing a circle of assignments and obligations."

Jesus promises that the Holy Spirit will guide us into all truth,[80] and this includes our efforts to discover and carry out God's will for us. As the stories of various saints show, sometimes this process may involve surprising or even dramatic events. More often our prayers, reflection, and even sacrifice will gradually give us a sense of what God wants. Occasionally our best efforts will result in misunderstanding, opposition, or failure. Even in such difficult instances, however, the Lord will graciously accept and reward our honest efforts to please Him, for He wants us not to be listeners who overdid their time (as did the unknown girl buried in the Roman catacombs), but faithful servants who have tried to do their duty. Ven. Charles de Foucald tells us, "In everything, ask yourself

[80] John 16:13.

only what the Master would have done, and do that." If we make this our rule of life during our time here on earth, we can approach our entry into the next life with confidence and peace.

For Further Reflection

"It is very clear that no virtue can come to full term or can endure without the grace of discernment. . . . For discernment is the mother, the guardian, and the guide of all virtues." — *St. John Cassian*

"For he who neglects to look forward by consideration to what he is about to do advances his steps with his eyes closed; proceeds on and accomplishes his journey, but goes not in advance of himself by looking forward; and therefore the sooner falls, because he gives no heed through the eyelid of counsel to where he should set the food of action." — *St. Gregory the Great*

"I am oppressed by the uncertainty of my future, but I cherish the lively hope of seeing my dreams fulfilled, because the Lord cannot place thoughts and desires in a person's soul if He does not really intend to fulfill them, to gratify these longings which He alone caused." — *St. Pio of Pietrelcina*

Something You Might Try

◆ St. Isaak of Syria advises us, "Sometimes a man desires something good, but God does not help him. This happens because at times a similar desire comes from the Devil and is harmful instead of useful; or because what we wish is beyond our powers, since we have not yet achieved a conformable life; or because it is alien to the form of endeavor we have accepted; or because the time has not yet come, when it can be fulfilled or begin to be fulfilled; or because we have neither knowledge nor physical strength sufficient for it; or because the present circumstances are not propitious. Yet the Devil uses all his wiles to offer this activity in a favorable light, to incite us to it and thus disturb our peace of soul or cause harm to the body. So we must carefully examine even our good desires. It is best to act in all things with advice." Thus, the apparent desirability of a certain course of action is no guarantee that it's actually God's will for us. When making important choices, we must give ourselves sufficient time to hear or discern the Lord's calling — making use of prayer, reflection, and consultation with others when appropriate. As long as we're honestly trying to discover and act upon the truth, the Lord will be patient with us.

◆ Discovering God's will is a very important subject for St. Ignatius of Loyola. His "Rules for the Discernment of Spirits" may be summarized as follows:

• *If we receive a direct, unmistakable revelation from God, we must act upon it.* This, however, is relatively rare.

• *We should use our intellects by analyzing the situation logically,* exploring our options and listing the advantages and disadvantages of each course of action; doing so may make the correct choice more apparent.

• *We should also use our feelings:* a sense of excitement or desire regarding one possibility may indicate God's favor; a feeling of dread or depression may suggest it's not the Lord's will.

• *Our imaginations may be helpful;* we might pretend someone asks us for advice on the same decision, or that we're on our deathbeds, looking back over our lives — what choice would we have wanted ourselves to make?

• *When we've done our best to make a good decision, we should prayerfully ask the Lord to give us a sign of confirmation.* If we later have doubts or second thoughts, we should never change our decision in a time of spiritual turmoil, but only when we feel God's peace.

Further Reading

Scripture: Wisdom 9:10-11; Psalm 25:4-5; Psalm 143:8.

Classics: St. Ignatius of Loyola, *Spiritual Exercises*; St. Alphonsus Liguori, *Conformity to the Will of God*.

Contemporary Works: Richard Gula, *Moral Discernment*; John Crossin, *Walking in Virtue: Moral Decisions and Spiritual Growth in Daily Life*; Germain Grisez and Russell Shaw, *Personal Vocation: God Calls Everyone by Name*.

I would gladly do good, my Jesus,
but I do not know how.
I would gladly seek You, my Jesus,
but I do not know the way.
I would gladly serve You, my Jesus,
but I do not know how.
I wish to love You, my Jesus,
but I know not how.
I seek You and cannot find You.
Come to me, my Jesus.
I cannot love You unless You help me, my Jesus.
Unless You help me, O my Jesus,
I know not what to do.
Jesus, be a Jesus to me.

St. Philip Neri

Unforgiveness

So speak and so act as those who are to be judged under
the law of liberty. For judgment is without mercy to one
who has shown no mercy; yet mercy triumphs over judgment.

James 2:12-13

World War II began on September 1, 1939 with the German invasion of Poland. After their rapid conquest of the country, the Nazis began persecuting not only Polish Jews, but other potential threats to their rule: intellectuals, military officers, politicians, and Church leaders. Poland's agriculture and economy were exploited for the benefit of Hitler's war effort, and every vestige of resistance was ruthlessly stamped out. Thousands of Polish citizens disappeared without a trace, and in 1940, the Germans began transforming a former Polish military encampment near the town of Oswiecim into a hell on earth: the first part of a vast and sprawling death camp commonly known as Auschwitz.

Early in 1941, a Polish Franciscan priest named Maximilian Kolbe was arrested by the Gestapo because of his opposition to the Nazi conquerors, and on May 28, he and 250 other prisoners were taken to Auschwitz, in southwestern Poland. Maximilian and other Catholic priests received particularly harsh treatment from the guards, being assigned to punishment details and enduring frequent beatings. Throughout this ordeal, Fr. Maximilian assured his companions that the Germans "will not kill our souls," and he constantly urged his fellow prisoners to forgive their tormenters, promising that "when we die, then we die pure and peaceful, resigned to God in our hearts." A Protestant doctor later testified, "From my observations . . . the virtues in the Servant of God [Fr. Maximilian] were no momentary impulse such as are often found in men; they sprang from a habitual practice, deeply woven into his personality. In Auschwitz, I knew of no other similar case of heroic love of neighbor."

At the beginning of August, a prisoner escaped, and the German commandant ordered ten men, chosen at random, to be taken to the starvation bunker and executed in retaliation. One of the ten cried out in despair, worrying over the fate of his family, so Father Maximilian stepped out of the ranks — something no one had ever dared to do — and, approaching the commandant, asked to die in the man's place. The speechless German officer nodded his agreement, and Maximilian and nine other prisoners were led away to building number 11, where they were stripped of their clothes and confined in the dark, stinking bunker without food or water.

Normally men in that hellish situation despaired, went insane, or attacked one another with animal-like fury, but under Fr. Maximilian's saintly influence, the prisoners prayed the Rosary, sang religious hymns in honor of our Lady, and remained calm and peaceful. The holy priest urged them to forgive their Nazi captors and heard their confessions.

After two weeks of this ordeal, Maximilian and two other prisoners were still alive, so on August 14, 1941, they were given lethal injections, and their remains were cremated the following day. On October 10, 1982, Pope John Paul II canonized his fellow countryman, declaring St. Maximilian Kolbe to be a martyr and naming him "patron of our difficult century."

St. Maximilian, who died praying for his enemies, gives us an amazing example of Christian forgiveness — yet, it's an example the Lord requires each of us to imitate in the particular circumstances of our lives. The great Christian author C. S. Lewis noted, "Everyone says forgiveness is a lovely idea, until they have something to forgive"; but this sort of inconsistent, "only when it's convenient" standard will not satisfy divine justice. Jesus makes it very clear that we will receive mercy from God only to the degree we extend it to others,[81] and He Himself prayed for the forgiveness of His executioners while dying on the Cross.[82] Showing mercy to our enemies is a very difficult part of the gospel message, but the saints prove such a way of life is possible, and by imitating their example, we will make major strides along the path of holiness.

As a young monk, St. Anselm was appointed prior (an important position of leadership) of the monastery of Bec, which he had entered just three years earlier. Naturally, there were objections to his appointment, particularly from an older monk named Osbern, who expressed his displeasure by being unkind and uncooperative. The saint responded with gentleness and understanding, granting Osbern many privileges and dispensations from the strict observance of the rule. He treated the monk with warmth and love, and after gradually winning his confidence, led him back to a more careful and correct monastic lifestyle. When Osbern became deathly ill, Anselm tended to him continually, and after the monk's death, constantly remembered him in prayer — even to the point of writing, "Wherever Osbern is, his soul and mine are one. . . . Do not forget the soul of my dear Osbern; and if I seem too troublesome, forget me and remember him."

We are to express mercy and kindness not only to those persons who are like us in temperament and lifestyle, but also to those

[81] Matt. 6:14-15; 18:21-35.
[82] Luke 23:34.

whose lives and values are quite different from our own. This, too, is illustrated in the life of St. Anselm, for he showed the same consideration to the irreligious King William Rufus ("the Red") of England that he had to his fellow monk Osbern. Anselm became Archbishop of Canterbury during William's reign, and over the next few years angered the king by resisting (for the most part unsuccessfully) royal efforts to extort money from the English Church. The king also insulted Anselm and bore a grudge against him, finally managing to have him exiled to Rome. The saint patiently bore this injustice, and when William died under suspicious circumstances, Anselm sincerely mourned and prayed for him, even though the king's death allowed him to return to England.

A legend about St. Cuthbert states that, while working in the fields, he once spied two crows harming the crops and shooed them away. As the saint continued working, one crow returned and landed nearby, hanging its head and cawing as if asking for Cuthbert's forgiveness. The monk smiled and nodded in agreement; the crow left for a moment and then returned with its partner, and both happily flew around the saint (and from then on were more careful about what they ate).

It's probably easier for us to forgive animals, which don't know any better, for the harm they do than it is to forgive our neighbor, but our Faith calls us to make the supreme effort of showing mercy to everyone who offends us, and the saints give us many examples of this.

The sixth-century bishop St. Gall of Clermont was known for turning the other cheek — figuratively and literally. On one occasion, for instance, a man who had a grievance against him expressed his anger by hitting him over the head. Gall didn't try to defend himself and showed no sign of resentment, thereby disarming his assailant and shaming him into asking forgiveness. Also, a priest named Evodius — a former senator — haughtily insulted his bishop during a banquet. Gall said nothing, but quietly left the hall and headed for a nearby church to pray. Touched by this example of meekness, Evodius ran after St. Gall and fell to his knees in the middle of the street, begging his pardon. The saint raised him to his feet and forgave him.

Turning the other cheek didn't come naturally to all the saints; some of them found it difficult to put our Lord's words[83] into practice. St. Gregory of Nazianzus and St. Basil the Great were very close friends, but a serious dispute occurred between them. The sensitive Gregory, feeling himself wronged, struggled for a long time before he was able to forgive his friend (and it was even longer before he could fully dismiss the incident from his mind).

In the sixth century, an illiterate Irish farmer named Aedh Mac Bricc was cheated out of his inheritance by his brothers. In revenge, he, in turn, kidnaped their serving girl, holding her for ransom; but St. Illathan, the local bishop, persuaded him to return her. The bishop also convinced Aedh — who was not a practicing Catholic — that God wanted him to start his own monastery. The farmer took this unexpected message to heart, acted upon it, and eventually became a bishop himself, gaining a reputation as a miracle worker — and today he's known as St. Aedh Mac Bricc.

Jesus expects His followers to forgive others in His Name. When the twelfth-century bishop St. Lawrence O'Toole went to Canterbury to visit the shrine of St. Thomas Becket, he was attacked for no apparent reason by a demented man, with a blow to the head rendering him temporarily unconscious. The king was furious when he heard of this assault on a visiting dignitary, and ordered the assailant to be hanged; but St. Lawrence intervened and managed to have his life spared.

Christian charity of a different sort was shown by the twentieth-century American religious foundress St. Katherine Drexel,

[83] Cf. Luke 6:29.

whose sisters worked with blacks in Harlem, New Orleans, and other cities. When the sisters described some of the racial taunting and insults they received from white bigots, Mother Drexel merely asked, "Did you pray for them?"

We're called not only to show mercy to others, but also to invite them to live by this higher standard, as shown by this example from the life of St. John the Almsgiver, a patriarch of Alexandria in Egypt. On one occasion, he spoke in opposition to a new tax being proposed by the governor, as it would impose great hardship on the poor; his unwelcome message caused the angry official to storm out of the room. Heeding our Lord's words about the need to be reconciled with those who hold a grudge against us,[84] John sent the governor a message late that afternoon: "The sun is about to set" (referring to the injunction that we should never let the sun set on our anger[85]). Fortunately, the governor took the hint and apologized, thereby resolving the issue.

Not all disputes are handled this easily, of course, and we can't compromise our efforts to uphold gospel values and the teachings of the Church just because some people are offended by them. When it comes to personal disputes, however, we're called to be understanding and forgiving, setting aside our anger and pride and resisting the temptation to brood over the injustices we've suffered. To the well-known saying "Revenge is sweet," we can rightly add the words, "until it leaves a bitter and deadly taste in our hearts." For this reason, St. Francis of Paolo instructs us, "Take pains to refrain from sharp words. Pardon one another so that later on you will not remember the injury. The recollection of an injury is itself wrong. It adds to our anger, nurtures our sin, and hates what is good. It is a rusty arrow and poison for the soul. It puts all virtue to flight."

[84] Cf. Matt. 5:23-24.
[85] Eph. 4:26.

A refusal to forgive is like a sharpened sword without a handle; those who try to wield it against their enemies end up harming themselves most of all. According to St. Ambrose, "No one heals himself by wounding another," and as St. Polycarp warns us, "If we pray to the Lord to forgive us, we ourselves must be forgiving; we are all under the eyes of our Lord and God, and every one of us must stand before the judgment-seat of Christ, where each of us will have to give an account of himself." Similarly, St. Vincent Ferrer reminds us, "If you wish God to forgive you your offenses against Him, forgive your enemies what they have done to injure you. At the very instant when you forgive your enemy, God will forgive you."

Many Christians find our Lord's teaching on the absolute necessity of forgiving others in His Name to be one of the most difficult parts of the gospel message, but in this very difficulty lies a great opportunity. St. Albert the Great informs us, "To forgive those who have injured us in our body, our reputation, our goods, is more advantageous to us than to cross the seas to go to venerate the sepulcher of the Lord." We don't have to make a pilgrimage to the Holy Land to follow in Christ's footsteps; we simply need to follow His example by forgiving those who wrong us. This radical, unworldly, humanly impossible act truly opens into our hearts a channel for Heaven's richest blessings — and gives us the absolute assurance of receiving a merciful reception ourselves on the Day of Judgment.

For Further Reflection

"This outpouring of [divine] mercy cannot penetrate our hearts as long as we have not forgiven those who have trespassed against us. Love, like the Body of Christ, is indivisible; we cannot love the God we cannot see if we do not love the brother or sister we do see. In refusing to forgive our brothers and sisters, our hearts are closed, and their hardness makes them impervious to the

Father's merciful love; but in confessing our sins, our hearts are opened to His grace." — *Catechism of the Catholic Church, par. 2840*

"What is mercy but a fellow feeling for another's misery, which prompts us to help him if we can. And this emotion is obedient to reason, when mercy is shown without violating justice, as when the poor are relieved, or the penitent forgiven." — *St. Augustine*

"It makes no difference whom you mistreat, a just person or an unjust one, since mistreatment is not permitted you. To punish others by doing the same things they do is spreading wickedness, not avenging it." — *St. Ambrose*

Something You Might Try

◆ According to the *Catechism of the Catholic Church*, "It is not in our power not to feel or to forget an offense; but the heart that offers itself to the Holy Spirit turns injury into compassion and purifies the memory in transforming the hurt into intercession."[86] It's only through God's grace that we're truly able to forgive others, but this grace will not be available to us unless we sincerely desire it. This means that when we find it impossible to show mercy toward someone who has hurt us, we must still *want* to forgive in Christ's Name, for this sincere desire on our part will allow the Holy Spirit to begin healing us and filling us with peace. If an injury seems too great or difficult for you to forgive, simply pray, "Lord Jesus, I know I must forgive this person, but I can't. So I ask You to forgive him [or her] for me."

◆ St. Teresa of Avila tells us, "The saints rejoiced at injuries and persecutions, because in forgiving them, they had something

---

[86] Par. 2843.

to present to God when they prayed to Him." It can be helpful to look at our sufferings at the hands of others in these terms: by forgiving those who wrong us, we're actually able to present a valuable and pleasing gift to God (while at the same time growing in grace more rapidly than we would otherwise).

Further Reading

Scripture: Proverbs 25:21; Sirach 28:1-7; Matthew 6:14-15; Matthew 18:21-35.

Classics: St. Francis of Assisi, *Admonitions*; St. Francis de Sales, *An Introduction to the Devout Life*.

Contemporary Works: Dennis Linn and Matthew Linn, S.J., *Healing Life's Hurts*; John Monbourquette, *How to Forgive: A Step-by-Step Guide*; Eamon Tobin, *How to Forgive Yourself and Others*.

O my Jesus,
You teach me from Your Cross
the feelings of love and forbearance
that I should have for my neighbors,
and the service that You would
have me render to them. . . .
What were Your first words
after the torments of the night and
of the day of Your bitter Passion?
They were words of deepest forbearance.
"Father, forgive them;
they know not what they do."
My Jesus, Infinite Goodness, You did
perceive that the passions of Your enemies

clouded their judgments and
was the cause of their ignorance.
What a lesson to teach us the forbearance
with which we should forgive
those who have injured us!

St. Louise de Marillac

Widowhood

Father of the fatherless and protector
of widows is God in His holy habitation.

Psalm 68:5

Husbands and wives rarely die together; thus, there's a high likelihood that a married person will eventually become a widow or widower. This, of course, is no reason not to marry in the first place. God wants husbands and wives to be united "until death do them part" so that they may assist each other in mutual sanctification and spiritual growth. Sooner or later, one of them will probably experience the profound grief associated with losing a beloved spouse. For persons of faith, however, this wrenching experience and immense sorrow is a temporary one, eventually to be followed by a joyous reunion. In the meantime, God provides the strength and courage needed to carry on in the world. Coping with grief is rarely easy, but it's never impossible.

Many of the saints experienced widowhood; quite often it was a very difficult adjustment, but — as in everything else — they learned to trust in the Lord and to offer Him their sorrows and pain.

St. Elizabeth of Hungary had only six very happy years of marriage before her husband died on one of the Crusades. Upon learning of her husband's death, Elizabeth, who was only twenty and had three children, is said to have run about her castle, screaming with grief.

Intense sorrow was also the fate of St. Jane Frances de Chantal, who was very happily married for eight years. Then, in 1601, her husband was accidentally shot while hunting. He suffered great pain before dying after nine days (although Jane had the consolation of seeing him die a happy death after receiving the last rites). Jane's grief was increased when her deceased husband's father, an embittered old man, insisted that Jane and her children live with him. He treated her unkindly, but she resolved to remain optimistic and hopeful in spite of him.

Widowhood also proved to be very challenging for St. Elizabeth Ann Seton. After her beloved husband's death, she converted to Catholicism — causing her Episcopalian family and friends to disown her. This created severe financial difficulties. To support herself and her children, Elizabeth opened a school, and this turned out to be the first step in God's plan for her: the founding of a new religious order named the Sisters of Charity. (Even as Elizabeth was engaged in this holy project, she later had to cope with the unexpected deaths of two of her daughters, ages sixteen and twelve.)

In the sixteenth century, St. Francis Borgia grieved deeply over the death of his wife, Eleanor, who was only thirty-seven; just a few weeks after she died, he sought admission into the Society of Jesus. St. Ignatius of Loyola wisely advised him to fulfill his responsibilities toward his eight children (ages eight through fifteen) first; only after several years had passed (allowing Francis to make arrangements for the care of his children, and to work through his grief) did Ignatius grant him permission to join the order.

Grief over the death of a spouse can be prolonged, but as the grief begins to lift, widowed persons may discover that this new (and often painful and lonely) stage of life also coincides with a different calling from God and new ways to serve Him. For example, St. Pammachius, a fourth-century Roman senator and friend of St. Jerome, lost his wife when she died giving birth; he spent the remaining years of his life using his wealth for good works. The wife of St. Pammachius, by the way, was a daughter of St. Paula, who — having been widowed with five children at the age of thirty-two — is considered the patron saints of widows. Paula's grief was intense and prolonged; only when her friend St. Marcella advised her to cope with her loss by serving God and other people did she start to become her normal self again.

A list of saints who experienced the death of a husband or wife includes St. Bridget of Sweden, who, after her husband died, established a religious order for women and tended to victims of the Black Plague; St. Rita of Cascia, who had married a crude and easily angered man at her parents' command and, after his violent death, finally achieved her desire of becoming a nun; St. Olympias, who, after becoming a widow at age twenty, was determined, in spite of her wealth and charm, not to remarry, but to be of service to the Church; St. Thomas More, who became a widower at twenty-seven when his beloved wife Jane died, and who decided to remarry so that his four children would have a mother; St. Alphonsus Rodriguez, who joined the Society of Jesus after the death of his wife, his young daughter, his mother, and later his son; St. Matilda, who lived as a widow for thirty-two years following the death of her royal husband; St. Joaquina, who established a religious order in nineteenth-century Spain some years after her husband's death; and St. Jutta, whose husband died while on a pilgrimage to the Holy Land, and who, after a period of deep grief, gave away her possessions and spent her remaining years caring for the poor.

Widowhood can be a heavy cross to bear, especially for persons who, like the saints, are capable of loving their spouses very deeply. This cross can be lessened, however, by taking steps to transform grief into service — perhaps by donating the possessions of a deceased spouse to the needy, becoming involved in efforts to prevent others from needlessly dying in the same way a spouse died, establishing a memorial scholarship in honor of one's spouse, and so on. These and similar efforts to help others please God, and allow Him to bless and sustain us in additional ways (and, if it's the Lord's will that a widow or widower remarry, activities of this sort make it easier to meet the right person).

As the saints knew, God never abandons us. He gives us the time we need to mourn our losses, but then He calls us to continue traveling the way of truth and life.

For Further Reflection

"A widow who enjoys sufficiently robust health should spend her life in works of zeal and solicitude, keeping in mind the words of the apostle [Paul] and the example of Dorcas"[87] — *St. Basil the Great*

"To hope in God while sustained by a husband is not so rare; but to hope in Him while destitute of that prop is highly praiseworthy." — *St. Francis de Sales*

"The true way to mourn the dead is to take care of the living who belong to them." — *Edmund Burke*

Something You Might Try

♦ According to the *Catechism of the Catholic Church*, "United with Christ by Baptism, believers already truly participate in the heavenly life of the risen Christ, but this life remains hidden with Christ in God. The Father has already 'raised us up with Him, and made us sit with Him in the heavenly places in Christ Jesus' (Ephesians 2:6). Nourished with His Body in the Eucharist, we already belong to the Body of Christ."[88] Thus, each time you attend

[87] Acts 9:36, 39; 1 Tim. 5:9-10.
[88] Par. 1003.

Mass and receive Holy Communion, you're allowing Jesus — the Source of all life — to live within you, and, if you choose, you can offer this experience as a prayer for and an experience of unity with your deceased spouse. At least once a week, attend Mass and receive Communion, and then, if practical, spend some time at the cemetery, talking to your spouse; this may give you a deeper sense of his or her presence, and you can be sure that through the love of Christ, "which conquers all things, even death itself,"[89] you and your spouse will be profoundly united in spirit.

♦ St. Jane Frances de Chantal, as a widow herself, knew how painful the loss of a spouse could be, so when her son-in-law died at an early age, she wrote her daughter these words: "My greatest wish is that you live like a true Christian widow, unpretentious in your dress and actions, and especially reserved in your relationships. . . . I know very well, darling, of course, that we can't live in the world without enjoying some of its pleasures, but take my word for it, dearest, you won't find any really lasting joys except in God, in living virtuously, raising your children well, looking after their affairs, and managing your household. If you seek happiness elsewhere, you will experience much anguish, as I well know." Living a simple, wholesome life, with a special emphasis on meeting the needs of one's children, has great value in the eyes of God; and as the years pass, the knowledge that you did your best to fulfill your responsibilities will prove to be a great consolation.

Further Reading

Scripture: Deuteronomy 24:17, 19; Sirach 35:14; Zechariah 7:10; Mark 12:41-44.

Classics: St. Francis de Sales, *An Introduction to the Devout Life*.

---

[89] Order of Christian Funerals.

More Saintly Solutions

Contemporary Works: Medard Laz, *Coping When Your Spouse Dies*; Cathleen Curry, *When Your Spouse Dies*; Beverly S. Gordon, *Toward Peace: Prayers for the Widowed*; Helen Reichert Lambin, *The Death of a Husband*; Robert L. Vogt, *The Death of a Wife*; Marta Felber, *Finding Your Way After Your Spouse Dies*.

Father of mercies and
God of all consolation,
You pursue us with untiring love
and dispel the shadow of death
with the bright dawn of life.
Comfort Your family in their loss and sorrow.
Be our refuge and our strength, O Lord,
and lift us from the depths of grief
into the peace and light of Your presence.
Your Son, our Lord Jesus Christ,
by dying has destroyed our death,
and by rising, restored our life.
Enable us, therefore, to press on toward Him,
so that, after our earthly course is run,
He may reunite us with those we love,
when every tear will be wiped away.
We ask this through Christ our Lord.

Order of Christian Funerals

Appendix

Special Novenas and Prayers

In a novena, prayers are offered for a particular intention for nine consecutive days. Novenas trace their origin back to the nine days our Lady and the Apostles spent together in prayer between the Ascension and Pentecost Sunday.

Any of the following novenas (or others you may be aware of) may be offered for your specific needs. Simply pray the prayer given here, either aloud or silently, once a day for nine days, while asking God to grant you wisdom and the ability to accept His will, whatever it may be.

Novena to the Sacred Heart of Jesus

Divine Jesus, You have said, "Ask and you shall receive; seek and you shall find; knock and it shall be opened to you." Behold me kneeling at Your feet, filled with a lively faith and confidence in the promises dictated by Your Sacred Heart to St. Margaret Mary. I come to ask this favor: *(mention your request)*.

To whom can I turn if not to You, whose Heart is the source of all graces and merits? Where should I seek if not in the treasure which contains all the riches of Your kindness and mercy? Where should I knock if not at the door through which God gives Himself to us and through which we go to God? I have recourse to You, Heart of Jesus. In You I find consolation when afflicted, protection when persecuted, strength when burdened with trials, and light in doubt and darkness.

Dear Jesus, I firmly believe that You can grant me the grace I implore, even if it should require a miracle. You have only to will it, and my prayer will be granted. I admit that I am most unworthy of Your favors, but this is not a reason for me to be discouraged. You are the God of mercy, and You will not refuse a contrite heart. Cast upon me a look of mercy, I beg of You, and Your kind Heart will find in my miseries and weakness a reason for granting my prayer.

Sacred Heart, whatever may be Your decision with regard to my request, I will never stop adoring, loving, praising, and serving You. My Jesus, be pleased to accept this my act of perfect resignation to the decrees of Your adorable Heart, which I sincerely desire may be fulfilled in and by me and all Your creatures forever.

Grant me the grace for which I humbly implore You through the Immaculate Heart of Your most sorrowful Mother. You entrusted me to her as her child, and her prayers are all-powerful with You. Amen.

Novena for the Help of the Holy Spirit

Holy Spirit, Third Person of the Blessed Trinity, Spirit of truth, love, and holiness, proceeding from the Father and the Son, and equal to Them in all things, I adore You and love You with all my heart.

Dearest Holy Spirit, confiding in Your deep, personal love for me, I am making this novena for the following request, if it should be Your holy will to grant it: (*mention your request*).

Teach me, Divine Spirit, to know and seek my last end; grant me the holy fear of God; grant me true contrition and patience. Do not let me fall into sin. Give me an increase of faith, hope, and charity, and bring forth in my soul all the virtues proper to my state of life.

Make me a faithful disciple of Jesus and an obedient child of the Church. Give me efficacious grace sufficient to keep the Commandments and to receive the sacraments worthily. Give me the four cardinal virtues, Your seven gifts, Your twelve fruits. Raise me to perfection in the state of life to which You have called me, and lead me through a happy death to everlasting life. I ask this through Christ our Lord. Amen.

Novena to Our Lady of Perpetual Help
by St. Alphonsus Liguori

Mother of Perpetual Help, behold at your feet a sinner who has recourse to you and has confidence in you. Mother of mercy, have pity on me. I hear all calling you the refuge and hope of sinners. Be, then, my refuge and my hope. For the love of Jesus Christ, your Son, help me.

Give your hand to a poor sinner who commends himself to you and dedicates himself to your lasting service. I praise and thank God, who, in His mercy, has given to me this confidence in you, a sure pledge of my eternal salvation.

It is true that in the past, I, miserable and wretched, have fallen into sin because I did not have recourse to you. But I know that with your help I shall be able to overcome myself. I know, too, that you will help me, if I commend myself to you. But I fear that in the occasions of sin, I may neglect to call upon you and thus run the risk of being lost.

This grace, then, I seek of you; for this I implore you as much as I know how and as much as I can: that in all the attacks of Hell I may ever have recourse to you and say to you, "O Mary, help me. O Mother of Perpetual Help, do not let me lose my God."

Three Hail Marys

Mother of Perpetual Help, aid me ever to call upon your powerful name, since your name is the help of the living and the salvation of the dying. Mary most pure, Mary most sweet, grant that your name from this day forth may be to me the very breath of life. Dear Lady, do not delay in coming to help me when I call upon you, for in all the temptations that trouble me, in all the needs of my life, I will ever call upon you, repeating, "Mary, Mary."

What comfort, what sweetness, what confidence, what consolation fills my soul at the sound of your name, at the very thought of you! I give thanks to our Lord, who, for my sake, has given you a name so sweet, so lovable, and so mighty. But I am not content only to speak your name; I will call upon you because I love you. I want that love to remind me always to call you Mother of Perpetual Help.

Three Hail Marys

Mother of Perpetual Help, you are the dispenser of every grace that God grants us in our misery. For this reason He has made you so powerful, so rich, and so kind that you might help us in our needs. You are the advocate of the most wretched and abandoned sinners, if they but come to you. Come to my aid, for I commend myself to you.

In your hands I place my eternal salvation; to you I entrust my soul. Count me among your most faithful servants. Take me under your protection; that is enough for me. If you protect me, I shall fear nothing. I shall not fear my sins, because you will obtain for me their pardon and remission. Neither shall I fear the evil spirits, because you are mightier than all the power of Hell.

I fear only that through my own negligence I may forget to commend myself to you and so lose my soul. My dear Lady, obtain for me the forgiveness of my sins, love for Jesus, final perseverance, and the grace to have recourse to you at all times, Mother of Perpetual Help.

Three Hail Marys

Novena to St. Joseph

O glorious St. Joseph, faithful follower of Jesus Christ, to you do we raise our hearts and hands to implore your powerful intercession in obtaining from the benign Heart of Jesus all the helps and graces necessary for our spiritual and temporal welfare, particularly the grace of a happy death, and the special favor we now implore: (*mention your request; then say the following prayer seven times in honor of the seven sorrows and joys of St. Joseph*).

O Glorious St. Joseph, through the love that you bore to Jesus Christ, and for the glory of His Holy Name, deign to hear our prayers and obtain for us our petitions. O Jesus, Mary, and Joseph, come to our assistance. Amen.

Novena to St. Anthony of Padua, the "Wonder Worker"

St. Anthony, glorious for the fame of your miracles, obtain for me from God's mercy this favor that I desire: (*mention your request*).

Since you were so gracious to poor sinners, do not regard my lack of virtue, but consider the glory of God which will be exalted once more through you by the granting of the petition that I now earnestly present to you.

Glorious Wonder Worker, St. Anthony, father of the poor and comforter of the afflicted, I ask for your help. You have come to my aid with such loving care and have comforted me so generously. I offer you my heartfelt thanks.

Accept this offering of my devotion and love and with it my earnest promise which I now renew, to live always in the love of God and my neighbor.

Continue to shield me graciously with your protection, and obtain for me the grace of being able one day to enter the kingdom of Heaven, there to praise with you the everlasting mercies of God. Amen.

Novena to St. Jude,
Patron of Lost Causes

Glorious St. Jude Thaddeus, by those sublime privileges with which you were adorned in your lifetime, namely, your relationship with our Lord Jesus Christ according to the flesh, and your vocation to be an apostle, and by that glory which now is yours in Heaven as the reward of your apostolic labors and your martyrdom, obtain for me from the Giver of every good and perfect gift all the graces of which I stand in need, and in particular: *(mention your request)*.

May I treasure up in my heart the divinely inspired doctrines that you have given us in your epistle: to build my edifice of holiness upon our most holy Faith, by praying for the grace of the Holy Spirit; to keep myself in the love of God, looking for the mercy of Jesus Christ unto eternal life; to strive by all means to help those who go astray.

May I thus praise the glory and majesty, the dominion and power of Him who is able to keep me without sin and to present me spotless with great joy at the coming of our divine Savior, the Lord Jesus Christ. Amen.

Novena to St. Thérèse of Lisieux

St. Thérèse of the Child Jesus, during your short life on earth, you became a mirror of angelic purity, of love strong as death, and of wholehearted abandonment to God. Now that you rejoice in the reward of your virtues, turn your eyes of mercy upon me, for I put all my confidence in you.

Obtain for me the grace to keep my heart and mind pure and clean like your own, and to abhor sincerely whatever may in any way tarnish the glorious virtue of purity, so dear to our Lord.

Most gracious Little Rose Queen, remember your promises of never letting any request made to you go unanswered, of sending down a shower of roses, and of coming down to earth to do good.

Full of confidence in your power with the Sacred Heart, I implore your intercession in my behalf and beg of you to obtain the request I so ardently desire: *(mention your request)*.

Holy "Little Thérèse," remember your promise "to do good upon earth" and shower down your "roses" on those who invoke you. Obtain for me from God the graces I hope for from His infinite goodness. Let me feel the power of your prayers in every need. Give me consolation in all the bitterness of this life, and especially at the hour of death, that I may be worthy to share eternal happiness with you in Heaven. Amen.

Novena to One's Patron Saint

Great St. N., at my Baptism you were chosen as a guardian and witness of my obligations, and under your name I then became an adopted child of God, and solemnly renounced Satan, his works, and his empty promises. Assist me by your powerful intercession in the fulfillment of these sacred promises. You also made them in the days of your earthly pilgrimage, and your fidelity in keeping them to the end has obtained for you an everlasting reward in Heaven. I am called to the same happiness that you enjoy. The same help is offered to me that enabled you to acquire eternal glory. You overcame temptations like those that I experience.

Pray for me, therefore, my holy patron, so that, being inspired by your example and assisted by your prayers, I may live a holy life, die a happy death, and reach eternal life to praise and thank God in Heaven with you.

I ask you to pray to God for this special request if it be God's holy will: *(mention your request)*.

Recommended Reading

The following books may be particularly helpful to those seeking either additional stories about the saints or insights from their writings applicable to daily life.

An Introduction to the Devout Life, St. Francis de Sales (TAN Books and Publishers, Inc., 1942, 1994). This classic by St. Francis de Sales is one of the greatest works on practical spirituality ever written; it stresses the idea (re-emphasized by the Second Vatican Council) that all Christians are called to holiness, and provides a wealth of information and advice on how to achieve this goal. If you can read only one book from this list, *An Introduction to the Devout Life* should be your choice.

Lessons from the Lives of the Saints, Rev. Joseph M. Esper (Basilica, 1999). A brief biography is given of each saint in the Church's liturgical year, along with two or three lessons for Christian living taken from his or her life.

The Little Way of Saint Thérèse of Lisieux, John Nelson (Liguori, 1997). "The Little Flower," or St. Thérèse of Lisieux, is surely one of the most popular saints in history, and this short book is a delightful collection of passages from *The Story of a Soul* (her spiritual autobiography), interspersed with scriptural quotations and other reflections. Those who have never read St.

Thérèse's writings will find this book to be a genuine spiritual treat.

Modern Saints: Their Lives and Faces, Ann Ball (TAN Books and Publishers, Inc., 1983; two volumes). The author presents short biographies of more than a hundred contemporary saints (of the eighteenth, nineteenth, and twentieth centuries) and servants of God, along with artistic renderings or, in many cases, actual photographs.

Saint of the Day, Leonard Foley, O.F.M. (St. Anthony Messenger Press, 1990). A revised, updated edition of the 1974 original, this work offers a short biography of each saint listed in the Church's liturgical calendar, along with an appropriate reflection, quotation, or story.

Saintly Solutions to Life's Common Problems — From Anger, Boredom, and Temptation to Gluttony, Gossip, and Greed, Rev. Joseph M. Esper (Sophia Institute Press, 2001). The precursor to this current book, *Saintly Solutions*, uses the same format given here, with saintly stories, anecdotes, and reflections on a variety of common experiences and difficulties in life, along with advice from the saints themselves, and recommended Scripture passages and other suggested readings. (Many of the chapters in this current book cover the same topics as those in the first, but they contain all new material. Also, each of the two books stands on its own; it's not necessary to have read one in order to benefit from the other.)

365 Saints, Woodeene Koenig-Bricker (Harper San Francisco, 1995). A brief description of one saint (often a little-known model of virtue) is given for each day of the year, along with a helpful and interesting reflection on a particular topic, followed by one or two reflection questions and a suggested resolution. This book can serve as a useful and enjoyable devotional aid for the average person.

Bibliography

An Introduction to the Devout Life, St. Francis de Sales (TAN Books and Publishers, Inc., 1942, 1994).

Antidotes & Stepping Stones, George W. Kosicki, C.S.B. (Spirit Song Ministries, 2000).

The Art of Choosing, Carlos G. Valles (Doubleday, 1986, 1989).

At Prayer with the Saints, Anthony F. Chiffolo (Liguori, 1998).

Augustine Day by Day, edited by John E. Rotelle, O.S.A. (Catholic Book Publishing Co., 1986).

The Avenel Dictionary of the Saints, Donald Attwater (Avenel Books, 1965).

Butler's Lives of the Saints, edited by Herbert J. Thurston, S.J. (Christian Classics, 1990).

The Complete Book of Christian Prayer (Continuum Publishing Company, 1996).

Conversations of the Saints, Bernard-Marie, O.S.F., and Jean Huscenot, F.E.C. (Liguori, 1999).

Daily Reflections with the Saints, Rev. Rawley Myers (Catholic Book Publishing Co., 1993).

A Dictionary of Quotes from the Saints, Paul Thigpen (Servant Publications, 2001).

Dominican Saints, by Dominican Novices (TAN Books and Publishers, Inc., 1921, 1940).

More Saintly Solutions

The Encyclopedia of Saints, Rosemary Ellen Guiley (Checkmark Books, 2001).

Father Solanus: The Story of Solanus Casey, O.F.M. Cap., Catherine M. Odell (Our Sunday Visitor, 1988, 1995).

Favorite Novenas to Jesus, Rev. Lawrence G. Lovasik, S.V.D. (Catholic Book Publishing Co., 1994).

Favorite Novenas to the Holy Spirit, Rev. Lawrence G. Lovasik, S.V.D. (Catholic Book Publishing Co., 1997).

Favorite Novenas to Mary, Rev. Lawrence G. Lovasik, S.V.D. (Catholic Book Publishing Co., 1993).

Favorite Novenas to the Saints, Rev. Lawrence G. Lovasik, S.V.D. (Catholic Book Publishing Co., 1992).

Fifty-Seven Saints, Eileen Heffernan, F.S.P. (Pauline Books and Media, 1994).

Finding Perfect Joy with St. Francis of Assisi, Kerry Walters (Servant Publications, 2002).

The Great Means of Salvation and of Perfection, St. Alphonsus Liguori (Redemptorist Fathers, 1927).

Great Spiritual Masters, John Farina (Paulist Press, 2002).

Heroic Sanctity and Insanity, Thomas Verner Moore (Grune and Stratton, 1959).

How to Live a Holy Life, St. Alphonsus Liguori, edited by Thomas M. Santa, C.Ss.R. (Liguori, 1999).

John Paul II's Book of Saints, Matthew Bunson, Margaret Bunson, and Stephen Bunson (Our Sunday Visitor, 1999).

The Ladder of the Beatitudes, Jim Forest (Orbis Books, 1999).

Lessons from the Lives of the Saints, Rev. Joseph M. Esper (Basilica, 1999).

The Little Way of Saint Thérèse of Lisieux, John Nelson (Liguori, 1997).

Lives of the Saints, Richard P. McBrien (Harper San Francisco, 2001).

Lives of the Saints for Every Day of the Year, Rev. Hugo Hoever (Catholic Book Publishing Co., 1993); two volumes.

Magic of a Mystic: Stories of Padre Pio, Suzanne St. Albans (Clarkson N. Potter, Inc., 1983).

Modern Saints: Their Lives and Faces (Books 1 and 2), Ann Ball (TAN Books and Publishers, Inc., 1983).

Ordinary Suffering of Extraordinary Saints, Vincent J. O'Malley, C.M. (Our Sunday Visitor, 2000).

Padre Pio's Words of Hope, edited by Eileen Dunn Bertanzetti (Our Sunday Visitor, 1999).

Paying Attention to God, William Barry (Ave Maria Press, 1990).

The Practice of the Love of Jesus Christ, Saint Alphonsus Liguori (Liguori, 1997).

Prayers and Heavenly Promises, Joan Carroll Cruz (TAN Books and Publishers, Inc., 1990).

The Quotable Saint, Rosemary Ellen Guiley (Checkmark Books, 2002).

Quotable Saints, Ronda De Sola Chervin (Servant Publications, 1992).

Saints at Prayer, Raymond E. F. Larson (Coward McCann, Inc., 1942).

Saint of the Day, Leonard Foley, O.F.M. (St. Anthony Messenger Press, 1990).

Saints for All Seasons, edited by John J. Delaney (Doubleday and Company, Inc., 1978).

The Saints, Humanly Speaking, Felicitas Corrigan, O.S.B. (Servant Publications, 2000).

Saints Preserve Us! Sean Kelly and Rosemary Rogers (Random House, 1993).

Saints Who Spoke English, Leo Knowles (Carillon Books, 1979).

The Secret of the Saints, Chris John-Terry (Alba House, 1999).

Secular Saints, Joan Carroll Cruz (TAN Books and Publishers, Inc., 1989).

Selected Writings and Prayers of Saint Alphonsus, edited by John Steingraeber, C.Ss.R. (Liguori, 1997).

Send Me Your Guardian Angel, Fr. Alessio Parente, O.F.M. Cap. (Editions Carlo Tozza Napoli-Dicembre 1984).

More Saintly Solutions

The Thirty-Three Doctors of the Church, Fr. Christopher Rengers, O.F.M. (TAN Books and Publishers, Inc., 2000).

The Voice of the Saints, edited by Francis W. Johnston (TAN Books and Publishers, Inc., 1965).

The Way of Salvation and of Perfection, St. Alphonsus Liguori (Redemptorist Fathers, 1926).

The Wisdom of the Saints, Jill Haak Adels (Oxford University Press, 1987).

Thoughts of the Curé D'Ars (TAN Books and Publishers, Inc., 1967).

365 Saints, Woodeene Koenig-Bricker (Harper San Francisco, 1995).

Touching the Risen Christ: Wisdom from the Fathers, edited by Patricia Mitchell (The Word Among Us Press, 1999).

Through the Year with the Saints, M. Basil Pennington O.C.S.O. (Doubleday, 1988).

Voices of the Saints: A Year of Readings, Bert Ghezzi (Doubleday, 2000).

Wisdom from Saint Bernard of Clairvaux, edited by Jeanne Kun (The Word Among Us, 2001).

Wisdom from Saints Francis de Sales and Jane de Chantal, edited by Louise Perrotta (The Word Among Us, 2000).

A Year With the Saints (Sisters of Mercy, 1891; TAN Books and Publishers, Inc.).

Saints Mentioned and Quoted

St. Adalbert of Prague (c. 956-997), bishop and martyr (April 23).

St. Aedh Mac Bricc (d. 589), Irish bishop (November 10).

St. Aelred of Rievaulx (1110-1167), Cistercian abbot and author of several treatises (March 3).

St. Afra (d. c. 304), martyr (August 5).

Bl. Agostina Pietrantoni (1864-1894), religious and nurse who was murdered by a patient (November 13).

Bl. Albert of Bergamo (d. 1279), Dominican tertiary and wonder-worker (May 11).

St. Albert the Great (c. 1200-1280), medieval theologian, philosopher, and scientist (November 15).

St. Aldobrandesca (1245-1310), widow and penitent (April 26).

St. Aloysius Gonzaga (1568-1591), young Jesuit who cared for plague victims (June 21).

Bl. Aloysius Stepinac (1898-1960), Croatian Cardinal imprisoned and martyred by the Communists (February 10).

Bl. Alphonsa Muttathupandatu (1910-1946), Indian mystic.

St. Alphonsus Liguori (1696-1787), bishop, Doctor, writer, and founder of the Redemptorists (August 1).

St. Alphonsus Rodriguez (d. 1617), Spanish wool merchant and Jesuit lay brother (October 30).

Bl. Alvarez of Cordova (d. c. 1430), Dominican preacher and royal adviser in Spain (February 19).

St. Amand of Maastricht (c. 584-679), missionary bishop (February 6).

More Saintly Solutions

St. Ambrose (c. 340-397), Bishop of Milan and Doctor (December 7).

St. Andrew, one of the Twelve Apostles and brother of St. Peter (November 30).

St. Andrew Avellino (1521-1608), Italian priest, missionary, and confessor (November 10).

Bl. Angela of Foligno (c. 1248-1309), widow and mystic (February 28).

St. Angela Merici (1474-1540), foundress of the Ursulines (January 27).

Bl. Anna Maria Taigi (1769-1837), wife, mother, and mystic (June 9).

Bl. Anne-Marie Janouvey (1779-1851), foundress of the Congregation of St. Joseph of Cluny (July 15).

St. Anselm (c. 1033-1109), Archbishop of Canterbury and Doctor (April 21).

St. Anterus (d. 236), Pope from 235 and martyr (January 3).

St. Anthony Claret (1807-1870), bishop and founder of the congregation of Missionary Sons of the Immaculate Heart of Mary, also known as the Claretians (October 24).

St. Anthony of Egypt (251-356), desert monk and father of Western monasticism (January 17).

St. Anthony Grassi (1592-1671), Oratorian priest (December 13).

St. Anthony of Padua (1195-1231), Franciscan friar and Doctor (June 13).

St. Anthony Zaccaria (1502-1539), founder of the Clerks Regular of St. Paul (July 5).

St. Antoninus (1389-1459), archbishop of Florence, moral theologian, and writer on local and international law (May 10).

St. Arnulf (d. c. 643), bishop of Metz (July 18).

Bl. Assunta Pallotta (1878-1905), Italian religious (April 7).

St. Athanasius (c. 297-373), Bishop of Alexandria and Doctor (May 2).

St. Augustine (354-430), Bishop of Hippo and Doctor (August 28).

St. Austreberta (d. 704), virgin (February 10).

St. Barsanuphius (d. c. 550), Egyptian hermit known for his austere lifestyle (April 11).

Bl. Bartolo Longo (1841-1926), former Satanist who, after his conversion, dedicated his life to promoting the Rosary (October 5).

St. Basil the Blessed (d. 1552), Russian Orthodox holy man (August 2).

St. Basil the Great (c. 329-379), Bishop of Cappadocia and Doctor (January 2).

St. Bede (673-735), English monk and scholar (May 27).

Bl. Benedetto Dusmet (1818-1894), Benedictine cardinal known for his extreme generosity to the poor (April 4).

St. Benedict (c. 480-c. 547), abbot who founded the monastery of Monte Cassino (July 11).

St. Benedict Joseph Labre (1748-1783), pilgrim and mendicant saint (April 16).

St. Bernadette (1844-1879), Sister of Notre Dame who, in 1858, received eighteen apparitions of the Blessed Virgin Mary at Lourdes in France (April 16).

St. Bernard of Clairvaux (1090-1153), abbot and Doctor (August 20).

St. Bernardine of Siena (1380-1444), Franciscan friar whose powerful preaching helped reform fifteenth-century society (May 20).

Bl. Bernardino of Feltre (1439-1494), Franciscan friar known for his preaching (September 28).

St. Bonaventure (1221-1274), Franciscan mystical theologian and scholastic, writer, bishop, and Doctor (July 15).

St. Boniface (c. 680-754), bishop, Primate of Germany, and martyr (June 5).

St. Brendan of Birr (sixth century), Irish bishop.

St. Bridget of Sweden (1304-1373), foundress of the Brigittine Order (July 23).

St. Brigid (c. 450-c.525), Abbess of Kildare (February 1).

St. Cadoc (sixth century), abbot and son of Sts. Gundleus and Gwladys (September 25).

St. Caesarius of Arles (470-543), bishop (August 27).

St. Cajetan (1480-1547), founder of the Theatine Order (August 7).

St. Camillus de Lellis (1550-1614), reformed soldier and gambler who directed a hospital and founded the nursing congregation of the Ministers of the Sick (July 14).

St. Catherine de Ricci (1522-1590), Dominican sister and visionary (February 13).

More Saintly Solutions

St. Catherine of Genoa (1447-1510), mystic and writer who ministered to the sick at a Genoese hospital (September 15).

St. Catherine Labouré (1806-1876), virgin and religious to whom
Our Lady appeared, resulting in devotion to the Miraculous Medal
(November 28).

St. Catherine of Palma (d. 1574), virgin and mystic (April 1).

St. Catherine of Siena (1347-1380), Dominican tertiary (April 29).

Bl. Ceferino Gimenez Malla (1861-1936), Gypsy martyred during
the Spanish Civil War (August 2).

St. Celestine V (1214-1296), hermit who reigned as Pope for four
months before resigning (May 19).

St. Chad (d. 672), bishop of the Mercians known for his humility
(March 2).

Bl. Charles of Blois (1320-1364), French noble killed in battle
(September 29).

St. Charles Borromeo (1538-1584), bishop who established the
Confraternity of Christian Doctrine (November 4).

Ven. Charles de Foucald (1858-1916), desert hermit whose ideals
inspired the founding of the Little Brothers of Jesus seventeen
years after his death.

St. Charles of Sezze (d. 1670), lay brother of the Observant branch
of the Franciscans (January 19).

St. Christina the Astonishing (1150-1224), virgin known for incredible mystical and religious experiences (July 24).

Bl. Christina of Spoleto (1436-1458), virgin (February 13).

St. Clare of Assisi (c. 1193-1253), foundress of the Poor Clares
(August 11).

Bl. Clare of Rimini (d. 1346), widow and Franciscan tertiary who
led a life of penance and almsgiving (February 10).

St. Claude de la Colombière (1641-1682), Jesuit priest and spiritual
director of St. Margaret Mary Alacoque (February 15).

St. Clement of Alexandria (c. 150-c.215), Church Father and theologian (December 4).

St. Clement Hofbauer (1751-1820), Redemptorist who opened an
orphanage and schools and established a Redemptorist congregation in Warsaw (March 15).

St. Clotilda (c. 474-545), wife of the Frankish king Clovis who spent her later years as a widow serving the poor and the suffering (June 3).

St. Colette (1381-1447), foundress of the Colettines, a branch of the Poor Clares (March 6).

St. Colman (d. 611), Abbot of Lann Elo (September 26).

St. Columba (c. 521-597), Irish abbot and missionary (June 9).

St. Columban (d. 615), Abbot of Bobbio (November 23).

St. Contardo (d. 1249), pilgrim (April 16).

Sts. Cosmas and Damian (d. c. 283), brothers who were physicians and martyrs (September 26).

St. Cunegund (d. 1033), wife of Emperor St. Henry II (March 3).

St. Cuthbert (c. 634-687), bishop (March 20).

St. Cyprian (c. 200-258), Bishop of Carthage and martyr (September 16).

St. Cyril (d. 869), priest and Apostle of the Slavs, with his brother St. Methodius (February 14).

St. Cyril of Alexandria (c. 376-444), bishop and Doctor (June 27).

St. Cyril of Jerusalem (c. 315-386), bishop and Doctor (March 18).

Bl. Damien de Veuster (1840-1889), priest who ministered among the lepers of Molokai (May 10).

St. Dativus (d. 304), a Roman senator who was arrested for being a Christian and who died in prison (February 11).

Bl. Diana d'Andalo (c. 1201-1236), virgin (June 9).

St. Dismas, the repentant criminal crucified with Christ and known as the "Good Thief" (March 25).

St. Dominic (c. 1170-1221), founder of the Dominican Order, also known as the Order of Preachers (August 8).

St. Dominic Savio (1842-1857), student of St. John Bosco known for doing even the smallest things out of love for God (March 9).

St. Donatus (d. c. 876), Bishop of Fiesole (October 22).

St. Dunstan (c. 909-988), bishop (May 19).

St. Dymphna (d. c. 620), a young woman martyred by her father for defending her purity (May 15).

St. Edith Stein (1891-1942), Jewish convert to the Catholic Faith who became a Carmelite nun and was martyred in Auschwitz (August 9).

More Saintly Solutions

St. Edmund (841-869), king and martyr; unsuccessfully defended England against a Viking invasion (November 20).

St. Edward (c. 1004-1066), King of England (October 13).

St. Edwin (d. 633), king and martyr (October 12).

St. Elisabeth of Schönau (1126-1164), virgin and mystic (June 18).

St. Elizabeth Ann Seton (1774-1821), the first American-born saint, who founded a school and the congregation of the Sisters of Charity of St. Joseph (later known as the Daughters of Charity of St. Joseph), of which she was the Superior (January 4).

St. Elizabeth Bichier des Ages (1773-1838), foundress of the Congregation of the Daughters of the Cross (August 26).

St. Elizabeth of Hungary (1207-1231), daughter of King Andreas II of Hungary, niece of St. Hedwig, and widow who became a Franciscan tertiary (November 17).

St. Elizabeth of Portugal (1271-1336), wife of King Denis of Portugal who became a Poor Clare tertiary after her husband's death (July 4).

Bl. Elizabeth of the Trinity (1880-1906), Carmelite nun known for her great mystical writings (November 9).

St. Ephrem (c. 306-373), theologian, preacher, Doctor, and writer of poems, hymns, and biblical commentaries (June 9).

St. Eustochium (c. 368-c. 419), virgin and pupil of St. Jerome (September 28).

St. Fabian (d. 250), Pope and martyr under Emperor Decius (January 20).

St. Fabiola (d. 399), Roman patrician who, after the death of her second husband, did public penance for their illicit marriage, devoted her time and money to charity, and established the first Christian public hospital in the West (December 27).

St. Faustina Kowalska (1905-1938), Sister of Our Lady of Mercy who spread the Divine Mercy devotion.

St. Felix of Cantalice (d. 1587), Capuchin lay brother (May 18).

St. Felix of Nola (d. c. 260), priest who miraculously escaped during a persecution and cared for the fugitive Bishop of Nola (January 14).

St. Fidelis of Sigmaringen (1577-1622), Capuchin who wrote and preached against Calvinism and was martyred (April 24).

St. Fillan (eighth century), monk renowned for his miracles (January 9).

St. Finnian of Moville (d. c. 579), bishop who established the monastery of Moville in Ireland (September 10).

St. Flannan (seventh century), Irish bishop (December 18).

St. Flavian (d. 449), Archbishop of Constantinople who died in exile after upholding Church doctrine (February 18).

Sts. Flora and Mary (d. 851), martyrs (November 24).

Bl. Fra Angelico (c. 1387-1455), famous Dominican painter (February 18).

St. Frances of Rome (1384-1440), foundress of the Benedictine Oblates of the Tor de' Specchi (March 9).

St. Frances Xavier Cabrini (1850-1917), Italian-born foundress of the Missionary Sisters of the Sacred Heart at Codogno in Lombardy and of orphanages and hospitals in North and South America; first United States citizen to be canonized (November 13).

St. Francis of Assisi (1182-1226), founder of the Franciscan Order, also known as the Order of Friars Minor (October 4).

St. Francis Borgia (1510-1572), Duke of Gandia who became a Jesuit, established the order throughout western Europe, and sent missionaries to the Americas (October 10).

Bl. Francis de Capillas (d. 1648), Jesuit missionary to China and martyr (January 15).

St. Francis de Sales (1567-1622), Bishop of Geneva, writer, and Doctor (January 24).

St. Francis di Girolamo (1642-1716), Jesuit priest known for his miracles and his work among the outcasts of society (May 11).

St. Francis of Paola (1416-1507), founder of the Order of Minim Friars (April 2).

St. Francis Xavier (1506-1552), Jesuit missionary to the East Indies (December 3).

St. Francis Xavier Bianchi (1743-1815), Barnabite known for his ministry to the poor and the neglected, his austerities, and his miracles; called the Apostle of Naples (January 31).

St. Gabriel Possenti (1838-1862), Passionist who sought to attain perfection in and through small things (February 27).

St. Gall of Clermont (c. 486-551), bishop known for his gentleness and humility (July 1).

St. Gaudentius (d. c. 410), bishop of Brescia in northern Italy and friend of St. Ambrose (October 25).

St. Genevieve (c. 420-c. 500), virgin and patroness of Paris (January 3).

St. Gengulf (d. 760), Burgundian knight murdered by his unfaithful wife's lover (May 11).

St. Germaine of Pibrac (c. 1579-1601), shepherdess (June 15).

Bl. Giles of Assisi (d. 1262), early follower of St. Francis of Assisi (April 23).

St. Godelive (c. 1045-1070), laywoman and victim of spousal abuse and murder (July 6).

St. Godric (c. 1065-1170), hermit (May 21).

St. Gregory the Great (d. 604), Pope from 590, writer, and Doctor (September 3).

St. Gregory of Nazianzus (c. 329-390), Bishop of Constantinople, theologian, and Doctor (January 2).

St. Gregory of Sinai (c. 1290-1346), monk and mystic (November 27).

Sts. Gundleus and Gwladys (sixth century), husband and wife who later repented of their sins and lived as hermits (March 29).

St. Hedwig (1174-1243), laywoman and aunt of St. Elizabeth of Hungary; known for her generosity to the poor (October 16).

St. Henry (972-1024), Holy Roman emperor and husband of St. Cunegund (July 13).

St. Henry de Osso (1840-1896), Spanish priest who founded the Society of St. Teresa of Jesus.

St. Henry Morse (1595-1645), Jesuit priest martyred at Tyburn (February 1).

Bl. Henry Suso (d. 1365), Dominican known for enduring extreme penances (March 2).

Bl. Herman Joseph (d. 1241), Premonstratensian priest known for his mystical experiences (April 7).

St. Hermenegild (d. 585), son of the Visigothic Spanish king Leovigild who was killed by his father for converting from Arianism to Christianity (April 13).

St. Hilarion (c. 291-371), abbot and first hermit of Palestine (October 21).

St. Hugh of Grenoble (1052-1132), bishop who was canonized only two years after his death (April 1).

St. Hugh of Lincoln (c. 1135-1200), bishop (November 17).

St. Hyancintha Mariscotti (d. 1640), religious who attained heroic virtue after her conversion from her lax observance of her rule (January 30).

St. Hypatius (d. c. 446), abbot (June 17).

St. Ignatius of Antioch (d. c. 107), disciple of John the Evangelist, bishop, and martyr (October 17).

St. Ignatius of Laconi (1701-1781), Capuchin lay brother (May 12).

St. Ignatius of Loyola (1491-1556), founder of the Jesuit Order, also known as the Society of Jesus (July 31).

St. Illathan (sixth century), Irish bishop.

St. Isaak of Syria (d. 439), Armenian bishop (September 9).

St. Isidore the Farmer (d. 1130), Spanish farm worker and example of Christian perfection (May 15).

St. Isidore of Seville (c. 560-636), Spanish bishop and scholar (April 4).

St. Ives (1253-1303), lawyer turned priest (May 19).

Bl. James of Lodi (d. 1404), Franciscan tertiary who was later ordained a priest (April 18).

St. Jane Frances de Chantal (1572-1641), foundress of the Visitation Order (August 18).

St. Jeanne de Lestonnac (1556-1640), widow and foundress (February 2).

St. Jerome (c. 342-420), Doctor who translated the Bible into Latin (September 30).

St. Jerome Emiliani (1481-1537), founder of the congregation of clerks regular known as the Somaschi, primarily to care for orphans (February 8).

St. Joan of Arc (1412-1431), French heroine who led the French army against English invaders and was burned to death for alleged heresy, but later declared innocent (May 30).

St. Joan of France (1464-1505), queen of France known for her patience amid great suffering (February 4).

More Saintly Solutions

St. Joaquina (1783-1854), Spanish widow and foundress of the Carmelites of Charity (August 28).

St. John, Evangelist and one of the Twelve Apostles (December 27).

Bl. John XXIII (1881-1963), Pope from 1958, who opened the Second Vatican Council.

St. John the Almsgiver (c. 560-619), patriarch of Alexandria (January 23).

St. John of Avila (d. 1569), Spanish secular priest, writer, adviser of saints and sinners, and missionary in Andalusia (May 10).

St. John the Baptist, cousin and forerunner of Christ (Birth: June 24; Martyrdom: August 29).

St. John Baptist de La Salle (1651-1719), founder of the Institute of the Brothers of Christian Schools (April 7).

St. John Berchmans (1599-1621), Jesuit who followed the "Little Way" (November 26).

St. John Bosco (1815-1888), founder of the Salesian Order (January 31).

Bl. John Buoni (c. 1168-1249), penitent and hermit (October 23).

St. John of Capistrano (1386-1456), Franciscan friar and missionary (October 23).

St. John Cassian (c. 360-433), abbot who wrote extensively on the monastic life (July 23).

St. John Chrysostom (c. 347-407), Archbishop of Constantinople and Doctor; name Chrysostom, or "Golden Mouth" for his eloquent preaching (September 13).

St. John Climacus (d. c. 649), abbot of the monastery of Mount Sinai and author of the mystical work *Ladder to Paradise* (March 30).

St. John of the Cross (1542-1591), Spanish Carmelite mystic, and reformer of the Carmelite Order (December 14).

Bl. John Dominici (1376-1419), Archbishop of Ragusa (June 10).

St. John of Dukla (1414-1484), Franciscan friar (September 28).

St. John the Dwarf (fifth century), monk (October 17).

St. John Eudes (1601-1680), priest who tended to victims of the plague and who founded the Sisters of Our Lady of Charity of the Refuge and a congregation for the sanctification of the clergy and those aspiring to the priesthood (August 19).

St. John Fisher (1469-1535), English bishop martyred under King Henry VIII (June 22).

St. John Gabriel Perboyre (1802-1840), Vincentian missionary martyred in China (September 11).

St. John of God (1495-1550), founder of the order of the Brothers Hospitallers (March 8).

St. John of Kanty (d. 1473), priest and professor at the University of Cracow who gave his goods to the poor (December 23).

St. John Leonardi (c. 1550-1609), priest who founded the congregation of Clerks Regular of the Mother of God and reformed the monks of Vallombrosa and Monte Vergine (October 9).

St. John of Matera (d. 1139), monk who faced persecution because of his austerity and who founded a monastery at Pulsano (June 20).

St. John of Matha (d. 1213), founder of the Order of Trinitarian Friars, whose mission was to ransom Christian prisoners captured by Muslims (February 8).

St. John Neumann (1811-1860), Bishop of Philadelphia and first American bishop to be canonized (January 5).

St. John Oglivie (1569-1615), Scottish convert to Catholicism, Jesuit priest, and martyr (March 10).

Bl. John Ruysbroeck (1293-1381), Flemish priest, theologian, and mystical author (December 2).

St. John the Silent (454-558), monk known for his great love of silence and recollection (May 13).

St. John Vianney (1786-1859), patron saint of parish priests; known as the Curé d'Ars (August 4).

Bl. Jordan of Saxony (d. 1237), second Master General of the Dominican Order, known for his eloquent preaching (February 15).

St. Josemaría Escrivá (1902-1975), Spanish priest and founder of Opus Dei (June 26).

St. Joseph, husband of Mary and foster-father of Jesus (March 19; Joseph the Worker: May 1).

St. Joseph Cafasso (1811-1860), priest known for his selfless devotion to others and to the needs of criminals and convicts (June 23).

St. Joseph of Cupertino (1603-1663), Franciscan tertiary (September 18).

Bl. Joseph de Anchieta (1534-1597), Jesuit missionary (June 9).

St. Jude, apostle, relative of Christ, and author of a New Testament letter (October 28).

St. Julia Billiart (1751-1816), virgin and cofoundress of the Institute of Notre Dame of Namur (April 8).

Bl. Julian of Norwich (d. c. 1423), recluse whose book, *Revelations of Divine Love,* in which she recounts her visions, speaks of God's loving dealings with man (May 13).

Bl. Julian of St. Augustine (d. 1606), Franciscan brother known for performing extreme penances (April 8).

Bl. Juliana of Mount Cornillon (1192-1258), virgin who helped institute the feast of Corpus Christi (April 5).

St. Jutta (d. 1260), widow (May 5).

Bl. Kateri Tekakwitha (1656-1680), Native American Christian known as the "Lily of the Mohawks" (July 14).

St. Katherine Drexel (1858-1955), wealthy Philadelphia native who founded the Sisters of the Most Holy Sacrament, numerous catechetical centers, and sixty schools and colleges (March 3).

St. Lawrence of Brindisi (1559-1619), Franciscan missionary, theologian, and Doctor (July 21).

St. Lawrence Giustiniani (1381-1455), Patriarch (Archbishop) of Venice (September 5).

St. Lawrence O'Toole (1128-1180), Archbishop of Dublin (November 14).

St. Leander (d. c. 600), Bishop of Seville and elder brother of St. Isidore (February 27).

St. Leo the Great (d. 461), Pope from 440-461 and Doctor (November 10).

St. Leonard of Port Maurice (1676-1751), Franciscan friar and missionary (November 26).

St. Leopold Castronovo (Mandic) (1866-1942), Capuchin priest who spent one year as a prisoner of war during World War I and afterward became known as a remarkable spiritual director and confessor (July 30).

St. Louis IX (1214-1270), King of France (August 25).

St. Louis de Montfort (1673-1716), secular priest who founded the Sisters of the Divine Wisdom and the Missionary Priests of Mary and is known for his book *True Devotion to Mary* (April 28).

Bl. Louis Guanella (1842-1915), Italian priest who cared for orphaned and mentally handicapped children (October 24).

St. Louise de Marillac (1591-1660), cofoundress of the Daughters of Charity (now known as the Sisters of Charity of St. Vincent de Paul) (March 15).

St. Lucy (d. c. 304), virgin and martyr (December 13).

St. Ludger of Münster (c. 744-809), missionary, bishop of Münster (March 26).

St. Lutgardis (d. 1246), Benedictine nun and mystic who took on the more austere Cistercian life (June 16).

St. Lydwina (1380-1433), virgin who bore patiently the painful symptoms of an illness that resulted from a skating accident and who later received visions (April 14).

St. Macarius the Elder (c. 300-390), priest who lived an austere life and ministered to his fellow hermits (January 15).

St. Marcella (d. 410), widow who gave her life to prayer and almsgiving after the early death of her husband (January 31).

St. Margaret Mary Alacoque (1647-1690), Visitation nun who received revelations of and promoted devotion to the Sacred Heart of Jesus (October 16).

Bl. Margaret of Castello (c. 1286-1320), virgin and victim of neglect (April 13).

St. Margaret of Cortona (d. 1297), mother who repented of an illicit relationship with a young nobleman when he died suddenly, became a Franciscan tertiary, received visions, and was the instrument of marvelous healings (February 22).

St. Margaret of Scotland (c. 1046-1093), wife of King Malcolm Canmore of Scotland who ministered to the spiritual and temporal needs of her people (November 16).

St. Maria de la Cabeza (twelfth century), wife of St. Isidore the Farmer (May 15).

St. Maria Goretti (1890-1902), twelve-year-old girl who was killed while resisting a young man's advances (July 6).

More Saintly Solutions

St. Mariana of Quito (1618-1645), virgin who publicly offered God her life if He would spare the city of Quito from an epidemic and earthquake, and who died soon afterward (May 26).

Bl. Marie of the Incarnation (1599-1672), French widow who became an Ursuline nun and served as a missionary in Canada (April 30).

St. Mark the Ascetic (d. c. 580), hermit in Italy (October 24).

St. Martha, friend of Jesus and sister of Mary and Lazarus (July 29).

St. Martin I (d. 656), Pope from 649 and martyr (April 13).

St. Martin de Porres (1579-1639), South American lay brother and infirmarian at the Dominican Friary of the Rosary in Lima, Peru, and friend to the poor (November 3).

Blessed Virgin Mary, Mother of Jesus and spouse of St. Joseph (Immaculate Conception: December 8; Birth: September 8; Mary, the Mother of God: January 1; Presentation of Mary: November 21; Assumption: August 15; Coronation: August 22; Seven Sorrows: September 15; Visitation: May 31; Our Lady of Lourdes: February 11; Our Lady of Mount Carmel: July 16; Holy Rosary: October 7).

St. Mary di Rosa (1813-1855), foundress of the Handmaids of Charity of Brescia (December 15).

St. Mary Frances of Naples (1715-1791), virgin and religious said to have been visited by many souls from Purgatory requesting her prayers (October 6).

St. Mary Joseph Rossello (1811-1880), foundress of the Daughters of Our Lady of Mercy (December 7).

St. Mary Magdalene, follower of Jesus and the first to whom He appeared after His Resurrection (July 22).

St. Mary Magdalene de Pazzi (1566-1607), Carmelite nun who patiently bore grievous trials of body and spirit (May 25).

St. Matilda (d. 968), wife of King Henry I of Germany and mother of St. Bruno (March 14).

St. Maximilian (d. 295), Roman soldier and martyr (March 12).

St. Maximilian Kolbe (1894-1941), Franciscan priest and founder of the Knights of the Immaculata; died as a martyr at the Nazi death camp of Auschwitz (August 14).

St. Maximus the Confessor (c. 580-662), abbot (August 13).

St. Maximus of Turin (c. 380-c. 467), Bishop of Turin (June 25).

St. Mechthild of Magdeburg (1210-1297), Dominican tertiary and mystic (November 19).

St. Melania the Younger (383-439), granddaughter of Melania the Older; married woman who joined a community of women in Jerusalem, where her husband had become a monk, and devoted herself to caring for the poor and copying books (December 31).

St. Michelina of Pesano (d. 1356), widow and penitent (June 20).

St. Miguel Cordero (1854-1910), Ecuadorian Christian Brother and scholar (February 9).

St. Molaise (d. 639), Bishop of Leighlin and papal legate to Ireland (April 18).

St. Monica (332-387), mother of St. Augustine (August 27).

St. Moses the Ethiopian (330-405), slave and thief who converted to Christianity and became a priest (August 28).

St. Narcissus (d. c. 304), bishop and martyr who converted St. Afra to Christianity.

St. Nicholas (d. c. 346), Bishop of Myra (December 6).

St. Nicholas of Flue (1417-1487), father of ten who, with the consent of his family, spent nineteen years as a hermit (March 22).

St. Nicholas of Tolentino (1245-1305), Augustinian friar known for his patience, humility, and selfless work (September 10).

St. Norbert (1080-1134), Bishop of Magdeburg and founder of the Premonstratensians, or Norbertines (June 6).

Bl. Notker Balbulus (912), monk known for his humble wisdom and contributions to Church music, in spite of a stuttering problem (April 6).

St. Odilia (d. c. 720), abbess (December 13).

St. Oliver Plunkett (1629-1681), Archbishop of Armagh, Primate of Ireland, martyr (July 11).

St. Olympias (c. 366-c. 408), widow and supporter of St. John Chrysostom (December 17).

Bl. Osanna of Mantua (1449-1505), virgin (June 20).

St. Pachomius (c. 290-c. 346), first monk to organize hermits around a written rule and shared community life (May 14).

More Saintly Solutions

St. Pammachius (d. 410), Roman senator and friend of St. Jerome who married St. Paula's daughter Paulina and, as a widower, with St. Fabiola, founded the first pilgrims' hostel in the West (August 30).

St. Pancras (d. c. 304), Roman martyr (May 12).

St. Paola Frassinetti (1809-1882), foundress of Sisters of St. Dorothy in Genoa (June 11).

St. Paschal Baylon (1540-1592), Franciscan friar (May 17).

St. Patrick (c. 389-c. 461), patron saint and apostle of Ireland (March 17).

St. Paul (d. 67), apostle and author of several New Testament letters (June 29).

St. Paul of the Cross (1694-1775), founder of the Passionist Order, who had gifts of prophecy and healing (October 19).

St. Paula (347-404), wife and mother of five — among them Sts. Blesilla and Eustochium — who, after her husband's death, formed a community of religious women and helped St. Jerome in his biblical work (January 26).

Bl. Paula Cerioli (1816-1865), widow, foundress of the Institute of the Holy Family of Bergamo (December 24).

St. Paulinus of Nola (c. 354-431), wealthy convert to Christianity who became a bishop and built churches, an aqueduct, and other public works in Nola, Italy (June 22).

St. Peter, one of the Twelve Apostles and the first Pope (June 29; Chair of Peter: February 22).

St. Peter of Alcantara (1499-1562), mystic and founder of a reformed order of Franciscans known as the Alcantarines (October 19).

St. Peter Armengol (d. 1304), converted brigand and thief who became a Mercedarian who worked tirelessly to ransom hostages (April 27).

St. Peter Canisius (1521-1597), Jesuit who worked to rebuild the Church after the Reformation and spent his time preaching, teaching, arbitrating, writing catechisms and other works, and reforming and establishing schools (December 21).

St. Peter Chrysologus (c. 400-450), bishop nicknamed Chrysologus ("golden speech") for his eloquent preaching (December 4).

St. Peter Claver (1580-1654), Jesuit who ministered to the slaves in South America (September 9).

St. Peter Damian (1007-1072), abbot, Cardinal-bishop of Ostia, and Doctor devoted to writing, preaching, and working against clerical abuses of his time (February 21).

St. Peter Julian Eymard (1811-1868), founder of the congregation of Priests of the Blessed Sacrament and writer (August 1).

St. Peter Fourier (1565-1640), founder of Augustinian Canonesses of Our Lady (December 9).

Bl. Peter Gonzalez (d. 1246), Dominican friar and popular preacher (April 14).

St. Peter of Mount Athos (c. eighth century), hermit who lived on Mount Athos in Macedonia (June 12).

St. Peter Nolasco (d. 1256), founder of Our Lady of Ransom (January 28).

St. Peter of Verona (1205-1252), Dominican who became a popular preacher, was murdered by a heretical assassin, and was canonized the year after his death (April 29).

St. Philastrius (d. c. 397), Bishop of Brescia in Italy and friend of St. Ambrose (July 18).

St. Philip Benizi (1233-1285), Servite priest who worked for peace between the Guelphs and the Ghibellines and assisted at the second general Council of Lyons (August 23).

Bl. Philippa Mareri (d. 1236), virgin and religious (February 16).

St. Philip Neri (1515-1595), Italian priest who founded the Congregation of the Oratory (May 26).

St. Philomena (d. c. 304), thirteen-year-old virgin martyred for refusing the advances of the Emperor Diocletian (August 11).

Bl. Pier-Giorgio Frassati (1901-1925), wealthy young Italian who devoted himself to caring for the poor and the sick (July 4).

St. Pio of Pietrelcina (1887-1968), Capuchin friar known as Padre Pio; famous for stigmata and other spiritual gifts (September 23).

St. Pior (d. 395), hermit in Egypt (January 17).

St. Pius V (1504-1572), Pope from 1565 (April 30).

St. Pius X (1835-1914), Pope from 1903 (August 21).

Bl. Placid Riccardi (d. 1915), Benedictine monk of the monastery of St. Paul Outside the Wall in Rome (March 14).

St. Polycarp (d. c. 155), bishop and martyr (February 23).

St. Prosper of Aquitaine (c. 390-c. 455), lay theologian who wrote a chronicle of the world from Creation to 455 AD (July 7).

St. Raphael Kalinowski (1835-1907), Carmelite priest known for his long hours in the confessional (November 15).

St. Raphaela Maria Porras (1850-1925), virgin and foundress of the Handmaids of the Sacred Heart (January 6).

St. Raymond of Penafort (1175-1275), Master General of the Dominicans and compiler of first organized collection of Church law (January 7).

St. Reinold (d. c. 960), monk and martyr (January 7).

St. Rita of Cascia (1381-1457), widow who became an Augustinian nun and experienced ecstasies while meditating on Our Lord's Passion (May 22).

St. Robert Bellarmine (1542-1621), Jesuit Cardinal, teacher, writer, and Doctor (September 17).

Bl. Robert Southwell (c. 1561-1595), English Jesuit martyred under Elizabeth I (February 21).

St. Roch (1295-1327), French pilgrim to Rome who cared for plague victims and was mistakenly accused of and imprisoned for espionage (August 16).

Bl. Roger LeFort (d. 1367), Bishop of Bourges (March 1).

St. Rose of Lima (1586-1617), Dominican tertiary and first canonized saint of the New World (August 23).

St. Rose Philippine Duchesne (1769-1852), French-born missionary to American Indians, called by them the "woman who always prays" (November 18).

Bl. Rudolph Aquaviva (d. 1583), Jesuit missionary and martyr (July 27).

St. Sabas (439-532), abbott, important influence on Eastern monasticism (December 5).

St. Seraphim of Sarov (1759-1833), Russian priest, hermit, and spiritual director (January 2).

St. Servulus (d. c. 590), layman and paraplegic (December 23).

St. Silas (first century), companion and fellow worker of St. Paul (July 13).

Bl. Silvester of Valdiseve (1278-1348), uneducated Camaldolese lay brother known for his extraordinary wisdom (June 9).

St. Simeon (c. 390-459), hermit (January 5).

St. Simon Salus (d. c. 590), monk and hermit (July 1).

Ven. Solanus Casey (1870-1957), American Capuchin friar (July 31).

St. Stanislaus (1030-1079), bishop of Krakow and martyr (April 11).

St. Stanislaus Kostka (1550-1568), model Jesuit who died during his novitiate (November 13).

St. Stephen of Hungary (969-1038), King of Hungary who helped build churches and defended the rights of the Holy See (August 16).

St. Sunniva (tenth century), virgin (July 8).

St. Symeon the New Theologian (949-1022), monk and mystic (March 12).

St. Syncletica (d. c. 400), wealthy Macedonia woman who gave away her fortune and lived as a hermitess (January 5).

St. Teresa of Avila (1515-1582), Spanish Carmelite nun, Doctor, and mystic who reformed her order (October 15).

Bl. Teresa of Calcutta (1910-1997), foundress of Missionaries of Charity; known as Mother Teresa and famous around the world for her work among the poor in India.

St. Theophan the Recluse (1815-1894), Russian bishop.

St. Théophane Vénard (d. 1861), priest of the Missions Étrangères of Paris who was sent to Western Tonking, where he suffered persecution, imprisonment, and martyrdom (February 2).

St. Thérèse Couderc (1805-1885), religious and foundress (September 26).

St. Thérèse of Lisieux (1873-1897), Carmelite nun and Doctor famous for her "Little Way" of spirituality (October 1).

St. Thomas Aquinas (c. 1225-1274), Dominican philosopher, theologian, and Doctor (January 28).

St. Thomas Becket (1118-1170), Archbishop of Canterbury and martyr (December 29).

St. Thomas More (1478-1535), Lord Chancellor of England and martyr (June 22).

St. Thomas of Villanova (d. 1555), Augustinian Archbishop of Valencia and writer who had a great love for the poor (September 22).

Sts. Timothy and Maura (d. c. 286), Christian married couple martyred together (May 3).

Bl. Torello (c. 1202-1282), penitent (March 16).

St. Turibius of Mongrovejo (1538-1606), Spanish-born Bishop of Lima, Peru (April 27).

St. Ulphia (d. c. 750), virgin (January 31).

St. Vincent de Paul (1580-1660), founder of the Lazarist Fathers and the Sisters of Charity (September 27).

St. Vincent Ferrer (1350-1419), Dominican mission preacher who helped to mend the Great Schism of the West (April 5).

St. Vincent of Lerins (d. c. 445), bishop (May 24).

St. Vincent Pallotti (1795-1850), Italian priest and founder of the Society of Catholic Apostleship, or the Pallottine Fathers (January 22).

St. Virgil (d. 784), abbot and bishop (November 27).

St. Vitalis of Gaza (d. c. 500), hermit who went to Alexandria to convert women of loose morals and was killed by a scandalized Christian who misunderstood his actions (January 11).

St. Volusian (d. 496), Bishop of Tours (January 18).

St. Walter of Pontoise (d. 1095), Abbot of Pontoise in France (April 8).

St. Wilgefortis (date unknown), virgin and martyr (July 20).

St. William of York (d. 1154), bishop (June 8).

St. Willibrord (658-739), Bishop of Utrecht and missionary (November 7).

St. Zita (c. 1218-1278), domestic servant (April 27).

St. Zosimus (c. 570-660), Bishop of Syracuse in Sicily (March 30).

Fr. Joseph M. Esper

Joseph Esper studied at Sacred Heart Seminary in Detroit and at St. John's Provincial Seminary in Plymouth, Michigan, and was ordained a priest of the Archdiocese of Detroit in 1982.

Fr. Esper has lectured at Marian conferences, spoken on Catholic radio, and written more than a dozen articles for *Fidelity*, *This Rock*, *Signs and Wonders*, *The Priest*, and *Homiletic and Pastoral Review*. He is the author of four other books: *Saintly Solutions to Life's Common Problems*, *After the Darkness*, *Lessons from the Lives of the Saints*, and *Why Is God Punishing Me?*

From his experience as a parish priest and his vast knowledge of and devotion to the saints — and of their strengths and weaknesses — Fr. Esper offers today's readers practical, encouraging, and inspiring wisdom to help them follow the countless holy men and women who have preceded them on the path to Heaven.

Index

Sophia Institute Press®

Sophia Institute® is a nonprofit institution that seeks to restore man's knowledge of eternal truth, including man's knowledge of his own nature, his relation to other persons, and his relation to God. Sophia Institute Press® serves this end in numerous ways: it publishes translations of foreign works to make them accessible to English-speaking readers; it brings out-of-print books back into print; and it publishes important new books that fulfill the ideals of Sophia Institute®. These books afford readers a rich source of the enduring wisdom of mankind.

Sophia Institute Press® makes these high-quality books available to the general public by using advanced technology and by soliciting donations to subsidize its general publishing costs. Your generosity can help Sophia Institute Press® to provide the public with editions of works containing the enduring wisdom of the ages. Please send your tax-deductible contribution to the address below. We also welcome your questions, comments, and suggestions.

For your free catalog, call:
Toll-free: 1-800-888-9344

Sophia Institute Press® • Box 5284 • Manchester, NH 03108
www.sophiainstitute.com

Sophia Institute® is a tax-exempt institution as defined by the
Internal Revenue Code, Section 501(c)(3). Tax I.D. 22-2548708.